NO MIDDLE GROUND

NO
MIDDLE
GROUND

How Informal Party Organizations Control Nominations and Polarize Legislatures

Seth E. Masket

THE UNIVERSITY OF MICHIGAN PRESS

Ann Arbor

First paperback edition 2011
Copyright © by the University of Michigan 2009
All rights reserved
Published in the United States of America by
The University of Michigan Press
Manufactured in the United States of America
⊗ Printed on acid-free paper

2014   2013   2012   2011   5   4   3   2

A CIP catalog record for this book is available from the British Library.

Library of Congress Cataloging-in-Publication Data

Masket, Seth E., 1969–
    No middle ground : how informal party organizations control
nominations and polarize legislatures / Seth E. Masket.
        p.   cm.
    Includes bibliographical references and index.
    ISBN-13: 978-0-472-11689-8 (cloth : alk. paper)
    ISBN-10: 0-472-11689-4 (cloth : alk. paper)
    1. Political parties—California.   2. Politics, Practical—California.
3. California. Legislature—History.   4. California—Politics and
government.   I. Title.
    JK2295.C3M37   2009
    328.794'0769—dc22   2008051146

ISBN 978-0-472-03467-3 (pbk. : alk. paper)
ISBN 978-0-472-02212-0 (e-book)

TO VIVIAN, ELI, AND SADIE

CONTENTS

ACKNOWLEDGMENTS

This book began as a small graduate school project. A professor saw my interest in parties and elections and my curiosity about California politics and encouraged me to dig a little bit. So I dug. I was astounded to find that, as recently as the 1950s, California had nearly nonexistent legislative parties, and it appeared that most state legislative elections were going uncontested. I was interested, as was my professor, who encouraged me to find out more.

That professor, who later became my mentor, colleague, and friend, is John Zaller. Although he is primarily known for his work in public opinion, he had come to develop an interest in party organization right around the time I started graduate school. The little research project he was prodding me to pursue ultimately became the book you are holding now. His encouragement, his enthusiasm for the project, and the high standards he sets for his own work and for that of his students fueled my long but fascinating journey into the history of California's political parties and helped me develop a deeper understanding of my home state. John Zaller's mentorship remains my touchstone as I work with students of my own.

I had a stroke of good fortune when Jeff Lewis joined the UCLA faculty and, a few hours later, my dissertation committee. An innovative methodologist with an interest in California politics, he is also a gifted teacher who is generous with his time. This book has profited tremendously from Jeff's skills and knowledge. In particular, he devised several clever methods of obtaining, inputting, and interpreting roll call votes that allowed us to develop a dataset of every roll call vote ever cast in the California Assembly. Findings from this dataset lie at the heart of this book's analysis. Had it not been for Jeff, I'd likely still be entering the votes for 1851 by hand and looking around for 1852.

I benefited from critical early advice on this project from Jim DeNardo, Frank Gilliam, and Dan Lowenstein, who kept me on task and helped give my project focus. I received support and some crucial course release time from the University of Denver that enabled me to move the project forward.

I remain indebted to the ragtag group of scholars known as the Klugies—Ken Gaalswyk, Phil Gussin, Wesley Hussey, Greg Koger, Hans Noel, and Darren Schreiber—for reading numerous drafts of various chapters and providing me with invaluable feedback. I particularly relied upon Wesley's encyclopedic knowledge of the politics of Orange County and of California.

This book was also markedly improved thanks to input and advice from John Aldrich, Kathy Bawn, Ben Bishin, Shaun Bowler, Marty Cohen, John Coleman, Gary Cox, Joe Doherty, Barbara Geddes, Elisabeth Gerber, Matt Gunning, Martin Johnson, David Karol, Marisa Kellam, Tom Knecht, Eric McGhee, Ellis Perlman, Jennifer Reich, Susan Schulten, Tom Schwartz, Susan Sterett, Jing Sun, Mike Thies, George Tsebelis, Lynn Vavreck, Nancy Wadsworth, Gerald Wright, and Demetria Zaller. Their willingness to read my drafts and listen to my "This one time, in California . . ." stories meant a lot to me.

The roll call data collection project was an enormous undertaking, and I am especially grateful to the National Science Foundation for providing the lion's share of the funding necessary to pull it off. (This material is based upon work supported by the National Science Foundation under Grant No. 0214514. Any opinions, findings, and conclusions or recommendations expressed in this material are those of the author and do not necessarily reflect the views of the National Science Foundation.)

Where the NSF's support fell short, John Zaller and Ken Schultz picked up the slack, for which I thank them. Mat McCubbins generously provided additional roll call votes, and Keith Poole helped me enormously in interpreting the data. I am also grateful for the flawless data entry and rapid turnaround time provided by Pranit Banthia, Hitesh Mistry, Herat Patel, and the other employees of Hi-Tech Export. I would be most remiss if I failed to acknowledge the small army of research assistants who inputted and proofread roll call votes: Thea Bernas, Andrew Bradley, Jules Butler, Chris Chin, Lauren Costales, Deanna Der, Janaki Dighe, Lauren Hansen, Irmak Ince, Viera Juarez, Andrew Kieser, Steve Kim, Kate Madden, Erica McWhorter, Nana Sogoian, Karl Su, and Bradley Whitworth.

Sheri Annis, Clea Benson, Jimmy Evans, Marc Herman, and Lark Park all deserve thanks for helping me to sort out some of the implications of my research. Jimmy and Lark get a special thank-you for letting me stay at their house while researching in Sacramento. Similar praise is due to my brother Harris and his wife Sirena for clearing a couch for me when I visited the San Francisco Bay Area.

I am deeply grateful to all of those who consented to be interviewed for this project. Their names appear in an appendix section. Finding the right people to talk to and figuring out how to approach them was not always an easy task, and I thank Barry Barnes, Jim Boren, Lou Cannon, Tony Castro, Richard DeLeon, Mary Hughes, Jean Pasco, Betty Pleasant, David Provost, Peter Skerry, and Erica Teasley for advising me and pointing me in the right directions. Ara Ogle and Jordan Cass-Boyle also helped me track people down at a crucial point in this project.

Several fine officers of the California state government volunteered their time to help me find the information I needed on numerous occasions. Ralph Romo of the Assembly Clerk's Office and Genevieve Troka of the State Archives are standouts as public servants and deserve both promotions and raises. I also wish to thank my old boss, state senator Joe Simitian, for consenting to several fascinating interviews and for getting me onto the floor of the Assembly during the 2001 budget stalemate. It was at that point that I had the chance to witness Senator John Burton (D-San Francisco) walk onto the floor, glance at the chaos, and then walk off, muttering, "I've lost control of this place." It was a sight I'll never forget.

I am grateful to Melody Herr, Scott Griffith, Jim Reische, and a number of anonymous reviewers at the University of Michigan Press for believing in this book and measurably improving it.

I wish to thank my parents, Barbara and Sam Masket, and my in-laws, Paula and Stuart Boxer, for being constant sources of encouragement (and occasional sources of free babysitting) throughout this process. Finally, my eternal thanks go out to my wife, Vivian, and my children, Eli and Sadie, who tolerated my odd hours and chronic workaholism and cheered me on when I needed it most. They helped me in more ways than they can ever know.

INTRODUCTION: EXTREME PARTISANSHIP

In the summer of 2003, as California's state legislators attempted to close a $38 billion deficit in a $100 billion budget, the parties stayed about as ideologically distant from each other as possible. Democrats wanted only modest cuts in services, but higher income taxes on the wealthy, a tripling of the car registration fee, and a hike in the state sales tax, which, at 7.25 percent, was already the highest in the nation. Republicans, for their part, opposed *any* new taxes, and not a few wanted tax *cuts*. To close the budget deficit, they called for massive cuts in spending, including eliminating the Seismic Safety Commission, a subsidy to poor blind people to feed their seeing-eye dogs, and public payments for the burial of dead foster children (Nicholas and Halper 2003). It seemed unlikely that the Democrats would get the tax hikes they sought (particularly with the Democratic governor facing a Republican-led recall), and even less likely that the budget could be balanced by starving seeing-eye dogs or leaving dead foster children unburied. Yet the lines were thusly drawn, and they held.

Amid a downgrading of the state's credit rating to near junk-bond status and threats that all state employees would have to go on minimum wage, the impasse dragged on for weeks. A mid-July Field Poll (DiCamillo and Field 2003) showed only 19 percent of Californians approving of the legislature's performance—a record low. Public animosity toward the California government hadn't been so high since the anti-incumbent fervor that swept the state in the late 1980s and early 1990s, which resulted in term limits, campaign contribution restrictions, mandatory cuts in legislative staffs, and 14 incumbents getting tossed out of the 80-person assembly. Legislators seemed to be courting that kind of reaction again.

The Democrats maintained large majorities in both houses of the legislature but fell a few votes short of the two-thirds supermajority necessary to pass a budget. This put intense pressure on a handful of swing Republicans who could, in theory, win plaudits from constituents for working out a compromise with Democrats to end the standoff.

More effective pressure, however, came from state senator Jim Brulte of Rancho Cucamonga. Brulte, the acknowledged Republican leader in Sacramento, vowed to recruit and fund a primary opponent to any Republican of either house who voted with the Democrats. At the same time, the leader of the Club for Growth, an antitax political interest group, visited the Republican caucus and promised, "We've got the knives out for any Republicans who would agree to raise taxes and vote with [Democratic governor] Gray Davis" (Halper and Vogel 2003; Halper 2003).

These threats were credible because there was still blood on those knives from two years earlier. On the key budget vote for fiscal year 2001–2, four Republican assembly members had crossed party lines to approve the Democratic plan, which included both spending cuts and a $1.2 billion tax increase. That was the last assembly session for all four of them, although none would be defeated in a general election. Anthony Pescetti of Rancho Cordova was confronted with a serious primary challenger the following year and dropped out. Dave Kelley of Idyllwild retired when he found that his assembly district had been made hostile to him in what was otherwise a profoundly pro-incumbent redistricting. Mike Briggs of Fresno decided to run for an open congressional seat, but was defeated in the primary by the little-known Devin Nunes; conservative donors throughout the state chose to back the unknown candidate rather than help a heretic. Finally, Richard Dickerson of Redding attempted a run for state senate but was defeated in the primary by assemblyman Sam Aanestad solely on the issue of Republican loyalty. Twenty-three of Dickerson's Republican colleagues in the assembly and all but three Republican senators endorsed Aanestad, as did the Howard Jarvis Taxpayers Association and many local officials (Cannon 2002; *California Journal* Staff 2002; Jeffe 2003; *Orange County Register* Staff 2001; Wasserman 2001). The specter of these four moderate Republicans being dispatched to private life for supporting a Democratic budget no doubt weighed heavily on legislators' minds two years later.

This example would strike most observers as a clear-cut case of strong party behavior. Legislators stuck together in partisan blocs even though their behavior disappointed the general public and potentially lowered their chances of reelection. The example is particularly striking considering its locale. Until recently, California was not known as a particularly partisan state. Legislative party discipline was notably weak, and as recently as the 1960s, speakers of the state assembly were regularly elected on bipartisan votes.

And yet California's polarization differs only modestly from the polarization that has occurred in the U.S. Congress and across the nation. Since the late 1980s, one could scarcely set foot in the U.S. Capitol without immediately recognizing that party pervades nearly everything Congress does. On issue after issue, almost all Democratic members of Congress stand in firm opposition to almost all Republican members. Compromise is shunned as most members of Congress, Democrats as often as Republicans, take positions that are more partisan than the voters they purport to represent. And while it was once common for members of different parties to call each other friends, today that almost never happens; insults and even physical threats across party lines are becoming more common (Jamieson and Falk 2000). Extreme partisan politics— "total war," in the words of a leading journalist (Brownstein 2003)—is the norm in the U.S. Congress.

Following the dictum of former Speaker Thomas P. O'Neill that all politics is local, this book examines the local roots of the new extreme partisanship. It argues that party organization at the community level is responsible for partisan behavior not only in Congress but in many state legislatures across the country. Local parties are not merely more active, better staffed, and better funded than they used to be (Cotter et al. 1984); they also recruit candidates, dominate primaries, and demand a high level of partisanship from elected officials.

To grasp this essential feature of American politics, one must study legislative politics not as a world unto itself, but rather in terms of its relationship to local politics. One must, that is, study how party systems channel influence from the local grass roots to the centers of legislative power.

This book is an attempt to do this in one particular state: California. Utilizing firsthand observations of party organizations in five communities, more than 150 years of roll calls in the state legislature, and a fresh interpretation of historical case material, I seek to illuminate the most basic features of party politics, prominently including the dependence of legislative parties on local party organization.

Although I might have done this study in any of several locales, California makes a particularly good setting. Its party system is small enough to be studied holistically, but also large enough to constitute a real system. In addition, the state's unusual political history affords a rare but convenient natural experiment in party organization: Progressive reforms in the early twentieth century effectively cut off state legislators from their roots in local parties. Then, about forty years later, voters repealed these reforms through the initiative process. By studying how this sequence of events affected legislative politics, one can see how local organization matters to party politics.

This is not simply a study of local parties; it is a study of the local roots of national politics and, as such, our contemporary party system as it operates at the local, state, and national levels.

Partisanship has been increasing at the national level for more than two decades now. Milestones along this path include the dispute over the 1984 house race in Indiana's "Bloody Eighth" district, the rejection of arch-conservative jurist Robert Bork for the Supreme Court in 1987, the forced resignation of Speaker Jim Wright in 1989, and the 1995–96 federal budget shutdown. In all these instances, moderate politicians turned their back on constituent sentiment to vote with their parties.

I have depicted the polarization of congressional politics graphically in figure 1. The figure presents evidence from four legislative sessions— 1969, 1983, 1995, and 2001. In each period, we see the relationship between the vote for president in a congressional district and the floor voting behavior of its member of Congress. The Republican presidential candidate's vote share in each district is on the horizontal axis, and roll call liberalism/conservatism, as measured by the Poole-Rosenthal NOM-INATE score (Poole and Rosenthal 1997), is on the vertical axis. In each time period, the members from districts that vote Republican for president are, as would be expected, somewhat more conservative than members from districts carried by Democratic presidential candidates. But the relationship goes from anemic in 1969 to overwhelmingly strong in 2001.

Indeed, the relationship seems arguably *too strong* in the 2001 session. Districts that are strongly Democratic or Republican in their presidential votes have, unsurprisingly, members of Congress that are extremely liberal or extremely conservative. But districts that are only barely Democratic or barely Republican elect people that are almost as extreme. Indeed, even districts that are almost evenly split between Democrats and Republicans in presidential elections are represented by

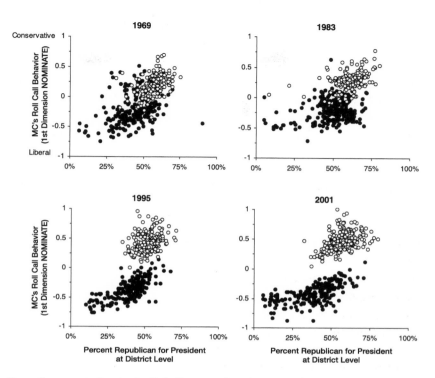

Fig. 1. Representation in the U.S. House at four time periods. Each data point indicates a member of Congress (MC). Hollow dots depict Republican House members; solid dots depict Democratic House members. Members are plotted horizontally by the conservatism of their district (as measured by the Republican vote for president) and vertically by their roll call conservatism (as measured by NOMINATE ideal points). (Adapted from Cohen, Noel, and Zaller 2004.)

members of Congress who are either extremely liberal or conservative. Where is the middle? Why is it missing?

Voters have noticed this change, and they don't particularly like it. Journalist E. J. Dionne (1991) argues that parties have caused Americans to hate the political system by creating a "false polarization":

> Liberalism and conservatism are framing political issues as a series of false choices. Wracked by contradiction and responsive mainly to the needs of their various constituencies, liberalism and conservatism *prevent* the nation from settling the questions that most trouble it. (11)

Similarly, Fiorina (1999b: 4) notes that today's politicians seem to have become insensitive to the appeals of the centrist voters who, according to much evidence, determine election outcomes. "Whatever happened to the median voter?" he asks. "Rather than attempt to move her 'off the fence' or 'swing' her from one party to another, today's campaigners seem to be ignoring her. Instead, they see their task as making sure that strong partisans and ideologues don't pout and stay home." Many political observers today are clearly concerned that the nation's political system is becoming too partisan. Even David Broder, who just a few decades ago penned *The Party's Over* (1972), now complains that "partisan excess" is contributing to the "perversion of representative government" (Broder 2003).

This trend is decidedly not limited to the federal level. In 2003, Republican legislators in Colorado and Texas attempted to redraw congressional districts for the second time in two years to exploit their partisan advantages following the 2002 elections. Although the Colorado Supreme Court decided such activity was unconstitutional in that state, the successful redistricting in Texas resulted in five new Republican districts for the 2004 elections. These actions represented the first time in the past half century that any state attempted a mid-decade redistricting for reasons other than a court order. Democrats then threatened to retaliate by redistricting Democratic-controlled Oklahoma and New Mexico (Reid 2003; Marshall 2003). Even as voters and journalists complained that such behavior was petty and disgusting, politicians seized every chance to eke out even a small victory for their party.

These examples and others are jarring for the generation of students assigned to read David Mayhew's influential *Congress: The Electoral Connection* (1974). That book famously described members of Congress as single-minded seekers of reelection and legislative parties as all but meaningless entities with little desire and less power to compel members to vote contrary to their districts' wishes. Mayhew's book was but one part of a vast literature that saw politicians as craven protectors of their own hides and parties as laughable in their impotence.

Clearly something has changed in the decades since that book was penned. Indeed, in recent years, a new literature has arisen to explain why strongly partisan behavior by members of Congress is entirely logical and expected. These titles, including John Aldrich's *Why Parties?* (1995) and Cox and McCubbins's *Legislative Leviathan* (1993), depict an almost totally different political system from the one Mayhew described just a few decades earlier. How could such astute observers of the political system see things so differently? What has changed?

One possible explanation is that the nature of politicians has changed. That, however, seems inherently unlikely, and as I shall show in a later chapter, the evidence is strongly against this view. Much more likely, politicians are operating in an environment that is somehow different from that of their predecessors. One major difference is that general elections don't matter as much as they once did. In recent years, House incumbents have won upward of 95 percent of their reelection battles. Ninety-nine percent of incumbents retained their seats in 2002, and the 2006 election—a "thumpin'" of President Bush that saw the Democrats take over both houses of Congress—only involved 30 seats changing hands. Whether one attributes it to redistricting, realignment, or increasingly strategic parties, far fewer congressional districts are in play today than at any time in recent history (Jacobson 2001; Abramowitz and Alexander 2004; Abramowitz 2004; Krasno 2007).

What's more, the major parties aren't even bothering to put up a fight for most districts, particularly when there's an incumbent involved. Only a handful of incumbents have encountered significant spending by the opposing party in recent elections. Even prior to the 2006 elections, as pundits broadly predicted the best environment for Democrats in a generation, the most optimistic Democratic strategists targeted 50 Republican incumbents, leaving the other 182 unmolested (VandeHei 2006). Incumbents, by and large, are being left alone.

That most congressional seats go essentially uncontested in general elections tells us something about why officeholders would be ignoring voters. But it doesn't tell us everything. Defeats do still occur, and, as Thomas Mann (1978) has famously argued, members of Congress feel "unsafe at any margin" because they know that political tides can turn quickly. Or, as Mayhew has put it, "Congressman Smith is unbeatable as long as he continues to do the things he is doing" (Mayhew 1974: 37).

It is, moreover, the case that electoral extremity still carries electoral risk. Members of Congress who take ideologically extreme stances significantly dampen their reelection prospects (Erickson 1971; Canes-Wrone, Brady, and Cogan 2002; Wright and Berkman 1986). And yet such risky behavior is apparently acceptable today, and historically, as well. According to Ansolabehere, Snyder, and Stewart (2001), the custom of voting one's district from the 1940s through the 1970s was actually an aberration in American history. Today, and for most of the time since the mid–nineteenth century, candidates for Congress have regularly deviated from their districts' median voters. In other words, politicians are intentionally pursuing behavior that angers the bulk of their constituents and decreases their chances of electoral success.

We have, then, a small mystery. Members of Congress are partisan—indeed, extremely so—even when they come from relatively moderate districts. The risks of extremism are diminished as a result of declining competitiveness in congressional elections. But risk still exists, and just in the past few years, dozens of members of Congress have flouted district opinion on issues from the Iraq War to Terri Schiavo—exposing themselves to greater risk of an adverse partisan tide than, by all appearances, they have any reason to.

The most likely explanation for this new state of affairs is the resurgence of party organization at the local level. While members have grown less fearful of challenges from the other party, they have become more concerned with threats from within their own party.

I cannot prove this thesis for the nation as a whole, because I cannot investigate local party organization on a national scale. But I can offer supporting evidence from the local party organizations that I have studied in California—organizations that send a substantial number of representatives to Washington.

Yet a striking feature of local party organization is that it is not organized by congressional district boundaries, state legislative district lines, or any other legal description. Legal boundaries do, of course, influence party structure (Aistrup 1993), but the main boundaries are those of organic political communities. Hence, there is a local party organization for the Latinos of Eastside Los Angeles County, the African Americans of South Los Angeles, the well-off Republicans of Orange County, and so forth. These organizations do not specialize by office; rather, they are concerned with all offices within their boundaries, from city council to state legislature to Congress. They may also become active in gubernatorial and presidential campaigns, but their bread-and-butter concern is the locally elected public official. The rules that apply to filling one of these offices tend to apply to all.

The natural political communities that are at the base of local party organization are often politically (and racially) homogeneous. Hence the parties tend to be concerned more with party nominations, which are often wide-open contests, than with general elections, where the results are foregone conclusions. But even in those few places where the general election outcome is in doubt, the role of local parties in nomination politics is too important for even sitting officeholders to ignore.

Nominations are made in primaries that typically have low turnout, little advertising, no rival party labels among which to choose, and virtually no media attention until they are over. For these reasons, nominations are often easily controlled by political insiders, including legislative leaders, interest groups, activists, and others. I call this collection of actors the *informal party organization,* or IPO, and I argue that these IPOs are the heart, soul, and backbone of contemporary political parties. Since activists are a prominent and energetic component of these organizations, IPOs tend to seek the most ideologically extreme candidate they feel they can get elected in a general election. And, since most general elections are not seriously contested today, winning at that stage is often not much of a constraint.

My claim, then, is that the parties control the public behavior of their officeholders by acting as gatekeepers to political office. Just as it is nearly impossible to win office without the nomination of a major political party, so is it nearly impossible to win the nomination of a major political party without the backing of a local IPO. Those interested in being candidates must work their way up through the IPO, proving their abilities to win votes and return public goods to their backers. Those who pass these tests receive the campaign resources—money, endorsements, Election Day labor—needed to prevail in a primary. And if they fail to deliver once in office, those resources will not be there for them the next time around. Incumbents are the most responsive to those with the greatest capacity to fire them. Today, thanks to the organizational abilities of activists and the declining importance of the general election, those who control party nominations are more terrifying to incumbents than the median voter is.

IPOs stay involved after the election, monitoring officeholders more carefully than ordinary voters can and pressuring them to enact a partisan agenda. Officeholders who drift toward the center after their initial election may face punishment by IPO leaders. A vast, poorly informed general electorate that leans toward the incumbent's own party does not instill as much fear among incumbents as a smaller, tightly controlled primary electorate. To be sure, few politicians are defeated in primaries. But few need to be if politicians are risk averse—one or two examples are usually sufficient to keep members in line. The end product of these political arrangements is a highly polarized government whose elected officials are often ideologically steadfast and unwilling to compromise, even in cases in which they might win a few more general election votes by doing so.

E. E. Schattschneider (1942: 35) defined a party as "an organized attempt to get . . . control of the government." This is precisely what these informal party organizations are. They pick the candidates who are capable of winning and endow these candidates with the resources—campaign funds, workers, and political cues such as endorsements—that make it possible to gain office. Because IPOs are active across levels of government—local, state, and national—they may be able to satisfy a wide range of demands, including those of benefit seekers for government aid and of career politicians for upward mobility.

Since these informal party organizations function primarily at the local level, and since it is at the local level that nomination battles are fought and won, this is where I focus my study. Although this study centers largely on the state of California, I develop arguments that are entirely general and test them in conditions that are common throughout the nation. California is like the nation in that it has achieved high levels of partisanship despite the weakness of its formal party organizations. And it is like the nation in that its voters are frequently frustrated by partisan acrimony but cannot seem to do anything about it. As we will see in chapter 3, the increasing polarization of legislators in Washington, DC—even among those representing moderate legislative districts—has been occurring in the California assembly, as well.

Another trait California shares with the nation is that most of its legislature's general elections are predetermined. As will be examined in greater detail in the next chapter, assembly election results are wildly lopsided. Candidates are either winning by huge margins or losing by them, even in districts in which the two parties are evenly matched in terms of presidential voting or voter registration. Indeed, the *California Journal* declared a mere two of the state's eighty assembly districts to be toss-ups in the 2004 election; the rest were safely in the hands of one party or another (*California Journal* Editors 2004). No assembly incumbents have lost in the past five general elections.

And as with the U.S. Congress, California assembly general elections are not seriously contested by the two parties. The number of open-seat races in which the two major party candidates spend roughly equal amounts has been declining since the 1970s, and incumbents have never faced many serious challenges over this time span. Thanks to term limits, there are more open seats (roughly a third of the chamber) in assembly elections than there are in most U.S. House elections, but there is much less competition for those open assembly seats. In the 2002 general election, only two incumbent-held seats and three open seats saw candidates spending even roughly similar amounts. As at the federal level, with few exceptions, California's general legislative elections are not serious contests.

One way in which California stands out from the nation is that it has achieved its current high level of partisanship despite an unusual history of nonpartisanship. As late as 1984, a leading textbook on the state described its parties as existing solely on paper (Christensen and Gerston 1984: 37). This reputation is largely attributable to the state's experiences with the Progressive movement of the early twentieth century. Some of the most radical Progressive reforms in the country's history—cross-filing chief among them—were enacted in this state. Many forms of party organization taken for granted in other states were made illegal in California for the first half of the twentieth century. Furthermore, traditional forms of patronage (public jobs and cash payments available to large numbers of regime supporters), which have been in decline across the nation for decades, were never much of a fixture in California, forcing political actors to organize politics without such help. Despite the state's antiparty legacy, today it has two of the most ideologically polarized legislatures in the country (Wright and Osborn 2002).

California's nonpartisan history is actually a boon to understanding current partisanship. It means that a state's current vibrant partisanship cannot be explained as simply an inheritance of the past. And cross-filing, which was implemented in 1914 and eliminated in 1959, uniquely focuses attention on party control of nominations as the key to understanding how parties work and why they are important.

Another important distinction between California and the United States is the existence of term limits on officeholders. Like the declining contestation of general elections, term limits have had the effect of making the nominations stage even more important. By compelling career politicians to change offices regularly, term limits force them into primary elections in which they must run as nonincumbents. With their incumbency advantage gone, these candidates become more dependent upon and subservient to IPOs for assistance in winning office.

A central part of my argument is that legislators are behaving like partisans because (1) they are chosen for such behavior, and (2) they fear the wrath of the activists and other political actors who control the primaries more than they fear the judgment of voters in the general election. This book is not, however, a study of extreme partisanship per se. Rather, it uses this extreme partisanship as a jumping-off point to understand what parties are and how they function, both in California and, as more limited evidence suggests, many other parts of the nation. The most distinctive element of this study is that it examines parties both in government and in the local community and relates the two venues of party activity to one another.

My study argues that we need a new framework for understanding what exactly political parties are. The existing views of parties in their relation to politicians can be divided into two main competing camps. One sees politicians as ambitious, self-interested actors who care about nothing except winning and remaining in office, and views parties as having little or no power to compel them to act otherwise. Issues are either ignored or cynically exploited to win votes. As a congressional staffer famously claimed, "The point on Capitol Hill is not to win on issues, it's to get reelected. Issues are checker chips. You give some away, you take some back" (Jackley 1992: 179). Politicians' convictions shift with the wind, conforming to whatever some narrow majority of voters believes. Politicians, in this view, run politics by themselves—they may construct weak parties as service organizations to help them get reelected, but such parties could never force them to vote against their wishes or those of their constituents.

The other main view sees politicians as the parties' willing warriors, eagerly submitting to whatever their legislative party leaders want them to do or say. If a Republican leader claims that torture is a necessary component of modern warfare, then all other Republican members of Congress are expected to say the same thing. Likewise, virtually all Democrats stood up to be counted with a philandering president in 1998 because that's what the party demanded. Advancing the party's goals takes precedence above truth or principle, and certainly above the wishes of one's district. What's more, these partisan politicians are willing participants in this arrangement; they constructed the parties to serve their careers and their ideological goals.

To be sure, there are plenty of anecdotes available to support either of these claims, and many political observers frequently make both claims simultaneously. Author Ron Suskind, for example, has, in separate works, characterized Bush administration officials as both "Mayberry Machiavellis" who force their policy shop to conform to poll-tested political considerations (2003) and ideological warriors who advance ideals without consideration of political feasibility (2004). What such observers often fail to recognize is that these views are incompatible. Politicians are either poll-watching risk-minimizers or they are staunch ideologues who ignore their constituents—they cannot simultaneously be both.

So which is it? Are politicians just in it for themselves? If so, how could that explain the Clinton impeachment vote, in which many Republican House members acceded to party pressure to vote for impeachment against the clear wishes of their constituents? But are they blind partisans? If so, how did parties change from being little more than convenient labels to the organizing force behind much legislative voting? And why would these politicians manufacture and willingly submit to a party that puts their own careers in jeopardy?

The problem with this puzzle is that it's a false dichotomy. It's false because it looks to politicians to understand parties. Both theories proceed from the assumption that the "party is the creature of the politicians" (Aldrich 1995: 4). In fact, as I shall argue, quite the opposite is true. Politicians, like all professionals, would like to keep their jobs and the attendant privileges, but they must conform to a political institutional environment *that they do not control* in order to do so. That is, politicians may be craven individualists or devoted partisan foot soldiers, depending upon who is controlling politics and how they are doing it.

Years ago, the common practice for understanding parties was to look not at the legislators in Washington but at the people in the home districts—party bosses, business interests, newspaper editors, and so forth—who sent them there in the first place (Mayhew 1986; Dahl 1961; Wolfinger 1972; Kent 1924). The typical finding of such studies was that traditional party organizations (TPOs), in the style of Chicago under Richard J. Daley and New York City under Boss Tweed, control the behavior of elected officials by handpicking candidates for nomination, manipulating nominations through patronage, and credibly threatening denomination as a punishment for disloyalty. This model obviously has some traction for explaining modern politics, since it accepts an expanded view of parties with multiple types of actors (bosses and politicians) and paints a picture of politicians who are sometimes compelled to behave in ways they don't wish to. It helps resolve the question of why politicians appear to be party warriors at some times and median-hugging centrists at others by arguing that partisan forces come from outside the legislature; when these forces are strong and ideologically motivated, incumbents will be compelled to construct party institutions and march as ideological foot soldiers; when they are weak, legislators will eschew partisanship and individualism will reign.

A problem for this third view, however, is that few believe that there are national political machines operating today, if such a thing can even be said to exist at the national level. There are some problems with applying this model to California, as well. For one, California lacks strong formal party organizations—TPOs simply don't exist there, by scholarly consensus. Second, who's the boss? There are obviously influential figures in California politics today, including congresswoman Maxine Waters, former assembly Speaker and San Francisco mayor Willie Brown, and governor Arnold Schwarzenegger. But it would be difficult to match any of them up with the classic definition of *boss*.

Yet, despite the state's weak formal party structure, there is a great deal of party organization going on in California. Politicians are compelled to hold a party line and are punished—sometimes terminally—for failure to do so. They may also be rewarded for going along with what's asked of them. This control is being exerted by forces inside and outside the legislature, perhaps a combination of officeholders, activists, and benefit seekers who are capable of influencing the party nomination process. The dominant influence, however, comes from outside the government, and to the extent politicians are able, they attempt to insulate themselves from it. This is not the kind of relationship described by most modern studies of political parties.

The reason, I suspect, that existing models of political parties miss so much of the party action in California and elsewhere in the United States is that much of this action occurs out of plain sight and leaves little trace of quantifiable data. It occurs in local communities, at odd hours, behind closed doors, and occasionally outside the law. Because local organization is central to my argument, I have gone into the field to learn about it. Some of what I have found includes the following:

- A group of wealthy conservative activists, land developers, and officeholders has effectively controlled Republican nominations in Orange County for decades, and maintains a large presence in the state Republican Party. Some of these conservatives work in activist groups or on the county's Republican Central Committee. Many of the developers work through an organization known as the Lincoln Club, which uses its members' $3,500 annual dues to fund conservative candidates for state offices and to groom future candidates who can help their businesses. Through the centralization of money and the coordination of efforts, these conservative activists have played no small role in keeping the state's Republican elected officials well to the right of most Republican voters. Not only do they actively recruit conservative candidates and discourage or even threaten moderates who run for party nominations, but they also punish Republican officeholders who deviate from the party line. Members of the Lincoln Club were behind the 1995 recall of Speaker Dorris Allen—the assembly's first Republican Speaker in twenty-five years and first female Speaker ever—because she had made a deal with outgoing Speaker Willie Brown and the other assembly Democrats to win her position with their support. The Lincoln Club also backed a successful primary challenger to unseat her replacement, Brian Setencich (R-Fresno), who had become Speaker by a similar arrangement. In the minds of these activists and benefit seekers, bipartisanship is a punishable offense.

- In South Los Angeles, Democratic candidates for local, state, and federal offices all compete for the endorsement of Congresswoman Maxine Waters in primary elections. This endorsement brings with it access to Waters's benefit-seeking allies (often Los Angeles business leaders outside her congressional district), who donate substantial sums to her anointed candidates. Her endorsement also comes with the Election Day labor of activists in friendly unions, clubs, and churches. Finally, Waters publicizes her choices in her highly influential slate mailer, which alone can move thousands of voters toward one candidate or another (Lewis 2003). Locals describe Waters's grip on politics in the same way that Chicagoans have described Mayor Richard J. Daley's reign. "If she supports a candidate," a Democratic club member explains about Waters's political style, "as a rule, they will win, because that's how strong her influence is in her district."

- For more than two decades, aspiring Democratic politicians in Los Angeles County's Eastside have had to choose between aligning with the organization run by County Supervisor Gloria Molina or with the Alatorre-Torres-Polanco machine. Each of these organizations works closely with its affiliated activists in the labor unions and political action committees to elect dependable candidates who are typically well to the left of most Democratic voters in the area. The public offices of these principal elected officials and those of their close allies are filled with young aspirants waiting their turn for a chance to run for office, knowing that they will only receive their leaders' blessings—and accompanying donor lists and Election Day labor—if they stay in the queue. Winning office without the backing of one of these organizations, or switching between these organizations, is considered nearly impossible due to their control over the nominations process and their demand for loyalty.

- In rural Fresno County, weak formal party organizations of both parties have yielded to coalitions of elected officials (such as former Democratic congressman Cal Dooley and former Republican state senator Chuck Poochigian); benefit seekers, including wealthy agribusiness people and land developers; and passionate activists, including unions and business and law enforcement organizations. The success of these organizations is more impressive on the right than the left. In a county where the two parties roughly parallel each other in voter registration (and the median voter is thus quite moderate), the Republicans elected from this area are fiercely conservative, in part due to the influence of these organizations. Local conservative activists have proven their willingness to punish those Republican officeholders who vote with Democrats once too often. They were behind the 2002 primary defeat of Republican assembly member Mike Briggs after he supported a tax increase to balance the state budget in 2001.

As these examples suggest, party politics in California is driven by informal alliances between officeholders, benefit seekers, activists, and the candidates they back—alliances that center on party nominations. Nominations weigh heavily on the minds of incumbents and candidates, compelling them to deviate from the typical voter in their district even when experience, career-mindedness, and common sense might tell them to do otherwise. None of the leading views of parties does a good job explaining this phenomenon.

In the model I propose, candidates, officeholders, activists, and benefit seekers have a variety of incentives for working together to form informal party organizations. These actors understand that they can achieve more in politics by working together than they can on their own. For candidates, the organizations offer a chance at a stable support structure; the higher they wish to go in the hierarchy of offices, or the more often term limits force them to change offices, the more they need help from IPOs in primaries. For ideological activists and benefit seekers, IPOs ensure that campaign donations will be more effective. Instead of spreading money over a broad range of candidates, they can learn who has the support of insiders and who, therefore, is most likely to win. And even if that candidate doesn't win, their support will be remembered by IPO leaders. There is no such solace for the unaffiliated donor who contributes to a losing campaign. Finally, these organizations also arise because ambitious officeholders realize they can use them to build their own power bases, deliver for their constituents, and achieve more while in office.

A substantial and influential literature today argues that politicians themselves build parties to solve certain problems, including the unpredictability of careers, the instability of legislative majorities, and the difficulty of passing legislation they care about (Aldrich 1995; Schwartz 1989). I argue that political actors outside the government have precisely the same motivations. They need things from government—changes in social policy, public contracts for sympathetic businesses, and so on—but can't get those things by themselves. To meet their goals, they follow the logic of the minimal winning coalition (just as legislators are said to do) by finding just enough allies to control nominations. Indeed, these local actors are much better able to form durable coalitions than legislators are because they are closer to the voters and understand the appeals and issues that will turn elections. Once they have formed such a coalition, they are the gatekeepers to political office; no one can hold office without meeting their standards and owing them something in return. Thus do these informal party organizations control the government, or at least part of it.

Would-be candidates accede to this system not because they want to but because, except for a few characters with atypically high name recognition and large personal fortunes, they have to. The system is designed to produce ideologically polarized candidates, but officeholders may often resist party control from the outside. For example, when urged to abolish the Progressive reforms that made it difficult for activists to control primaries, legislators repeatedly refused to do so. Even legislators whose party would have benefited from the end of these reforms resisted ending them.

Evidence from other states suggests that this nomination-centered model with IPOs at its center has at least some validity in other parts of the nation. In Nebraska, for example, we find a unicameral state legislature that has forgone parties altogether. Reviewing the existing literature on parties, we might expect Nebraska's incumbents to have created weak parties to help them win reelection; they haven't. Or we might expect that incumbents have built disciplined parties to enable them to carry out the ideological agendas that their members run on and presumably believe in. They haven't done that, either (Wright and Schaffner 2002). Nor do there appear to be any local party bosses. Interestingly, a conservative group of activists recently approached the Nebraska legislature's leaders and urged them to make it a partisan institution, promising that the Republican Party would be able to hold it for the foreseeable future. Incumbents, however, rejected the suggestion, concluding that the nonpartisan environment to which they were accustomed was preferable (Sittig 1997: 196).

My interpretation of this story is that, consistent with my theory of party organization, informal forces outside the government were attempting to impose partisan control but that officeholders resisted. It seems obvious why legislators—even those in the dominant party— would resist external control, but this is not the dynamic envisioned by the leading theory of legislative partisanship. According to this theory, legislators of the dominant party should have seized the opportunity to create a durable, long-term coalition for policies they believed in.

By no means do I suggest that existing models of parties are without merit. Each has been appropriate to certain places and times in history. Mayhew's (1974) book, for example, is an excellent description of politics when it is actually candidate-centered, as it was nationally from the 1950s through the early 1980s, and in California during the first half of the twentieth century. But the nub of the problem is this: It is certainly correct that if legislators want to get things done, they need to create a legislative party organization to do it. What many scholars miss, however, is that legislators don't necessarily want to get things done—they just want to stay in office. That explanation, however, misses the fact that *somebody* may want to get things done, and that these somebodies can sometimes organize politics, control nominations at the local level, and force officeholders to pursue partisan goals. The traditional party organization model captures all this. What it misses, though, is that people who want to get things done don't need to work through the formal party structures to do it; informal party organizations can be just as effective.

This is where my nomination-centered approach to parties makes its contribution. It is essentially a more general version of the traditional party organization model, in that it sees control of the nominations process as the key to control of the parties. But if formal party organizations are not available or powerful enough to do that job, those interested in controlling government will find another means of doing it. Specifically, they will band together as informal party organizations (IPOs). These IPOs—coalitions of top elected officials, activists, and benefit seekers—are the modern equivalents of the old-fashioned political party, doing what it did by other means. When TPOs or IPOs are strong, party organization develops within the legislature because the external party leaders insist on getting things done, and strong legislative organization is a useful means of doing so. And when TPOs or IPOs are strong, the view of officeholders as single-minded seekers of reelection has little relevance, not because officeholders don't care about the electoral connection as Mayhew describes it, but because, unlike the situation Mayhew describes, parties interpose themselves between officeholders and voters and often thoroughly dominate the relationship.

My study proceeds as follows. Chapter 1 addresses the key question of why parties appear to be weak at some points and strong at others, laying out in greater detail my theory of nomination-centered politics. As I argue, the modern political party is remarkably similar to the machines that once dominated places like Chicago and New York City. Then, the behavior of officeholders was determined by the actions of those outside government, and those seeking to understand parties examined the local hierarchies of ward bosses and precinct captains who slated candidates for office and made sure they won. Although the shape of the modern party is more of a network than a machine hierarchy, the function is essentially the same: a small group of people operating only barely within the law manages to control elections and thereby the government. The major difference between these modern informal party organizations (IPOs) and their machine forebears is the existence of ideological activists. Machines distrusted ideologues; IPOs rely on them. The result is extreme candidates and highly polarized politics.

The notion that parties are not lying in service to elected officials but are, rather, controlling them from outside the government runs counter to the views of many modern scholars. However, I show exactly this to be the case in chapter 2, using California's unusual history to illuminate the nature of parties. Specifically, I examine the California assembly's responses to several state antiparty reforms enacted during the Progressive Era. The most influential of these reforms was cross-filing, which allowed candidates for partisan office to run in multiple party primaries without their party label appearing on the ballot. The Progressives' aim in creating cross-filing was to kill parties, and their theory of party was essentially mine: if parties could be severed from nominations and those who control them, party activity would wither and die. And indeed, the legislative parties collapsed in the aftermath of cross-filing. No longer needing to appease their partisan primary constituencies, legislators eagerly voted across party lines even on such crucial issues as the election of the assembly Speaker. Incumbents in the cross-filing era not only failed to develop partisan institutions but also rejected efforts to reintroduce partisanship to the legislature. When an anti-cross-filing initiative made it onto the ballot, legislators of both parties conspired to defeat it by advancing a watered-down compromise that they claimed to be superior. Legislators did not seek to build partisan institutions to "whip themselves"; parties and party discipline had to be imposed by forces outside the legislature.

While chapter 2 focuses on legislative behavior surrounding the imposition and removal of cross-filing, chapter 3 takes advantage of more than 150 years of legislative roll call data to examine a much broader range of incumbent activity. In this chapter, I examine the power of various influences on legislative behavior. The evidence in this chapter testifies to the profound dampening effect that cross-filing had on partisanship and the strong polarization that has occurred since cross-filing's demise. It also captures some of the ephemeral coalitions—often led by bosses, ideological activists, and other people outside the legislature who could affect incumbents' careers—that arose to influence legislative behavior when the formal parties were weak or nonexistent. This chapter provides further evidence that legislators will only act like partisans when people outside the government compel them to.

The evidence presented thus far has supported the notion that party groups outside the government control nominations and compel the behavior of elected officials. But how do they do it? Finding out how these groups function requires leaving the legislature and talking to the folks at the local level who actually structure politics. This is what I do in chapter 4, going inside the informal party organizations that exist throughout California today by means of dozens of interviews with key local political figures. I show how officeholders, donors, activists, and brokers form alliances and conspire to control nominations and elect people who will be faithful to them while in office. These organizations do not function the same way in every part of the state or every race; sometimes they will help a little-known but promising candidate, other times they may rally around a very well-known candidate who would likely win anyway. But they are always doing something to influence nominations and fill government with people who will bring public goods to them and their allies.

Chapter 5 complements the previous chapter's interviews and anecdotes with some quantitative evidence for the existence and influence of IPOs. I start with a discussion of the challenges in distinguishing between a candidate-centered political system and a party-centered one, using several historical examples of ambitious candidates within strong party systems to illuminate the analysis. I then investigate the paths that many current California officeholders took to power—whether, that is, they received the assistance of IPOs or jumped into politics on their own. The evidence confirms the role of IPOs as the gatekeepers to political offices. Current officeholders are overwhelmingly recruited by activists or other officeholders, or worked their way up within a political organization. The evidence also demonstrates that candidates with ties to IPOs are greatly advantaged in nomination races over those who are not. I then attempt to measure the influence of IPO endorsements in primary elections while controlling for the influence of campaign spending and candidate quality. The aim is to discover, for example, whether an IPO simply uses fundraising to aid its candidates or enlists Election Day labor to boost its candidates' performance. The evidence in this chapter firmly rejects the idea that candidates and incumbents are their own bosses; they depend upon outsiders to obtain and retain power.

The book's concluding chapter assesses the normative implications of my findings about political parties. Is California—or the country, for that matter—better off with stronger parties or weaker ones? I assess the advantages and disadvantages of each system, concluding that citizens have little direct control over politics in either system, but that stronger parties generally provide greater accountability by elected officials. I further suggest some avenues for reform to improve governmental responsiveness and performance.

A note about terminology: The informal party organization (IPO) I have described is a network, in the sense that it is, in Tichy's (1981: 225) respected definition, "a system of participants—people, groups, organizations—joining by a variety of relationships." Nonetheless, I have avoided using the term *network* in the label. *Network analysis* in the social sciences has come to mean a large study of points of contact between multitudes of actors. In theory, this is the correct approach for my study, and a few researchers have attempted this approach for studying parties (Schwartz 1990; Koger, Masket, and Noel 2009; Dominguez 2005). However, because I endeavor to study these organizations throughout the state of California, and because many of these organizations involve city council members from small towns, reclusive donors, busy activists, and others about whom little is generally known, the type of data collection necessary for quantitative network analysis is simply not available. I do attempt to get under the skin of these organizations to discover how they work and what motivates their members, but I am not capable of doing a statistical network analysis in a way that would satisfy adherents of that field.

I also offer a note about abbreviations. Although I will frequently refer to informal party organizations as IPOs, I will try to avoid excessive use of abbreviated terms so to spare those readers possessing fine literary sensibilities the pain that acronyms can inflict. When I do use acronyms, it will be only to avoid excess verbiage on terms for which the reader is already familiar.

Finally, I offer a remark about methodological pluralism. Studying the dynamics of political parties, particularly the more expanded, informal parties I describe herein, is a murky process. No one piece of evidence is likely to jump off the page as irrefutable proof of the existence and power of IPOs or any other form of party. I therefore employ a variety of methods—historical, statistical, qualitative—to examine the party phenomenon from all available angles. I believe that the preponderance of evidence, collected and presented methodically over the course of this study, persuasively supports my arguments and significantly advances our understanding of political parties at the local, state, and federal levels. The final verdict, of course, is the province of the reader.

CHAPTER 1

The Modern Political Party

For decades after its 1974 publication, David Mayhew's *Congress: The Electoral Connection* was considered the premier text for anyone wishing to understand how members of Congress behaved. The description was not a pretty one for anyone who believed in the value of party government. According to Mayhew, it was easiest to think of members of Congress as "single-minded seekers of reelection." Candidates, he found, didn't have much use for parties other than to help mobilize voters. Attention to party agendas didn't change much once politicians got into Congress, either. "To a remarkable degree," Mayhew noted, "members can successfully engage in electorally useful activities without denying other members the opportunity to successfully engage in them" (82). Why didn't members of Congress press a party agenda? Apparently, it was a matter of choice, and they chose not to. "American congressmen," Mayhew wrote, "could immediately and permanently array themselves in disciplined legions for the purpose of programmatic combat. They do not" (98). Any party battles that occurred were, for the most part, theater; members of Congress maintained strong friendships across party lines and hewed closely to the median voters in their districts. Reelection was far more important than the advancement of any ideological agenda.

Mayhew's descriptions were merely the most eloquent of an era of scholarship extending from the early 1950s to the early 1990s that depicted American politicians as nonideological poll-watchers, sticking closely to the median voter in their districts and avoiding any stances that would offend the general electorate. The beginnings of this period are marked by the American Political Science Association's report "Toward a

More Responsible Two-Party System," which decried the lack of responsibility in the weak party system. "Alternatives between the parties are defined so badly," the authors claimed, "that it is often difficult to determine what the election has decided even in the broadest terms" (APSA 1950: 3–4). One of the last gasps of such depictions was *Hill Rat*, an entertaining tell-all from a former Capitol Hill staffer. As the author described congressional committee work, "You sit around a table and divide up the money. Anything that gets in the way of that process—philosophy, conscience, and so on—gets checked at the door" (Jackley 1992: 103).

The literature of this period generally describes a Congress full of ambitious, nonideological politicians. Interestingly, it closely charts an unusual period in congressional elections during which candidates actually tended, on average, to represent the median voter. An innovative study by Ansolabehere, Snyder, and Stewart (2001) demonstrated that, at least since the mid–nineteenth century, candidates for Congress have deviated strongly from their districts' median voters, stubbornly defying Downs's (1957) prediction of convergence. The exception seems to be a period from the late 1940s to the early 1980s.

Despite the relative oddity of this weak party period, its view of nonideological politicians is the one that is most ingrained in American popular culture. Notably, one of the most common epithets in modern political discourse is "flip-flopper," directed at those who appear to have no core beliefs. The essential plotline of 1990s political movies like *Bullworth*, *Dave*, and *The American President* is that a politician has lost his way, abandoning the issues and agenda that drove him to run for office in the first place, and is now "so busy keeping my job I forgot to do my job." Only when the politician has some sort of catharsis (a near-death experience, falling in love, etc.) does he remember to "fight the fights that need fighting," rather than the fights he can win (Reiner 1995).

This view of politics is hardly confined to Washington. Many state governments went through a similar period of weak partisanship, avoiding the most controversial issues in order to protect their political class. "I've been on a tour of state legislatures," humorist Mark Russell joked in 1991. "Mostly they are a bunch of fat white guys pretending to hurt each other" (Richardson 1996: 360).

The pretense, for the most part, is gone. The literature from that weak party era is difficult to reconcile with the modern Congress and state legislatures. Today, by virtual consensus, the parties in Congress and in many state legislatures have diverged (Poole and Rosenthal 1997).

Candidates no longer converge on the median voter. They have returned to their old historical pattern of representing the ideologically extreme elements within their parties, despite the electoral risk that this strategy carries (Canes-Wrone, Brady, and Cogan 2002; Wright and Berkman 1986). While it was once common for members of different parties to call each other friends, today that almost never happens, and insults and even physical threats across party lines are becoming more common in Congress (Jamieson and Falk 2000).

The new version of *Homo politicus* is the eager party warrior; legislators recognize the advantages of partisan action and willingly engage in it. As with any other form of legislative organization, this one exacts a price: sometimes legislators must take stances that differ from their personal opinions or those of their constituents. A moderate Republican may feel that his party's deficit spending is endangering the country's fiscal standing and wish to oppose a tax cut, but he knows that he must stand with his colleagues. Similarly, a moderate Democrat may stand with his copartisans in opposing Social Security reforms even if he believes they are important for the program's long-term stability. Both these politicians recognize that they will, in the long run, do better, both in terms of their policy goals and their reelection efforts, if they stick with their party coalition. Even if they are derided for hackery, this is a decision that rational politicians will make.

Indeed, in recent years, an entire literature has evolved to explain why rational legislators would participate in strong parties rather than eschew them (Cox and McCubbins 2005; Aldrich 1995; Cox 1987; Cox and McCubbins 1993; Kiewiet and McCubbins 1991; Schwartz 1989; Volden and Bergman 2006). Parties, in this view, are "institutional solutions to the instability of majority rule" (Aldrich 1995: 72). Deliberative chambers are inherently chaotic—to get a bill passed, one must cobble together a majority and hold it together over numerous votes, any one of which could doom the bill. The easiest outcome in such a chamber is for nothing to get done. Parties, however, provide a solution. As standing coalitions that don't have to be constantly reassembled, parties make it possible for individual legislators to pass bills while providing a path for career advancement. Incumbents submit to parties because they make it easier to get legislative work done.

But why is it important to get work done? Cox and McCubbins elaborate on this with their theory of parties as legislative cartels (1993, 2005). According to cartel theory, politicians recognize that their reelection prospects rise and fall with those of their fellow partisans, so they seek to create and enhance their party's brand name, "the commonly accepted summary of the past actions, beliefs, and outcomes with which it is associated" (1993: 110). They do so by ceding power to a party leadership that can manipulate the legislative agenda, which it does in a way that helps their collective party reputation. Thus members can run in the next general election on a collective party label that resonates with a sizable chunk—ideally a majority—of the voters.

A key question, however, remains: Why has the behavior of politicians changed? Why are legislators who, by their nature, prefer to avoid real partisanship increasingly behaving as partisan warriors? This question is all the more puzzling since, as surveys show, voters increasingly claim to dislike parties and partisanship. If neither legislators nor voters like strong parties, who does?

As suggested in the introduction, these questions proceed from the wrong assumption: that parties are a function of politicians' preferences. When Aldrich (1995: 4) says that "the major political party is the creature of the politicians, the ambitious office seeker and officeholder," he is saying something of a piece with Mayhew's (1974: 98) claim that members of Congress "could immediately and permanently array themselves in disciplined legions for the purpose of programmatic combat" but "do not." Both, that is, are saying that we should look at politicians if we want to understand parties.

An alternative to this approach comes from the traditional party organization literature, which tends to see parties as hierarchical, patronage-based groups whose power lies in the control of nominations (Mayhew 1986; Dahl 1961; Kent 1924; Wolfinger 1972). The key to Mayor Richard J. Daley's power in Cook County, Illinois, for example, was his control over party nominations. Daley routinely slated candidates for every office from the board of aldermen to county judgeships to the congressional seats within the county limits, and these candidates just as routinely won nomination in direct primary elections. According to one ward boss, "He moves us around like a bunch of chess pieces. He knows why he's doing it because he's like a Russian with a ten-year plan, but we never know" (Royko 1971: 82). Daley also exerted considerable control over the Democratic Party's choices for governor and senate during his tenure, and his reputation as a kingmaker in Democratic presidential nominations during the 1960s is legendary (Mayhew 1986: 74–75).

Studying parties as organizations or machines that try to elect people helps us understand why the same politicians that are soulless poll-watchers in one era can be fierce party warriors in another. But it doesn't explain the dilemma at hand. That is, by virtual consensus, the party machines in the model of Daley's Chicago or Tammany Hall's New York don't exist anymore. Why would partisanship among elected officials increase as the machines go extinct?

We gain some purchase on this question from a strain of literature known as conditional party government (CPG) theory, which has the virtue of focusing both on events within the legislature as well as on forces outside it. As this theory describes, legislative party leaders have an array of tools available to foster party discipline. They can enforce unit rule voting in the party caucus, they can employ party whips to cajole members, they can award office space, staff, or popular committee assignments to loyal party members, and they can deny such perks to mavericks. However, the theory continues, the leaders' ability to use such methods is conditional on electoral forces outside the legislature (Rohde 1991; Aldrich and Battista 2002; Aldrich and Rohde 2001; Rohde and Shepsle 1987). Specifically, if the electorate sends an ideologically coherent party contingent to Congress, that party can build on its coherence by enforcing discipline on roll call voting. An ideologically incoherent party, such as the post–World War II Democratic Party with its Northern liberals and Southern segregationists, will have little success in whipping its members into line.

It would seem that understanding these forces outside the chamber is at least as important as understanding partisan tools within the chamber if we truly want to comprehend what parties are and how they function. It is surprising, then, that more attention is not devoted to such extralegislative forces, and all the more important that we try to understand them. So what are these forces that determine the partisan nature of our elected governments? From the literature, it would seem that there are two of them, voters and elites.

It was voters that Rohde was speaking of when he described "the exogenous influence of electoral change" (1991: 162) as a cause of polarization or depolarization in a legislature. That is, voters shift their preferences from time to time and vote accordingly. If a party's voters are relatively unified on a set of issues, they will tend to elect a coherent party contingent to the Congress, which will vote consistently as a bloc. If a party's voters can't agree on much, they will elect leaders who can't agree on much, either. As Rohde notes, a good deal of the variation in unity among the congressional Democratic caucus on civil rights votes can be explained by voters' shifting preferences on racial issues. Jacobson (2004) and Aldrich et al. (2007) also find that much (though not all) of the recent polarization of the congressional parties can be explained by the increasing homogeneity of congressional districts. Indeed, the whole literature on party realignments is predicated on the notion that voters' preferences will occasionally shift in a dramatic, often unanticipated way, forcing elected partisans to change their behavior or risk electoral defeat (Burnham 1965; Schattschneider 1942; Sundquist 1983; Rogin and Shover 1970). Thanks to shifting voter preferences, for example, officeholders in the mid-1850s could no longer equivocate on slavery, as the Whig Party had essentially done for decades. You were either with the slaveholders or you were against them. An officeholder who preferred Whig economic policies but supported the institution of slavery suddenly had to make a choice, and had to make it quickly.

This view that voters determine changes in party coherence and agendas has a hard time surviving Bartels's (2000) observation that shifts in voter partisanship tend to follow, rather than precede, shifts in congressional partisanship. It seems, that is, that voters follow the cues of party leaders rather than the other way around (Hetherington 2001). These objections strongly suggest the importance of the second category of extralegislative forces: outside elites. This term refers to activists, party bosses, interest groups, and other key political actors outside the government with a strong interest in affecting government behavior. These outsiders wield power over legislators through their control over party nominations and the resources needed to win them. If such outsiders serve as gatekeepers to holding public office, we would expect that shifts in external party coalitions will lead to important changes in legislative voting behavior, even if there has been no concomitant shift in mass voting behavior.

Historically, these outside actors have been able to alter politicians' behavior without changes in the preferences of the mass public. For example, some Democratic officeholders' embrace of civil rights in the late 1940s was not an adjustment to voter demands. Rather, the interest group Americans for Democratic Action essentially forced the issue of racial equality on President Harry Truman, whose nomination in 1948 was far from assured. Truman sided with the ADA and won the nomination, but this led to the Dixiecrats bolting the Democratic Convention in 1948 (Bawn et al. 2006). Similarly, recent literature has cast doubt on the designation of the 1896 election as a critical realignment of the electorate (Mayhew 2004; Bartels 1998; Stonecash and Silina 2005). There were few changes in electoral behavior around that period. Instead, it was a matter of political activists seizing power: Western silver-coinage advocates took control of Democratic nominations from eastern gold-standard support- ers. Other examples of outsider-led (rather than electorate-induced) changes in party priorities include the creation of the Republican Party in the 1850s and the takeover of that party in 1964 by the conservative Gold- water wing. What is left of realignment theory is pretty well decimated by Mayhew's (2000) analysis, in which he concludes, "The claims of the re- alignments genre do not hold up well, and the genre's illuminative power has not proven to be great" (471). Specifically, valence issues (Stokes 1966) or even random coin-tosses will explain more of presidential elec- tion history than realignment theory will.

Note, then, where this leaves us. Party leaders in a legislature may de- sire strong party behavior, but ultimately they are at the mercy of forces outside the legislature. And while voters may wish to control their elected officials, only a few key elites outside the legislature have the power over party nominations to determine just what the legislative parties will look like and fight for. But in order for these key elites to actually exert such control, they need to coordinate their activities. They need to be orga- nized. So what does such an organization look like? What follows are two examples of modern party organizations in California.

MAXINE WATERS AND THE TOM BRADLEY ORGANIZATION

Democratic Congresswoman Maxine Waters is a well-established politi- cal powerhouse in Southern California. Although her reputation for ad- hering to somewhat extreme viewpoints (such as the CIA–crack cocaine connection) has limited her power in Washington, her status as a king- maker within California is not disputed. As described briefly in the intro- duction, Waters regularly selects candidates to run in primaries for local, state, and federal office in her area of Los Angeles and provides those candidates with valuable endorsements, funds, and a spot on her sample ballot, which is mailed to voters throughout the city and has been shown to be highly influential in local elections (Lewis 2003). Her alliances with local unions and churches can help produce substantial Election Day get-out-the-vote efforts on behalf of her favored candidates.

A notable feature of Waters's organization is that it was not originally hers. Indeed, she is more properly thought of as the heiress to an organization that her mentor, former Los Angeles mayor Tom Bradley, helped to build along with Democratic activists and donors in the 1960s and 1970s. As effectively described by Sonenshein (1984), Bradley's organization was, at its peak, something of a citywide machine that not only aided the mayor's reelection efforts but also supported campaigns for his allies on the city council and in the state assembly, groomed activists for eventual runs for office, forged links with state and federal officials to ensure a steady flow of patronage funds, and rewarded campaign supporters and activists from competitive precincts with prestigious city commissionerships and staff jobs.

Moreover, this organization didn't begin with Bradley. As a young activist in the 1950s, the future mayor had to work his way up within a loose political network in order to get a seat on the city council in the first place. Many of the people who would make up Bradley's inner circle when he became mayor (people like Maurice Weiner, a staffer for Democratic congressman Ed Roybal) were already important players in Los Angeles politics in the late 1950s when Bradley first became interested in running for office. Most were involved in Democratic club politics under the auspices of the California Democratic Council (CDC). Indeed, although Los Angeles was considered a nonpartisan city at that time (Banfield and Wilson 1965), CDC clubs were beginning to play an important role in local politics, slating and backing at least half a dozen city council candidates between 1953 and 1964 (Carney 1964).

Bradley distinguished himself among the members of his local Democratic club through his activism, through recruiting other members, and by building a following among local African American and Jewish voters. When he got involved in a high-profile city council recall campaign in 1961, and when he ran for a council seat in 1963, he won substantial backing from members of the CDC and even from Mayor Sam Yorty, with whom Bradley would have several bitter fights later in his career. This support allowed Bradley to stand out amid a slate of a few dozen local black candidates in his district. As Weiner described it, "People regarded Bradley as someone who had paid his dues. And they were glad, it seemed, to repay him" (Sonenshein 1984: 51). And in his 1969 mayoral race, many of Bradley's campaign staff slots were filled by people on loan from other elected officials. In other words, Bradley rose to power abetted by a network of activists and officeholders, and he built his organization on top of the existing partisan structure.

As the Bradley organization matured in the 1970s and 1980s, it took on the flavor of a political machine, dispensing patronage and influencing elections throughout the city. Through his appointment powers and his network of allies on the council, Bradley was able to reward donors and loyal campaign workers with prestigious city commissionerships and steady public jobs. Furthermore, Bradley regularly dispatched teams of advisers to run the campaigns of candidates he supported for city council and state legislative seats. One of these advisers was Maxine Waters, who, after working on several Bradley-backed campaigns, won her own assembly seat in 1976 through the assistance of Bradley and his allies. As one of Bradley's most effective protégés, Waters has built on the organization and perpetuated its influence over politics in Los Angeles.

BILL THOMAS AND THE CENTRAL VALLEY REPUBLICAN MACHINE

Republican Bill Thomas, who served in the U.S. Congress from 1979 to 2007, is in many ways a polar opposite to Maxine Waters. For one thing, when he was chair of the House Ways and Means Committee, he obviously exerted a great deal more power in Washington than Waters ever has. And the conservative, largely rural constituency in California's San Joaquin Valley that reelected him for more than two decades bears little similarity to Waters's liberal inner-city district.

Yet, in terms of their style of organizing local politics, both Thomas and Waters appear to be cut from similar cloth. Thomas is widely feared and revered as a kingmaker in Republican politics in Bakersfield and the surrounding valley communities. "In Kern County," one reporter notes, "most political figures are gauged by their relationship to the county's powerful but controversial congressman, Republican Bill Thomas" (Pollard 1999). He rose to power, interestingly enough, as a moderate Republican professor of political science at Bakersfield Community College, offering local Republican operatives suggestions for revitalizing their party organization and making their candidates more competitive (Bardella 2004). Thomas routinely selects and endorses candidates in primaries for state, local, and federal offices throughout the southern San

Joaquin Valley. His backing is widely sought by Republican office seekers as a symbol of political viability, often leading to donations and endorsements from other officeholders, as well as from local conservative groups and business leaders. Such assistance is widely credited with getting the little-known twenty-eight-year-old Devin Nunes, who had worked on one of Thomas's campaigns, elected to Congress in 2002 (Werner 2004). Those who have served on Thomas's staff, including U.S. representative Kevin McCarthy and state senator Roy Ashburn, have found paths cleared for them in their own quests for office.

Although Thomas's influence is considered strongest within his own community, it is felt throughout the conservative San Joaquin Valley. In a tightly contested primary race for an open congressional district in suburban Sacramento in 2004, for example, Thomas provided candidate Dan Lungren with copious funds and access to his own fund-raiser. This assistance helped Lungren edge out state senator Rico Oller by less than 3,000 votes (Werner 2004).

What do we make of the Waters and Thomas organizations as parties? They are, notably, not legislative coalitions. Thomas was capable as a legislative mechanic—Waters is somewhat less so—but their power in California does not stem from their ability to craft or pass federal legislation. The collective action dilemmas they are trying to resolve do not originate in the House of Representatives. These organizations are also not traditional party groups in the model of Tammany Hall. Waters and Thomas are not bosses, in the traditional sense of the word, in that they do not spend much of their days meting out patronage in exchange for favors. Finally, there is little evidence that these two are or ever have been single-minded seekers of reelection. Both Waters and Thomas are fierce partisan fighters, and they regularly slate candidates on the basis of their loyalty to a coherent ideology.

The sort of party politics in which Waters and Thomas are engaged is different from how we typically think of parties. They seem to derive some authority from their status as veteran members of Congress, yet their political power with California seems to stem mostly from their skill in picking candidates for primary elections and getting them elected. This skill involves building and utilizing alliances with donors, activists, and other prominent partisan figures throughout their respective communities.

Importantly, both Waters and Thomas are playing key roles in the continued polarization of American politics. Although moderate on such key social issues as abortion and gun control, Thomas doesn't shy away from bombastic rhetoric or tactics in supporting his party over the Democrats, and he was singularly partisan in his administration of his duties on Capitol Hill. Indeed, while chairing a raucous Ways and Means Committee session on a pension bill, Thomas famously called in the Capitol police to remove the committee's Democrats from a library where they were attempting to caucus (Eilperin and Crenshaw 2003). Maxine Waters, meanwhile, has championed numerous far-left causes throughout her career. Long before the public soured on the Iraq War, for example, she accused President Bush of sending "American military men and women to be killed and maimed in a war based on a web of lies and deceit" (Waters 2004). Her voting record has placed her among the six most liberal members of the House in the past eight consecutive congresses. Both Waters and Thomas have also made a point of working for the nomination of like-minded candidates in their home communities.

The Waters and Thomas organizations, as I will show in subsequent chapters, are far from unique. They are examples of what I call informal party organizations, or IPOs: loose coalitions of activists, donors, and key officeholders who exert control over party nominations. This seems to be the dominant form of party activity in California and, I believe, elsewhere. If this is what's going on, then we need to upgrade our understanding of party dynamics. This is what I seek to do in the remainder of this chapter. Before doing that, though, it is helpful to think carefully about why party organizations form in the first place.

SERIOUSLY, WHY PARTIES?

In his famous book *Why Parties?* John Aldrich (1995) builds an account of party origin that is based on the goals that politicians are trying to accomplish. I do much the same in this section, reaching many parallel conclusions—but with one major difference. I pose the *Why Parties?* question for the whole panoply of players involved in party politics, not simply for candidates and officeholders.

Supply and Demand

Party organizations can be viewed from both a supply and a demand side. From the supply side, a few key officeholders offer the promise of delivering what constituents want from government—everything from lost Social Security checks to special provisions in the law to fat contracts to new highways. They offer this help for the same reason that business entrepreneurs offer products to customers: because they expect to profit from meeting a market need. And, as in other market situations, the political entrepreneurs attempt to grow their market share, for the simple reason that greater market share generates greater returns to the entrepreneur. These returns may be material or ideological, or they may simply consist of the personal enjoyment of power. The last is not to be neglected. To no small degree, power is its own reward for many officeholders, and building up an organization allows one to obtain more of it.

Demand for party organization comes from two main groups of people: resource donors and candidates. Resource donors—and here I include not just financial supporters of candidates, but unions, clubs, and other groups that donate the time, labor, and expertise that can be crucial in an electoral campaign—want to be able to control some aspect of government behavior. In essence, they wish to "buy" a piece of the government. Doing so without organization, however, is virtually impossible. As Schattschneider (1942) notes, there are hundreds of thousands of interests in the United States, each with the desire to affect public policy in some way. But even the wealthiest government must eventually discriminate among solicitors, and members of an interest invariably have differing levels of commitment to their cause. Given the multitude of demands on government and the challenges of keeping an interest united and committed, it is nearly impossible for an individual or an interest to affect government behavior. This feat is only possible through organization.

This argument applies as strongly to issue activists seeking their ideal of "good public policy" from government as it does to businesspeople seeking material favors. That is, activists want to be in close contact with the people who make the decisions, to be able to aggregate their individually small contributions into something to which a politician must pay attention, and to avoid making wasteful contributions to losers. Parties have often disliked "doing business" with activists because activists care about issues that are divisive to machine organizations. But if the concerns of the issue activists are organized by ideology, which they nowadays are, the potential for internal division is lessened. And if the activists are willing to put their money or their labor on the line for the party, officeholders may be quite pleased to respond to their demands upon the political system.

Besides benefit seekers, a second source of demand for the creation of party organizations is staff members and aspiring candidates. Staffers, for their part, desire some stability and predictability in their careers. Given levels of turnover in government, many staff jobs only last two or four years, and campaign jobs just a few months. If the officeholder is not well tied to an established organization, it may be difficult to find a job with her in the first place. And if the staffer works for a losing campaign, it will be all the harder for her to find a new job if the candidate was unaffiliated. Informal party organizations can lend some order to this chaos. The loose affiliation among various officeholders, and the fact that members of legislative chambers often know one another quite well, means that individual workers can hope to move up a reasonably stable and meritocratic career ladder. Los Angeles mayor Tom Bradley, for example, did not have ample staff positions to hire all his loyal activists, but he was able to find jobs for supporters in the offices of some of his close city council allies (Sonenshein 1984: 146). By working for an affiliated politician, staffers can be sure that they will quickly be able to find a new job when their boss leaves office or when the campaign ends, even if it is an unsuccessful one.

The other source of demand for party organizations comes from people who aspire to run for office. More than anything, these people want a defined career path to office. One way to achieve that is to align oneself with a prominent officeholder by serving as a staffer, or as a trustworthy lobbyist, adviser, or fund-raiser. Such a relationship offers ready access to donors, activists, brokers, reporters, and other contacts necessary for a serious run for office. But there are drawbacks. The aspiring politician may have to wait until the officeholder retires or dies to get a shot at running for office, and there may be other apparatchiks with similar intentions. Similarly, if the officeholder commits some apostasy or crime or leaves office in disgrace, the aspirant's ambitions are thwarted.

Party organizations offer a solution to these problems. The aspiring politician can move from office to office, building contacts and experience along the way, without incurring the risks of being closely tied to just one officeholder. Plus, there are always openings for new candidates within an organization and a defined pecking order determining whose turn it is to run. Only established party organizations can credibly promise such a career path in politics.

Party organizations thus arise both because elected officials have an interest in supplying benefits from the government and because donors, workers, and candidates demand them. At the nexus of this supply and demand lies an organizational arrangement that meets the needs of all participants: long, profitable, and influential careers for officeholders; influence and efficiency for donors; and a career ladder for aspiring politicians.

A Digression on Patronage and Honest Graft in Their Modern Forms

The preceding discussion assumes that public officials still perform favors and provide preferential services to individual constituents. It assumes, that is, that patronage and graft still exist on a significant scale. One may legitimately object, then, if there is so much favoritism and graft occurring, why do we not hear of more arrests?

The answer is that favoritism and graft can occur without running technically afoul of the law. To understand this, one merely need to reflect on the lessons of George Washington Plunkitt, a New York state legislator of the late 1800s and ranking member of the Tammany organization. Plunkitt's greatest contribution to our political lexicon was the term *honest graft*, by which he meant the legal (if ethically questionable) means for politicians to enrich themselves personally through their connections. For example, when, through his political contacts, Plunkitt learned a public park was to be built in a certain area of New York, he rushed out and bought up the land for a song. The taxpayers then needed to buy the land from him. "Ain't it perfectly honest to charge a good price and make a profit on my investment and foresight?" asked Plunkitt. "Of course, it is. Well, that's honest graft" (Riordan 1963). Plunkitt's motto (which he encouraged others to adopt) was simply "I seen my opportunities and I took 'em."

Is there any reason to believe that modern politicians are constitutionally different from Plunkitt and his peers? Outright favoritism, theft of public treasuries, or giving out public jobs for political favors are certainly illegal in their most blatant forms. But it is reasonable to assume that public officials will engage in similar activities that fall just short of criminality, particularly when such activities ensure political success. "Every good man looks after his friends," Plunkitt reminds us, "and any man who doesn't isn't likely to be popular" (Riordan 1963).

Patronage, defined broadly, is nothing more than "the manipulation of public authority for the special benefit of officeholders, their sponsors, business associates, and friends" (Mansfield 1965: 118). Mansfield notes that the modern spoils system may come in a variety of shapes and sizes, including

> unduly restrictive specifications for contract bidding, favoritism in contract awards, and preference or discrimination in the inspection of contract performance; special treatment for inmates of institutions; discriminatory enforcement of the criminal law and of building, health, zoning, and other codes; differential tax assessments; tariff, franchise, and license privileges; "honest graft" in the acquisition of real estate; and the like. (118)

This definition echoes Wilson's (1973: 97) description of patronage as jobs, contracts, professional opportunities, and legal exemptions resulting from one's contact with and loyalty to a local regime. So defined, patronage is alive and well, as are the organizations that specialize in dealing in these forms of patronage.

Consider, for example, a land developer who wants to encourage businesses and homeowners to relocate to an uninhabited area that she happens to own. The presence of roads and running water would certainly relieve potential investors' anxieties about the project. Securing roads and plumbing, however, requires approval and funding from either city or county government (or both). If the land development is near a coastline or some other protected land, the project may require approval from the state or federal government (or both). And depending on local spending rules, a bond or tax measure may need to be passed by the electorate to help fund the venture. The developer is probably wealthy and may gain some access to officeholders through generous campaign donations, but how can she win support from all the key people at the right time to make the development a worthwhile venture? How does she know how to allocate her money and lobbying efforts, or does she just contribute equally (and no doubt wastefully) to all the officeholders in her area? And how does she make her voice heard among the din of other developers, environmental protection organizations, suburban sprawl opponents, and the myriad other groups demanding attention and funds from their governments? She might have potential allies in the form of other land developers, but they may be more committed to other projects and not be willing to back her at key junctures. What is an influence seeker to do?

This problem, and one possible solution, was outlined by Tammany Hall boss Richard Croker, who was asked by reform-minded journalist Lincoln Steffens, "Why should there be bosses when cities had mayors, council, and judges?" Croker replied, "It's because there's a mayor *and* a council *and* judges *and*—a hundred other men to deal with. . . . A business man wants to do business with one man, and one who is always there to remember and carry out the—business." As Walsh (1972: 4) explains, "The boss, while normally holding no public office, served as an unofficial nervous system for a decapitated monster whose ever extending extremities might otherwise flay unknowing bystanders with total unpredictability. The boss, at least, was predictable."

In his early-twentieth-century treatise on machine politics, Kent (1924) finds similar value in the party boss:

> What, for instance, would these business interests do without the machine boss? Where, when legislative action of a disastrous kind threatens, would they go, if there were no boss? How would they stop a bill that affected them adversely, or pass one that they wanted passed? They could do it, of course, but not easily. It would mean going to the seat of the legislative body themselves, or employing expensive lawyers and lobbyists, making a hard, costly, and disagreeable fight, getting down into the mess of politics personally and fighting their way out. They would have to deal with all sorts of sub-bosses, ward executives, district leaders, and county overlords. They would have to count noses, pore over roll calls, locate the controlling influence over delegations. (90–91)

Of course, bossism isn't necessarily the solution to this problem. The solution is *organization,* and bossism is but one of its forms.

As these authors suggest, one vital function that party organizations perform is the coordination of activities across multiple levels of government. Without such coordination, it is nearly impossible to get most projects done. As Schattschneider (1942) argued, the thousands of interest groups peppering the national landscape also desire party organizations because parties give them an edge when competing for the government's attention and resources. Although Schattschneider didn't say it specifically, it follows that if a group is going to get what it wants out of the public sector, it will need compliance among several different levels of government. Thus the members of an informal party organization will try to support candidates at the federal, state, county, and municipal levels of government.

For ideologically motivated members, the commitment to various issues does not end at the state or city border—all levels of government are important to the organization. For those with more material motivations, access to many levels of government is important because their support-ers regularly have needs from those various levels. Transportation policy is just one example of the need for intergovernmental cooperation. Local officeholders may be the first to recognize the need for a bridge, train, or freeway in an area, but they need the support of state and federal office-holders to get ample funding and land use privileges. The funds will change governmental hands multiple times over the course of the proj-ect. A special purpose government, such as a local transit authority or port authority, may even be created in the process to build and maintain the project. If a business group wants to ensure that the new construction project serves the right communities, hires the right companies who em-ploy the right unions, and wins plaudits for the right officeholders, coor-dination across many levels of government is essential.

This need for coordination among multiple governments leads to an emphasis on local control. An informal party organization exerts the most leverage over those officeholders who rely upon it for election or reelec-tion (or, more specifically, nomination and renomination), and it exerts the most influence over those voters who are familiar with its public lead-ers. If an IPO wants to control nominations at the federal, state, and mu-nicipal levels and extract benefits from the incumbents it supports, it will really only be able to do so by operating locally.

At this point, the reader may object to my claim that patronage—even if legal—exists on a widespread basis today. Some authors claim that the conditions that allowed patronage to prosper no longer exist. As Sorauf (1960: 31) has argued, "Rising levels of prosperity, higher educational levels, declining numbers of unassimilated groups, and greater concern by government for the unfortunate all point to a decline of the boss and machine and of the patronage they relied on." Residents of East Los An-geles, Brooklyn's Bedford-Stuyvesant neighborhood, and Chicago's South Side would no doubt take issue with this report. If machines de-pend on the presence of urban poverty and poorly assimilated immigrant groups, then there is plenty to sustain them in essentially all major Amer-ican cities and many minor ones.

Nontraditional forms of patronage may also provide a basis for politi-cal organizations. Although the typical view of patronage is one of low-paying spoils jobs and charity payments that can be handed out to regime supporters, officeholders can reward adherents in many other ways. Staff positions in the offices of city, county, state, and federal elected officials, while not as numerous as the old bureaucratic positions now in the hands of civil service employees, have grown substantially in number in recent decades and provide livelihoods to dozens or even hundreds of an urban machine's key supporters. These staffers supply vital campaign assistance to their bosses and sometimes—but not always—go off the clock to aid friendly candidates for other offices. As Macartney (1975: 194) found in his survey of Los Angeles area elected officials, "Staff campaigning on government time is both widespread and illegal." Guerra (2002) adds, "In some respects [staff campaigning is] much more effective [than the Chicago machines], politically speaking, not in terms of political patronage, but in terms of delivering the vote. . . . These are professional, political, and public servants, who, on a moment's notice, can shift gears from politics to policy, back and forth."

The increasing size of public staffs in recent decades makes for more effective casework. For constituents in need of assistance with Social Security benefits, Medicaid coverage, law enforcement, or land use disputes, their local public officials have staff members who are at the ready (Fiorina 1977). As Wolfinger (1972: 385) notes, the growth of the welfare state has not lessened the responsibilities of the old political machines. Rather, "continuing growth in the scope, complexity, and impersonality of institutional life [may] produce greater need for politicians to mediate between individuals and their government."

"For holders of local office," says Macartney (1975: 202), "and increasingly for congressmen and state legislators, the district office is becoming a patronage-dispensing-station, not unlike the clubhouses of the old machines." Macartney (228) sums up the influence of staffers by noting, "Staffing can and does fulfill . . . traditional party 'functions,' such as political recruitment, tending to the public's political education and socialization (through the efforts of public relations aides), acting as a linkage between governors and governed, and even dispensing welfare (casework) as the party's machines used to."

In short, the decline of traditional forms of patronage, material benefits, and what Plunkitt called "honest graft" since the golden age of the TPO does not mean that most patronage has disappeared. Nor does it signify a more general decline in the incentives of individuals to be active in political parties. Purposive incentives, while carrying their own sets of challenges, can and have been used to sustain political organizations. And other, less traditional forms of patronage—including public staff positions, casework, and public works projects—can substitute for the traditional ones.

This discussion suggests the need for a theory of parties that accounts for the coordination of various actors both inside and outside the government. Before describing how this coordination occurs, it would be helpful for me to be more concrete about the individuals who inhabit modern political parties. In my taxonomy, there are four basic types:

1. *Officeholders and candidates.* Informal party organizations are usually identified with the one or two prominent officeholders who lead them. These officeholders leverage their relationships with other incumbents, their control over government machinery, and their name recognition among voters to influence elections and procure benefits for the IPO's supporters. Candidates often emerge from the activist community or the officeholder's staff. They are selected for their loyalty to an IPO and for various candidate qualities (name recognition, access to campaign money, etc.). They receive assistance from the IPO, including additional campaign funds and endorsements, that all but assures them the nomination. In return, they are expected to remain loyal to the IPO's backers once in office—they may be de-nominated if they stray too far from a particular agenda.

2. *Benefit seekers.* These actors include businesses, unions, civic organizations, and ordinary voters who wish to control government output. They may have ideological concerns of their own, but those concerns usually come second to more pragmatic issues of how to secure material government benefits for themselves or their membership. Benefit seekers often have considerable sums of money to contribute directly to candidates or to IPO leaders, although sometimes they will donate labor or advice. Through such donations, benefit seekers hope to curry favor with the IPO leaders and their anointed candidates, giving them influence over or at least access to the political process and an edge over rival organizations that do not make such contributions.

3. *Political activists.* These individuals, who can usually be found in volunteer associations or in local formal party organizations, are usually driven by ideological motivations to try to influence government to move in some direction or to address some pressing public issue. Activists may also enjoy solidary (social) benefits from simply associating with their like-minded peers (Wilson 1973). Others may hope to rise in politics, perhaps to the status of officeholder. Activists are usually less pragmatic and more purposive than benefit seekers; they do not tolerate compro-

mise among the elected officials they support, and they usually support the more ideologically extreme candidates. Activists usually contribute to candidates and IPOs through their labor, serving as campaign staffers and Election Day canvassers.

4. *Brokers.* These actors help coordinate actions among the other three types. Brokers are seasoned political players, usually experienced officeholders, lobbyists, or campaign consultants, who help maintain the organization's connections. They perform the essential function of centralizing and dispensing money and other resources necessary to campaign for office. For example, money brokers arrange small fund-raisers that put many individual donors in touch with credible candidates. Although the money they give to any particular candidate may be too small to gain much influence, regular giving through a broker assures that, when donors need help, the broker will remember them. The broker, who knows several officeholders well, may then have the pull to obtain the desired benefit on behalf of the donor. Candidates like brokers because they are a centralized source of campaign resources. Individual donors like brokers because they are a way of leveraging their donations.

One particular type of broker is the archetypal political "boss." Even if this person is not a prominent officeholder, he or she may be in a position to decide which candidates to recruit or support and to deploy other people's time, labor, and money accordingly. Brokers of all types are highly attuned to the political environment and follow the cues of local leaders to know which candidates have the support to run credible races. Brokers may be motivated by a combination of ideological and material goals; they can't operate if they can't turn a profit, but politics is often not their main source of income. Rather, they become so involved because they desire to achieve some goal in politics.

Individual actors may and occasionally do occupy more than one role (Clark and Wilson 1961). For example, an officeholder may, by involving herself in multiple campaigns, also be an activist. A businessperson may, as a benefit seeker, donate cash or other resources to a campaign, and may also work for that campaign for ideological reasons. The organization that these different actors form may be large and somewhat loosely defined, but it can usually be identified by the one or two high-profile personalities who lead it.

These informal organizations exist for the sole purpose of controlling government—or at least a piece of it. The distinction between holding an office, as an individual politician might want to do, and controlling a part of the government is critical. Controlling part of the government allows a group to actually deliver goods: ideological goods to activists, special benefits to donors, jobs to party workers. Because many goods require action across levels of government, and also because party supporters may want discrete goods out of multiple levels of government, control of government must span levels. Control need not be total. It merely needs to be sufficient to supply party supporters with the particular goods they require to remain part of the IPO.

Parties and Nominations

Following Schattschneider (1942), I offer a model of parties that sees control of nominations as the key to control of the government. My contribution is to adapt this idea to contemporary conditions. If *formal* party organizations are not capable of controlling the nominations process (as appears increasingly to be the case), others will do the job. I propose that the job will be filled by informal party organizations (IPOs): loose affiliations among political actors, including candidates, officeholders, benefit seekers, activists, and brokers who facilitate relationships among the others.

My approach resonates with other important strands in the parties literature. Schlesinger (1985) and Aldrich (1983, 1995), for example, have suggested that the definition of party organization should include both ambitious office seekers and benefit seekers who "hold, or have access to, critical resources that office seekers need" (Aldrich 1995: 20). Aldrich's activists or "policy demanders" tend to be ideologically extreme and demand no small degree of extremity from prospective nominees. Candidates recognize that moving away from the median voter may be costly in terms of votes, but that cost may be outweighed by the resources they receive from pleased activists. Similarly, Miller and Schofield (2003) see activists, rather than voters, as the main cause of party realignments. Schwartz's (1990) study of Illinois Republicans and Monroe's (2001) analysis of Los Angeles politicians, meanwhile, suggest that the network concept of party captures more truth than the older hierarchical model. Bernstein (1999) and Doherty (2006) find that political consultants form part of an "expanded party." Cohen et al. (2008) provide a powerful critique of the candidate-centered school of American politics, demonstrating that an alliance of donors and elite endorsers in each party have controlled presidential nominations since 1980. Recently, Dominguez (2005) has found evidence of a network of donors and endorsers who coordinate to promote some candidates in congressional primaries and prevent others from winning, and Koger, Masket, and Noel (2008) have used the direct mail address market to chart out the contours of extended party networks.

I draw from many of these works in my research. However, most of these studies focus on national politics, and Schwartz's (1990) otherwise compelling study of a state party does not delve much into a generalizable theory of local party organization. Indeed, there have been relatively few studies of parties that have actually gotten inside a local party organization to understand how it is run. This is understandable—the research is difficult and time-consuming, and the resulting scholarship is often descriptive rather than theoretical. Ehrenhalt's (1991) sketches of power in communities from Concord, California, to Sioux City, South Dakota, for example, give us some idea of the range of organizational structures that can govern a local community, although they don't give us much of a framework for understanding why a type of structure would emerge in one place and not another.

Epstein's (1958) rich descriptions of politics in Wisconsin, while admittedly atheoretical, provide some interesting points of comparison for California. After all, the Badger State was also home to a particularly strong variant of Progressivism in the first half of the twentieth century, producing an antiparty ideology similar to that found on the West Coast: "Wisconsin law treats parties as though they might pervert the real will of the voters," notes Epstein (31). Epstein's study demonstrates how party elites will often work outside of the formal party organizations to get what they need out of politics:

> For over twenty years, the regular or conservative Republicans had found it convenient to focus their activities, not in the statutory party, but the Republican Voluntary Committee (later called the Republican Party of Wisconsin). In the 1920s, the Voluntary Committee was necessary because the La Follettes controlled the statutory organization, but later (and to some extent always) the unofficial vehicle was useful as a means of avoiding the financial limitations imposed by law on the official party. Similarly the Democrats, when they wanted in 1948 to build a liberal-oriented organization, chose the unofficial form in order to have a less closely regulated kind of party. (51)

Clarence Stone offers something of a theory of local political organization in his analysis of Atlanta (1989), helping us understand why informal organizations emerge and how they are sustained. Stone's postwar Atlanta is a city run by an informal, biracial coalition of government officials and downtown business elites. Its leadership has helped avoid the racial strife encountered by many other Southern cities, but at a cost: poverty and other social maladies have gone largely unaddressed and have festered. Stone's study is specific to Atlanta, but his regime theory is certainly generalizable. Urban areas around the globe, after all, are marked by institutional sectors (government, business, entertainment, civic associations, etc.) that have no official unifying command structure. In such places, often an informal "regime" will emerge, proving itself very useful to members of different sectors who want to get things done. As Stone (1989) explains,

> The regime is purposive, created and maintained as a way of facilitating action. In a very important sense, *a regime is empowering*. Its supporters see it as a means for achieving coordinated efforts that might not otherwise be realized. (4–5; emphasis in original)

This certainly helps us understand why people get involved in politics and how important informal associations can be. However, there is little examination of parties per se, and neither Stone, Epstein, nor Ehrenhalt pays much attention to the dynamics of party nominations (although Epstein does note intraparty factionalism among Republicans). Here I must improvise.

Controlling Nominations

Given the interests of IPOs in controlling government, they fall within the classic definitions of parties provided by Schattschneider and Wilson. The former refers to a party as an organized attempt to seize power (Schattschneider 1942), the latter calls it "a group of persons who consciously coordinate their activities so as to influence the choice of candidates for elective office" (Wilson 1973: 95). These esteemed authors notably do not demand that this group of persons belong to some official party organization. So long as they are coordinating to influence the choice of candidates and thereby control government, they *are* the party organization.

Controlling government, of course, is no small task. To achieve that, the group must agree on good candidates for office. Members of IPOs attempt to find candidates who will work with them rather than competing organizations, and will try to create a united front to support these candidates (Schattschneider 1942).

Although much research on parties focuses on their performance in general elections, it is the primary election—or caucus, convention, or whatever means by which candidates are nominated—that determines who and what the party is. General elections obviously matter, but, as we saw in the introductory chapter, their outcomes are usually assured well in advance. In both the U.S. Congress and the California assembly, usually far fewer than 10 percent of legislative seats are considered "in play" in a given election.

Primary elections, by contrast, are far less predictable and far more open to manipulation. Voters choosing among candidates in a primary lack the party cue to guide them, relying on what information they can cheaply find to help them distinguish between candidates. Advertisements, yard signs, endorsements, slate mailers—all things that informal party organizations can produce—thus become much more powerful electoral tools, and the organization that can dominate those forms of communication holds an enormous advantage.

In addition, there are fewer voters to influence in a primary. In the 2002 primary election, for example, only 25 percent of California's eligible voters made it to the polls, as compared with 36 percent in the general election that year. In a hotly contested Democratic primary in the state's Forty-eighth Assembly District that year, only 26,108 of the district's 104,046 registered Democrats bothered to vote. A few thousand or even a few hundred votes in one direction or another can often change the outcome of a primary, and indeed in the Forty-eighth District, Mark Ridley Thomas beat Mike Davis by a mere 1,452 votes. As Kent (1924) argues, low turnout in primaries

> plays directly into the hands of the machine. This is what makes it possible for the machine to limit our choice in the general election to its choice in the primaries. This is the reason machines are powerful and a sufficient explanation of why so many unfit men are in public office. It can all be summed up in the single statement: The voters will not take part in the primaries. (4–5)

It is no accident that during the 2003 California budget crisis, Senator Jim Brulte (R-Rancho Cucamonga) threatened wavering Republicans in primaries. The primary election, with its low turnout and low information environment, is much easier for a party organization to manipulate than the general election. Moreover, the primary is usually the only election that matters, since the general election for both state and federal legislatures is often a fait accompli. And even if general elections were more dynamic, the primary would still be the place to study party politics. A political organization, notes Kent (1924: 11), "can lose its candidate time after time in the general election without greatly diminishing its strength or loosing the grip of its leaders. . . . But if it loses in the primaries, it is out of business. Any organization that cannot carry the primary election is a defunct organization." Kent (1924) persuasively argues for the importance of primaries when he states,

> Primaries are really the key to politics. There is no way for party candidates to get on the general election ballot except through the primaries. Primaries are the exclusive gate through which all party candidates must pass. Control of that gate in any community means control of the political situation in that community. It makes no difference whether the candidates who pass through the gate are knocked down in the general election or not, the next set of candidates must pass through the primary gate just the same. It ought to be plain, then, that so long as the machine controls the primaries, it is in a position to limit the choice of the voters in the general election to its choice in the primaries. That is the real secret of its power, and, so long as it holds that power, it cannot be put out of business. (7)

Although Kent was describing the machines of his day, his description could well be applied to any organization seeking to influence public affairs. If an organization wants to control a part of government, it must ensure that its candidate can win the primary. The nomination fight is therefore the appropriate place to study local party strength and character.

IPOs thus control government by controlling the nomination process. But how do they do that? Quite simply, they follow the same logic that Aldrich (1995) and Schwartz (1989) outlined for members of legislatures: they form minimal winning coalitions. That is, they work with just enough people—but no more—to control the outcome of a primary. An ideological activist will form an alliance with enough major donors so that the candidates she backs will receive sufficient funds to prevail in a contested primary. A business leader will find enough prominent local citizens who can make the endorsements that will tip an election. Having too few people in an IPO is futile since they won't be able to control a primary. Too many means that the individual members have to compromise more than necessary to achieve what they want. Trial and error will tell the members of these groups just how many people they need to involve.

Assembling these coalitions and figuring out just how many people to involve are, of course, costly exercises. The leaders of these groups would rather not have to do these tasks every election cycle. It makes far more sense for these organizations to be relatively permanent. Thus will they continue over the years from election to election, holding the same leaders and slating roughly the same group of candidates, albeit for different positions.

The payoff for installing a slate of candidates—the control of a portion of government and the attendant subsidies, ideological benefits, and preferential treatment—is potentially very large. It is therefore reasonable to expect that those community actors not included in the IPO will form their own alliance. And since primaries are, for the most part, winner-take-all events, and since most legislative districts in the United States are single-member districts, Duverger's Law would lead us to expect just two factions to emerge. And because these factions share a party identification, there will not be an enormous ideological difference between the two. As Key (1949: 304) described factional disputes in the one-party South, "campaigns often are the emptiest sorts of debates over personalities, over means for the achievement of what everybody agrees on." We can expect such trivial distinctions between intraparty groups in any functionally one-party region. But the distinction between the two groups is real: if you are with Group A, you will suffer when Group B wins, and vice versa.

The degree to which these factions can work together depends largely on how competitive a given district is. If a district is winnable by either political party, then the two factions within a party may attempt to bridge differences for that race, rather than have a costly primary that ends up handing the seat to the other party. However, if the area strongly leans toward one party, there is no particular need for factions within that party to work past their differences. The latter appears to be the typical situation in the vast majority of congressional and state legislative districts across the country.

Because these alliances are located in the communities where voting occurs, they are better able to control politics than alliances located within a legislature. That is, within a legislature, leaders hold coalitional lines together through the use of whips and caucuses, by rewarding or denying members privileges, chairmanships, and office resources, and by directly persuading members. Even the most obstinate legislative coalition member must be tolerated, though; a legislative leader cannot fire another legislator.

Conversely, an IPO maintains its grip on politics by serving as the gatekeeper to office. If an officeholder is acting in a manner that the IPO leaders find unacceptable, that officeholder will not be cajoled or denied resources; she will be fired. IPO leaders can find a more suitable candidate and provide her with the funds, endorsements, and Election Day labor she needs to defeat the incumbent.

By serving as the gatekeeper to party nominations, IPOs ensure that only the sorts of people they like—people who will vote in a certain ideological fashion or will provide particular benefits to their backers—will be able to serve in government. And once the IPO has filled the local, state, and federal offices in its region with supportive politicians, it can fulfill the desires of its participating members: patronage jobs, construction projects, preferential regulatory or tax policies, and so forth.

Two recent trends have made primary elections even more important to the political process. The first is the increasing polarization of legislative districts, whether due to partisan redistricting (Eilperin 2006) or self-sorting by voters (Abramowitz and Alexander 2004; Oppenheimer 2005). A few decades ago, when districts contained more equal proportions of Republicans and Democrats, it was a challenge for officeholders to please both the median voter in the primary and the median voter in the general election. The former was likely a strong partisan of her own party and the latter was often an independent or weakly attached partisan. It was this tension that prompted Richard Nixon's advice to anyone interested in winning a Republican nomination: "You have to run as far as you can to the right. But to get elected, you have to run as fast as you can back towards the middle" (Cornwell 1995). In a "safe" district, however, the median general election voter is a partisan rather than an unattached independent; the tension between pleasing both the primary and general median voters is largely alleviated. Thus there is even less incentive to deviate from the wishes of the ideological extremists who run IPOs—the reward for centrist behavior is reduced.

Some have argued that the effect of district polarization is a reduction in political accountability (see, e.g., Eilperin 2006; *Los Angeles Times* Staff 2005). However, in my model, the locus of accountability has merely been shifted from the general to the primary election, making officeholders more responsive to primary electorates and the IPOs that influence them.

The second trend that has increased the importance of primaries is term limits, which were enacted in California and twenty other states starting in the early 1990s. Term limits further increase the importance of primaries by forcing career politicians out of their current office at regular intervals. To maintain their careers, these politicians must frequently run in contested primaries as nonincumbents. With their incumbency advantage gone, these candidates become more dependent upon and subservient to IPOs for assistance in winning office.

Candidate Selection

The method by which IPOs select candidates to back for nomination is complicated and not normally directly observable by outsiders. Their aim, however, is always to find candidates who can win and who will cooperate with them while in office. The old conception of a strong party machine picking candidates from obscurity and getting them elected is, for the most part, an unrealistic one. Selecting a candidate with no public reputation, no money, and few personal contacts requires the organization to do all the political work of electing her. It is far more efficient for the organization to coordinate on someone with access to campaign funds and who carries some standing with at least a small section of the electorate.

Members of officeholders' staffs generally make very good candidates. Because they have worked closely with IPO leaders or their close affiliates, staffers are usually a known quantity; strengths and potential embarrassments can be assessed prior to running. Staffers, particularly district representatives, are usually on cordial terms with the key local figures—including donors, activists, and reporters—who can make a nomination campaign go smoothly. Elected officials from small towns may also make promising candidates, since they are familiar with the habits of running and have probably forged ties to voters, local activist groups, and wealthy contributors. Business leaders and otherwise wealthy individuals may be chosen, but only if they have ties to some established donors or activists within an IPO. The wealthy didn't become wealthy by throwing away their money, and such candidates cannot always be relied upon to spend what is necessary to win a nomination; an ability to get other people to spend their money is a far more desirable trait in politics.

Just because candidates nominated by IPOs are willing to work within organizations does not mean that they are pragmatic or centrist. Indeed, the candidate-selection process works systematically to produce polarized partisan officeholders. Organizations, as I have suggested, choose among the serious activists, public staff members, and local officeholders steeped in the political community. These potential recruits, having learned about and debated political issues for some time through their activities in politics, tend to be relatively extreme in their outlook. Two separate processes may account for this extremism, either jointly or independently. The first is best described by Zaller's (1992) work on political polarization. As people are exposed to greater levels of political information, they tend to seek messages that reinforce their predispositions while filtering out countervailing information. Because candidate recruits have been immersed in politics for some time, they have been exposed to large doses of political information, becoming ideologically polarized through the learning process.

Another reason that candidates are extreme is that so many of them got involved in politics as activists or with their help. As has been widely reported (Carsey and Layman 2005; Abramowitz, McGlennon, and Rapoport 1983; Miller and Schofield 2003; Layman and Carsey 2002), activists are far more partisan and ideologically polarized than the general population. This is because, as Aldrich (1983) suggests, only those who perceive serious differences between the two parties will take on the costly task of becoming activists, a considerably costlier task than simply voting. If the policy outcomes appear the same regardless of which party wins, there is little advantage to helping one of them. Similarly, if the parties are ideologically equidistant from the prospective activist, that individual becomes indifferent as to which one wins. Therefore, ideologically centrist individuals, who see the two parties as equally extreme, have little incentive to become activists. Only those already close to one party see any value to getting involved. Thus activists—a major source of political candidates and party elites—tend to be relatively extreme.

The result of these two mechanisms is that political organizations select from a highly skewed sample of public political sentiments. The organization will have its own set of policy goals. If it is dominated by business leaders, it may recruit the most centrist candidates it can find among the ideologically polarized candidate pool. If it is dominated by programmatic partisans, the candidates recruited may tend to be more extreme. Yet these partisans will not be foolish enough to slate candidates too extreme to win. Even the most ardent of the parties' activists tend to look toward electability when recruiting (Stone and Abramowitz 1983). Indeed, organizations face a trade-off between pleasing themselves and winning elections. As Kent (1924: 105) described it, "What [the boss] does is to try so to load the ticket in the primary with the precise proportion of 'Muldoons' [loyal organization people] that can get by in the general election—but no more." How the organization's leaders manage this trade-off is unclear, but a good assumption is that they will nominate as ideologically extreme a candidate as they feel they can get away with. As King (2003) suggests, even ideologically moderate districts often end up with extremist elected officials because of the influence of activist organizations. Regardless of the goals of the organization, because it selects from a pool of people with political experience, it will tend to produce candidates whose preferences diverge from those of the constituency at large.

Disciplining Slackards and Apostates

In theory, if candidate selection is done properly, no behavioral reinforcement is necessary. That is, informal party organizations generally want to slate a candidate who will work to enact a certain ideological agenda. If they're good enough at finding such a person, they should be able to trust that candidate to work for their agenda throughout her career. However, one can never be sure. Most of these candidates have never held high office before, and the temptation to drift toward the ideological center to protect one's career may surpass the desire to stay faithful to one's early backers.

Knowing this, IPO leaders will complement the carrots of funding and endorsements with the stick of de-nomination. If an elected official strays too far from the agenda of her original backers, they can respond by "primarying" her, backing a more dependable rival for the party nomination in the next election. An incumbent may develop some resistance to these threats by cultivating a personal following and a war chest, but it can be difficult to beat a high-quality, well-financed challenger in a primary if word has gotten out that the incumbent has betrayed the party's principles. Most incumbents would rather avoid the challenge. If an incumbent's transgression occurs early in a term, a more immediate and effective remedy to de-nomination may be the recall, at least in those states where it is available. Although the recall has recently become famous thanks to California's 2003 example, nearly half of the United States have some recall provision, although few have as easy ballot qualification requirements as California does.

De-nomination and recall are powerful weapons in an IPO's arsenal and are not taken lightly by those who wield them or by their possible targets. Like any powerful weapon, they are not employed often. They do not have to be. Even one or two examples per decade may be enough for incumbents to realize that the threat is credible and that they deviate from their backers' wishes at their own peril.

CONCLUSION

This chapter proposed a new way of thinking about political parties. I suggested that the best way to understand a party was not as a legislative coalition or a hierarchical organization or a group of like-minded voters, although these features are typically important components of parties. Rather, my model sees parties as loose alliances of policy demanders (activists, officeholders, donors) often operating at the local level, outside the legislature, who manipulate party nominations to control the government. They do so by coordinating on a preferred set of candidates and channeling vital resources—money, endorsements, expertise—to those candidates to help them prevail in primaries. They maintain leverage over officeholders by threatening to withhold those resources or to channel them toward a more faithful candidate. It is these outside actors, I posited, that are responsible for the party polarization we have seen in recent years.

How can we determine that it is these outside actors, and not the legislators themselves, inducing legislative partisanship? In the next chapter, I take advantage of a unique natural experiment offered by California's political history to address this question. Conveniently for the purposes of this study, outside party actors were functionally removed from the electoral process through Progressive Era institutional reforms. The consequences of those reforms, as we will see, were profound: elected officials moderated, and legislative party discipline collapsed. A review of legislative roll call voting history shows that political activity at the local level is the key to party discipline in the capitol. Real legislative partisanship only exists when actors outside the chamber can enforce it.

CHAPTER 2

The True Character of Politicians

Character, it is said, is how one behaves when nobody is looking. What, then, is the character of a politician? Moral implications aside, we may use this line of thought to inquire about the nature of partisanship among politicians. Are legislators natural partisans? Do they, as some political scientists argue, freely choose partisan institutions and discipline to organize their legislative activity? Or, do they actually resist partisanship, preferring an undisciplined chamber of loose, temporary coalitions? That is, do politicians create strong parties or simply try to survive them?

This question is nearly impossible to answer in a functioning party system. After parties are established, one cannot tell what keeps them going—the commitment of party politicians, pressure from activists, or perhaps just their own momentum. How politicians might organize legislative activity if they could start over, free of either institutional momentum or outsider pressure, is usually impossible to say.

However, the Progressive takeover of the California government in the 1910s gives us an unusual historical opportunity to examine this question. Progressive reformers did everything they could to crush parties and to prevent them from returning. In particular, they made it nearly impossible for party activists outside government to organize, coordinate actions, keep informed about legislative activities, or, perhaps most importantly, influence party nominations to office.

Under these conditions, in which the normal party activity had been thoroughly disrupted, California politicians revealed their true character. What they revealed is that they are fair-weather partisans—happy to use partisan affiliations when it is useful to do so but unwilling to organize the legislature for partisan purposes or to pursue a genuinely partisan agenda. Nor were they sorry about this state of affairs. Rather, they enjoyed and sought to perpetuate their nonpartisan legislature. Only when partisan activists outside the government regained influence over the nominating process did elected officials begin behaving like partisans, voting in coherent party blocs and trying to advance a partisan agenda.

In this chapter and the one that follows, I describe these findings that reveal the character of politicians and the necessity of outside activists to enforce partisan discipline. The present chapter focuses on the impact of Progressive antiparty reforms from their imposition in the 1910s until their removal in the 1950s. I examine the behavior of both voters and legislators in the years surrounding these crucial events. For the reader to understand these reforms and their impact, a brief history lesson is necessary, which I provide in this chapter. The subsequent chapter details legislative behavior over more than 150 years, showing how incumbents responded to a variety of institutional changes, again concluding that, when insulated from party activists, incumbents prefer nonpartisanship to the challenges of enacting a legislative agenda.

Both these chapters draw upon a new dataset consisting of every roll call vote cast in the California assembly between 1849 and 2003. The collection of this dataset was funded in large part by the National Science Foundation (Grant No. 0214514).

PUTTING THEORY TO THE TEST: PROGRESSIVE ERA CALIFORNIA, 1910–1952

At the turn of the twentieth century, California politics was dominated by two major political machines. One was local, based in San Francisco, and under the leadership of Abraham Ruef. Boss Ruef had few ideological impulses but controlled essentially all of the elected officials and convention delegates in San Francisco (then the largest city in the state) for the purpose of graft. He sold utility franchises and licenses for exorbitant sums until his conviction for bribery in 1908.

The other machine was a statewide organization run by the Southern Pacific Railroad. This machine had but one legislative goal: to protect the railroad industry. Indeed, representatives of the railroad company literally wrote the state Republican Party's 1902 platform. An observer of the 1907 legislative session reported, "Scarcely a vote was cast in either house that did not show some aspect of Southern Pacific ownership, petty vengeance, or legislative blackmail." And when an editorial cartoonist for the *San Francisco Examiner* drew images critical of the machine and its grip on the state, the legislature passed a law prohibiting the publication of such drawings (Mowry 1951: 16, 19–20, 63). Through its effective control of state politics, the railroad managed to avoid paying millions of dollars in taxes, appropriated land at will, and regularly subverted legislation locals believed necessary.

The Southern Pacific machine (and, to a lesser extent, the Ruef organization) was unpopular and the frequent object of reform. But state law required candidates to be nominated by parties, and parties made these nominations in party conventions that were easily controlled by machine loyalists. For example, the railroad quashed the 1904 renomination bid of U.S. senator Thomas R. Bard because of his occasional votes against the railroad. This move outraged many loyal conservative Republicans, who held Senator Bard in high esteem. In 1906, the railroad paid Boss Ruef $20,000 to deliver San Francisco's votes to the Republican convention in Santa Cruz, securing the nomination of a machine-friendly candidate for governor (Mowry 1951: 20, 29). "In every county in California," reported the *San Francisco Call,* "the railroad company maintained an expert political manager whose employment was to see that the right men were chosen as convention delegates, the right kind of candidates named and elected, and the right things done by the men in office" (quoted in Cannon 1969: 47). So long as this control over nominations held, voters had no true choice in the general election. Veteran newspaperman Franklin Hichborn (1959–60) explained:

> In California, the Railroad Machine probably never controlled the electorate or had a compelling influence upon a majority of it. The Machine's grip upon the state was made possible by partisan election laws which required that the candidate's party be stated. This was generally recognized and resented. All candidates for office, from township constable to Governor, were nominated by partisan convention. . . . The railroad machine usually controlled the conventions, but when it did not, with several candidates running for each office, could, and usually did, by centering its vote upon a dependable candidate, elect its choice by minority vote. By such procedure, the machine, broadly speaking, controlled official California from city hall to state capitol. (353–54)

Indeed, through its control over the party nomination system, the railroad machine had for years handpicked and funded not only its adherents in the legislature but its purported opponents, as well. The chief lawyer for the Southern Pacific once bragged that the secret to the machine's staying power was "its control of reform movements" (Hichborn 1922: 9).

The railroad machine ultimately met defeat at the hands of a group of Republican activists who were not part of the government or the formal party system. Reporters, including the *Los Angeles Express*'s Edward Dickson and the *Fresno Morning Republican*'s Chester Rowell, worked with small groups of like-minded fellow journalists, attorneys, and wealthy benefactors who were determined to overthrow the Southern Pacific machine. Their reform organization, regularly holding secret meetings at restaurants or clubhouses, operated primarily at the local level. As Mowry (1951) wrote in his study of the California Progressives,

> If the [Progressive Lincoln-Roosevelt] League were to be the influential force that its sponsors hoped, its enemies had to be answered, its funds built up, and most important—it had to be organized on a local level in every corner of the state. And since the most promising way of keeping a political organization together is to provide jobs for the faithful, local elections had to be fought and won. (73)

Dickson's organization slated 25 candidates for Los Angeles city elections in 1906 and got 17 of them elected. Good government groups in San Jose, Fresno, and Palo Alto all worked to take over their local Republican Party organizations that year, as well. From there, the Progressive activists attempted to win citywide elections in the machine strongholds of Oakland, Sacramento, and San Francisco, and met with considerable success. ✱ New PaRty

By the 1909 session, the Progressives were a force to be reckoned with in the state legislature. Their control of various Republican (and a few Democratic) local organizations meant that the railroad machine's threats of retribution against wayward legislators were losing their credibility. Even on the direct primary bill, which machine leaders rightly saw as a threat to their control over politics, the machine was losing its grip:

> "Threats, persuasions, and promises" were offered to legislators to change their votes, and it was made clear that their support of the bill would hurt them "in a business way at home." Instead of submitting to this pressure in the traditional fashion, fifteen anti-machine Republicans and a small number of like-minded Democrats left their parties' caucuses and held a bipartisan reform meeting of their own. (Mowry 1951: 82)

As a result of this antimachine activity, the direct primary bill passed, ending the era of nominations by convention in California. Repeatedly frustrated by the difficulty of nominating their own kind at machine-brokered conventions, reform-minded activists ended the convention system altogether.

Under the direct primary system, the Progressives won enough seats in 1910 to capture the legislature. Progressives also sent Hiram Johnson, who had been a prosecuting attorney in the trial of Boss Ruef, to the governor's mansion. Thus ensconced in power, the reformers began an all-out effort to rid state politics of corruption by routing the more established political parties. They created initiatives, referenda, and the recall. They also formally separated local party organizations from the state parties and granted home rule to the counties, preventing parties from developing their farm teams at the local level and institutionalizing intra-party tensions that weakened the formal party organizations (Wilson 1966; Owens, Costantini, and Weschler 1970). In a later session, the legislature would establish nonpartisan elections for county and judicial offices throughout the state. Progressive reforms also made it virtually impossible for anyone other than a candidate or officeholder to be a member of the formal party (Turner and Vieg 1967). This reform was designed to minimize the influence of informal political actors, mainly bosses and railroads. Yet, whether intended or not, the law drove out party activists, as well.

The sharpest blow to parties was a procedure called cross-filing (McHenry 1946; Leary 1957). Under this rule, candidates for state and federal offices could run in the primaries of multiple parties without specifying to which party they belonged. With no party labels next to the candidates' names on the primary ballot, many—and probably most—voters could not tell whether they were voting for a Democrat or a Republican. The only information on the ballot other than the candidates' names was their occupations. In particular, officeholders could list their status as incumbents, and their names would always appear first (Cresap 1954). Hence it was common for voters in both parties' low-key primary election contests to be confronted with a field that included only one recognizable name—that of the incumbent officeholder, helpfully labeled as such. A candidate who won both party primaries would stand alone on the general ballot with a hybrid party label ("Dem-Rep" or "Rep-Dem"), rendering the general election meaningless and significantly reducing the campaigning time and expenses of the cross-filer.

It is difficult to overstate the destructive effect cross-filing had on local party organizations. One of the key powers that a local party enjoys is control over the ballot. A party organization determines or strongly influences who may or may not run for that party's nomination. Ideally, the party organization will limit ballot access to just the candidate it prefers. Occasionally, an undesired candidate may qualify for the ballot. This is usually not a major problem for the party; that candidate can be deprived of the money, endorsements, and expertise she would need to be competitive.

Under cross-filing as it existed in California from 1914 to 1952, however, ballot control was functionally nonexistent. It was possible for a high-profile candidate (even an incumbent) from another political party to appear on a party's primary ballot. And with no party label next to her name, party voters would become confused in the primary to the point that they could not coordinate.

Imagine, then, a situation in which a Republican Party organization is dissatisfied with one of its incumbents, to the point that it has selected, and amply funded, a lesser-known but more ideologically pure challenger to run against her. The incumbent will get a healthy share of the vote by virtue of name recognition. It therefore falls to the party organization to get the message out to party voters that the incumbent has been a poor public servant and that the challenger is worthy of support. Now imagine that, thanks to cross-filing, a well-known Democrat within the district has decided to run for the same office. He runs in the Republican primary, but his party affiliation does not appear on the ballot. This Democrat will likely siphon off many of the anti-incumbent Republican votes in that primary, to the point where the Republican challenger cannot hope to achieve a plurality of the vote. Thus did cross-filing strip the party organization of its ability to control the ballot and, by extension, to punish wayward incumbents.

Few records exist today indicating true Progressive intentions with regard to cross-filing. The provision was not in the original version of Speaker C. C. Young's election reform bill, nor was it even part of the Progressives' stated platform (Rusco 1961: 478). The cross-filing rule was buried among thirty-seven other amendments to the bill and prompted no discussion by its author, journalists, or political commentators of the day (Findley 1959; Rowe 1961). However, the historical evidence suggests that the Progressives' reasons for creating this institution were twofold: they didn't think that the direct primary could, on its own, defeat the machines, and they wanted to preserve themselves in office.

As for the first motive, evidence from other states indicated that the direct primary would not be enough to drive the machine from politics. Direct primary systems in Oklahoma and Texas, for example, had apparently *increased* the importance of money in elections, encouraging graft and empowering those party organizations capable of providing it (Ford 1909: 6). A contemporary study of Boston politics found that the city's direct primary system had "practically handed the city over to the ward politician" (quoted in Ford 1909: 10). R. S. Boots's survey of New Jersey politics in the 1910s discovered that, despite the direct primary, "in almost all of the important primary contests the party organization puts up a slate of candidates for the lucrative offices. . . . [I]n an overwhelming majority of cases the organization slate is successful [and] in a large number of cases there is no contest against the organizational slate" (quoted in Key 1952: 416). Indeed, recent works by Ware (2002) and Reynolds (2006) suggest that political leaders saw the direct primary as a way to *preserve* their control of party nominations. This helps explain why so many machine-controlled legislatures enacted direct primaries in such a short time span.

Even early evidence from California's direct primary system suggested that the more democratic nominating system would not keep the machines at bay. In the 1909 San Francisco municipal elections, Francis Heney, a Progressive reformer who distinguished himself through his prosecution of Boss Ruef and others during the city's celebrated graft trials, ran for district attorney. However, remnants of Ruef's machine organized to stop Heney and packed the Republican registration with a "collection of miscellaneous scum" (Hichborn 1911: 72). Although Heney won the Democratic nomination by write-in vote, partisan voting patterns of the day made election of a Democrat in San Francisco next to impossible. The machine had prevailed, even in the age of the direct primary (Findley 1959). With the evidence available to them even in the 1910s, the California Progressives may have come to the same disheartening conclusion reached by political scientist Henry Jones Ford (1909):

One continually hears the declaration that the direct primary will take power from the politicians and give it to the people. This is pure nonsense. Politics has been, is and always will be carried on by politicians, just as art is carried on by artists, engineering by engineers, business by business men. . . . The direct primary may take advantage and opportunity from one set of politicians and confer them upon another set, but politicians there will always be so long as there is politics. The only thing that is open to control is the sort of politicians we shall have. (2)

Concerns about the direct primary's shortcomings may not have been the only motivation for California's Progressives. Several historians have suggested that Progressive officeholders quickly acquired a taste for power and wished to remain in office as long as possible. Yet the 1914 elections nationwide showed that voters were fickle. The Progressive Party's leading candidates lost overwhelmingly everywhere except in California, where they had come to power somewhat later than in other states. Efforts to create a viable third party or to replace one of the two major parties had also failed. For the Progressive Party to survive, California leaders therefore reasoned, its incumbents would have to reintegrate into the Republican and Democratic Parties from which they sprang, taking over the leadership of those parties if at all possible (Gendzel 2003).

Cross-filing gave them a way to do just that. With the advantage they had as incumbents, Progressive officeholders could likely beat conservative (or "Standpat") Republican challengers in the GOP primary, and they could win the Democratic primary as well thanks to Democratic voters who sympathized with the Progressive agenda. Standpat assemblyman Milton Schmitt (R-San Francisco) argued during the debate on the creation of cross-filing:

> The present administration was elected on party lines, the Progressive. Why this sudden ambition to abandon their party fealty? Is it not because they know that the Progressive party as a national organization is about gasping its last breath? Is it not because of this belief, that they are endeavoring to securely intrench themselves in office here, while their party passes into history? (quoted in Gaylord 1977: 32)

As an instrument of incumbency protection, cross-filing was a brilliant success. Figure 2 shows that as early as 1918, 60 percent of assembly members succeeded in avoiding a general election contest by winning the nominations of both parties. Most of the rest were freshmen vying for open seats (and hence lacking the incumbency cue on the ballot). By the

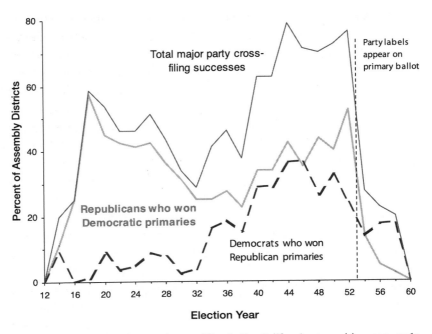

Fig. 2. Successful incidence of cross-filing in the California assembly, 1912–1960

1940s, nearly every incumbent in the legislature cross-filed to avoid a general election contest.

If, under this system, aggrieved constituents or activists wished to challenge an incumbent of the other party, their first task was to seize control of their own primary. To do this, they had to find a candidate who would be better known than the incumbent of the other party in the primary election. This was normally rather difficult. State legislative primaries are too low-key to attract well-known politicians, strong campaigners, or an abundance of campaign resources. Voters, forced to choose between a mess of challengers of various (unlabeled) parties and the incumbent, normally chose the incumbent. Hence, challengers favored by local activists—the same sorts of activists who had brought about the Progressive reforms in the first place—had little chance.

Detailed information about how local activists responded to their plight is scarce. Most likely this is because there was little reason for local party organization to exist at all. The tiny bit of evidence that exists is, however, revealing. It is the early political history of Jesse Marvin Unruh, who served as assembly Speaker from 1961–69. Unruh got involved in politics while still in college, one of a handful of students and alumni of the University of Southern California who formed the California Democratic Guild in 1949. Unruh ran for assembly in 1952. This was the last year that primary ballots were nonpartisan and seven years before cross-filing was abolished altogether. In that election, the impoverished Unruh and his Guild colleagues tried to organize and raise money for the race, but they weren't able to cull together more than $15. Unruh did not cross-file in the Republican primary simply because he couldn't afford the $30 filing fee. He lost in the Democratic primary to the incumbent, Republican (and former Democrat) John Evans, who had been cross-filing for most of his fourteen-year career in the assembly.

Things could hardly have been more different when Unruh ran again in 1954. Under pressure from liberal activists, the state legislature had authorized a ballot initiative to put party labels back on primary ballots. Cross-filing was still allowed, but the incumbent was required to reveal his party affiliation on the ballot. Under these conditions, Democratic Party activists deemed Evans's Inglewood district to be winnable by a Democrat (the district split evenly between Eisenhower and Stevenson in the 1956 presidential election), and labor unions helped Unruh raise $1,615 in the primary race, which he won. In the general election, labor unions and Democratic activists were even more generous toward Unruh, providing him with $2,495. This money supported an effective precinct organization, which enabled Unruh to unseat the eight-term incumbent by a 52-48 margin (Cannon 1969: 61–67).

Unruh's 1952 and 1954 campaigns are the only on-the-ground information I have about how cross-filing and its elimination affected party nominations. But as far as it goes, the evidence is clear: Even an extremely talented politician who enjoyed the backing of what passed at the time for local party organization was unable to prevail in his own party's primary when an incumbent of the other party could cross-file against him without revealing party attachment. The incumbency cue was more powerful than anything the candidate and his band of activists could muster.

The practice of cross-filing thus makes for an interesting examination of sources of legislative partisanship, since it allows us to examine the behavior of legislators unpoliced by activists. Left to their own devices, did incumbents organize themselves into disciplined teams to allow for the easier passage of legislation? Or did they simply not worry about these sorts of issues?

One way to investigate these questions is to compare a session of the California assembly with a simultaneous one from a chamber with no cross-filing provisions, the U.S. Congress. For this comparison, I use complete sets of roll call votes for the 1947 sessions of both chambers. I have employed Keith Poole's W-NOMINATE program (Poole and Rosenthal 1997) to calculate ideal points for legislators based on their roll call voting. The Poole program is a sophisticated computer algorithm that uses every single roll call vote cast by every legislator as its input. The output is a single "ideal point" estimate for each legislator, ranging from –1 (the most liberal position) to +1 (the most conservative position). These scores are substantively similar to interest group scores, with several distinct advantages. For example, because the NOMINATE program uses every roll call vote, and not those selected by a particular interest group, it avoids a major source of bias. NOMINATE also allows us to measure members' ideal points in several dimensions, and it produces a variety of indicators to describe partisanship in a legislature.

In several ways, the 1947 session is a natural high-water mark for the effects of cross-filing and nonpartisanship: the 1946 election that produced it also saw the successful cross-filing of Governor Earl Warren, the only California governor to be the nominee of both major parties. The assembly's choice for Speaker that year, Republican Sam Collins, won thanks to a bipartisan coalition—the majority of the chamber's Republicans actually voted against him.

Figure 3 shows the distribution of the first dimension of ideal points in the 1947 assembly chamber and the concurrent session of the U.S. House of Representatives. I have removed California's delegation from the House data because they were also elected through the cross-filing rules. As can be seen, there was at least some partisan division in each chamber; distributions for both chambers are bimodal, indicating that the bulk of members are voting regularly in either a liberal or conservative fashion. However, there is a notable gap between the liberals and conservatives in the U.S. House—almost no members exist at the zero mark. There is no such gap in the middle of the assembly distribution. In fact, a sizable number of assembly Republicans were voting more liberally than the chamber's Democrats, and vice versa. Although the 1947 U.S. House was not an exceptionally partisan chamber, partisanship in the concurrent California assembly clearly falls well short of even that mark. This is not a chamber that one would recognize as polarized today.

This comparison from 1947 suggests that California politicians mod-

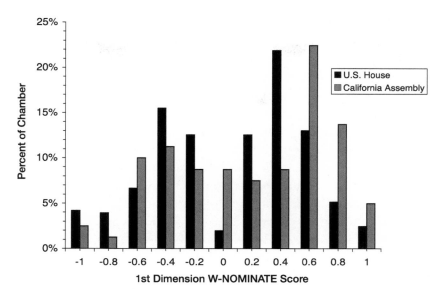

Fig. 3. Distribution of legislator ideal points in 1947. (Keith Poole provided the roll call votes for U.S. House members. The calculated ideal points for U.S. House members omit those from the California delegation.)

erated under the cross-filing regime. To further test this possibility, I have utilized Poole's DW-NOMINATE scaling program (Poole and Rosenthal 1997) to produce dynamic ideal points for each member. DW-NOMINATE ideal points have the virtue of being comparable from year to year; we can see how a legislature or individual legislators change over time.

After calculating these ideal points, I then used the first dimension DW-NOMINATE scores as a dependent variable in a multivariate regression equation. To predict these coordinates, I used each member's party affiliation (Democratic = −1, Republican = 1; third party members were excluded). I also used the assembly district's Republican vote for president in a recent presidential election as a measure of district ideology. I included a dummy variable for cross-filing (equaling 1 from 1915 through 1959 and 0 at all other times), and I interacted that variable with party. To compensate for influences on members' voting behavior other than party, I included variables measuring how urban each district was, whether the legislator was from a Northern or Southern district, and the district's tax burden to the state. Legislative professionalization is another matter that required consideration, since professionalization is associated with greater partisanship (Fiorina 1999a, 1994) and since Speaker Unruh's efforts to professionalize the chamber roughly corresponded with a jump in legislative partisanship (Squire 1992). To control for legislative professionalization, I have included a variable measuring the length of each legislative session in days. I have also interacted that variable with the party variable to determine whether Democrats become more liberal and Republicans more conservative as sessions grow longer.

Since the size of the majority party has been shown to affect chamber partisanship (Aldrich and Battista 2002), I also included a variable measuring the size of the chamber's majority party (as a percentage of the whole chamber) and interacted that variable with the party variable to control for the expected decline in partisanship in an imbalanced chamber. Finally, I have included a control for whether the member is part of the majority party and interacted that with the party variable, on the chance that membership in the majority party may encourage greater party discipline. Unfortunately, because district ideology data is only available from 1913 on, I cannot include evidence from prior to that year.

The party variable is predicted to have a strongly positive coefficient; since DW-NOMINATE scores are scaled such that −1 is the most liberal position and +1 the most conservative, Republicans should tend to have higher scores. However, if cross-filing did, in fact, suppress partisanship, the interaction of party and cross-filing should be negative. That is, Democrats will tend to be more conservative, and Republicans more liberal, during cross-filing. District ideology should have a positive coefficient, as members from conservative districts should tend to have higher scores. The interaction of party and majority size is expected to be negative, as Democrats will tend to be more conservative, and Republicans more liberal, when there is less numerical parity among the two parties. Conversely, near-parity between the parties should encourage greater party discipline. There are no predictions for the other control variables.

I have performed a fixed-effects regression on these variables, controlling for decade and district. The results of this regression can be seen in table 1. The results strongly support my predictions about cross-filing. Party is, unsurprisingly, a strong predictor of first dimension DW-NOMINATE scores, even controlling for district ideology. Both those measures are highly statistically significant and in the expected directions. The main interaction between party and cross-filing is also in the expected direction and is statistically significant at the .001 level. In other words, controlling for ideological predispositions and other characteristics of members and their districts, members were notably more moderate during the cross-filing era, moving .12 points away from the extreme poles on the −1 to +1 scale.

More evidence of such moderation can be seen in table 2. Here, I compare cross-filers with single-filers during the cross-filing years 1915 and 1959. The key variable is the interaction between party and cross-filing. I have included all the other control variables seen in table 1. As this shows, legislators who cross-filed were, on average, .045 points more

TABLE 1. Moderation during the Cross-Filing Years: Predictors of 1st Dimension DW-NOMINATE Scores in the California Assembly, 1913–2003

VARIABLE	COEFFICIENT
Constant	−0.240°°°
	(0.073)
Party	0.574°°°
(Dem = −1, Rep = 1, else missing)	(0.040)
Cross-filing era	0.167°°°
(1915–59 = 1, else = 0)	(0.028)
Party × cross-filing era	−0.122°°°
	(0.017)
District ideology	0.240°°°
(Republican percentage of vote in recent presidential election)	(0.057)
Session length	0.000
(in days)	(0.000)
Party × session length	0.0001
	(0.000)
Majority size	−0.060
(Percentage of whole chamber)	(0.063)
Party × majority size	−0.359°°°
	(0.047)
Majority party member	0.007
(1 = yes, 0 = no)	(0.010)
Party × majority party member	−0.008
	(0.011)
R-squared	.681
Number of cases	3,472

Source: Biennial Report of the State Treasurer (1902–44), the State Controller's *Annual Counties Report* (1956–2002), *California Assembly Handbook, 2005–06,* U.S. Census.

Note: Cell entries are regression coefficients, using a fixed effects model that controls for decade and district. Coefficients for region, district urbanism, and district tax burden are not shown. Standard errors appear in parentheses. Statistical significance is indicated by asterisks (°$p \leq$ .05, °°$p \leq$ .01, °°°$p \leq$ .001). District ideology was calculated from the Republican share of the presidential vote in a recent presidential election. Those presidential elections were 1920 (1913–31 assembly session), 1932 (1933–39), 1944 (1941–51), 1956 (1953–61), 1964 (1963–67), 1968 (1969–71), 1972 (1973–75), 1976 (1977–79), 1980 (1981), 1984 (1983–87), 1988 (1989–91), 1992 (1992–95), 1996 (1997–99), 2000 (2001), and the 2002 gubernatorial election (2003).

moderate than those who did not cross-file, and that result is statistically significant at the .001 level. This is not an enormous coefficient on a scale that ranges from −1 to +1, but given how little distance there was between the parties at this time, it could have made the difference between voting with one's party or with the opposition on many votes.

Interestingly, this moderating effect is far more pronounced for Democrats than for Republicans. In the analysis comparing the cross-filing era with the post-cross-filing era, the marginal effect (Brambor, Clark, and Golder 2006) of cross-filing on Democrats is a statistically significant .289, while the effect for Republicans was .044, which is not statistically significant and is in the wrong direction. In the second analysis, the marginal effects of being a cross-filer were greater for Democrats (.093) than for Republicans (−.029), although both were in the expected directions and were statistically significant at the .05 level.

TABLE 2. Moderate Behavior among Cross-Filers: Predictors of 1st Dimension DW-NOMINATE Scores in the California Assembly, 1915–59

VARIABLE	COEFFICIENT
Constant	−0.079
	(0.105)
Party	0.365°°°
(Dem = −1, Rep = 1, else missing)	(0.066)
Cross-filer	0.018
(Won both major party nominations in previous election)	(0.014)
Party × cross-filer	−0.045°°°
	(0.014)
District ideology	0.122
(Republican percentage of vote in recent presidential election)	(0.108)
Session length	0.000
(in days)	(0.000)
Party × session length	0.001°°
	(0.000)
Majority size	−0.067
(Percentage of whole chamber)	(0.118)
Party × majority size	−0.301°°°
	(0.074)
Member of majority party	0.026
(1 = yes, 0 = no)	(0.017)
Party × member of majority party	−.001
	(0.017)
R-squared	.459
Number of cases	1,751

Note: Cell entries are regression coefficients, using a fixed effects model that controls for decade and district. Coefficients for region, district urbanism, and district tax burden are not shown. Standard errors appear in parentheses. Statistical significance is indicated by asterisks (°$p \leq$ .05, °°$p \leq$ .01, °°°$p \leq$ .001).

It is not entirely obvious why we'd see such a difference between the two parties. It is possible that Republicans were able to maintain somewhat greater party unity by virtue of being the majority party during much of the cross-filing era. In addition, the cross-filing era occurred at a time when Republican intraparty factionalism was at a low point (at least after the demise of the Progressive movement), while the Democratic Party was torn internally on its responses to the Great Depression and its later attitudes toward the Cold War. If being a Democratic officeholder meant appeasing the activists urging massive federal intervention in the economy in the 1930s and recognition of communist China in the 1950s, and cross-filing offered some kind of resistance from these activists, then it is not surprising that we'd see such a powerful moderating effect of cross-filing on Democrats.

The incentive to officeholders under cross-filing to avoid excessive partisanship is rather obvious. If one wishes to run as both a Democrat and a Republican, one cannot make a record that is too blatantly partisan in either direction. Middle-of-the-road politics—or what seems middle-of-the-road in one's own district—is the safest route.

But middle-of-the-road politics can take many forms, including accommodation of whatever special interest offers the highest price. It may also include legislative cycling and failure to form any real agenda at all. Thus, an ineffectual politics of incoherence and corruption may be hard for inattentive voters—or even political scientists focusing on quantitative data—to distinguish from a centrism based on genuine legislative accomplishment.

Let us therefore turn to qualitative evidence to evaluate coalitional patterns we have seen in the roll call data. Those who served in the assembly in the late 1940s and early 1950s describe it in language that scholars use to describe the state of nature that spurs party formation: a place where long coalitions do not form and majority voting is chaotic and cyclical. Lloyd Lowrey, a conservative northern California Democrat, characterized the cross-filing era assembly as "complete turmoil," saying, "We were continually having unpleasant incidents develop. In other words, we weren't coordinating to pass legislation, but most of the time it seemed like we were at each other's throats" (Reinier 1987: 13). John Moss, who served in the assembly in the cross-filing period and later in the U.S. Congress, contrasts his experiences in Washington with those in Sacramento. In Washington, he says, "We didn't have the endless partisan wrangling; we had a structure where we could bring issues finally and resolve them. Here [in California] you have endless bickering; you don't have that kind of structure" (Seney 1989: 102–3). An effort to elect a new assembly Speaker in 1953 amounted to one bipartisan coalition facing down another, with the insurgents conspiring to carefully cobble together a voting coalition. As Lowrey explains:

> It had to be done in one fell swoop and very quickly. We didn't falter because we had to keep this thing under wraps. We couldn't have leaks, because if there had been leaks, it would have been rather easy to tear our coalition apart. So when we had the votes, we moved fast and surprised the opposition. (Reinier 1987: 41–42)

John Moss similarly describes an effort to pass a bill that would make the Rules Committee elected, rather than chosen by the Speaker. Again, no predictable coalitions existed: "The way that came about it, we conspired very carefully, building our oaths, solid commitments, blood commitments, because if we had lost, we would have been in perdition. I guess we'd have been banished" (Seney 1989: 161). Such ad hoc coalitions had to be built from the ground up because there was little or no central partisan authority in the chamber at the time. One organization that might have provided such leadership, the Republican Assembly Caucus, was decidedly not interested in the job. Gordon Fleury, a Republican Assembly member in the late 1940s and early 1950s, reports, "We had caucuses, but never had a vote—a unit vote or a caucus vote. We could vote the way we wanted. I, as a Republican, probably voted more with liberal Democrats than any way. And nobody ever said, 'Gordon, you shouldn't do it.'" Fleury continued the Republican Caucus's tradition when he served as its chair: "I . . . never once took a vote on how we should vote. We just had lunch and had a couple of drinks" (Hicke 1987: 9, 16). Similarly, assembly Democrats maintained a caucus, but its decisions were not binding upon its members (Chinn 1958: 299).

Party leaders outside the legislature were not happy with these arrangements. Elizabeth Snyder, who chaired the Democratic State Central Committee between 1952 and 1954, lectured cross-filers of her party, "If you're on our ticket, that means you're representing the Party, not just yourself and your own personal ambitions" (Snyder 1996: 86). But as Jerry Waldie (2001), who served in the assembly just after the end of cross-filing, observed, cross-filing "limited the ability of each party to seek conformance with party policies and party positions." Republican leaders outside the legislature were upset as well. Activists formed the California Republican Assembly (CRA) in 1935 in an effort to coordinate resources on more conservative candidates in Republican primaries; yet despite their efforts, Republicans in the legislature remained as nonpartisan as before. Moreover, the legislature as a whole resisted every attempt to allow partisan activists back into electoral politics.

Cycling, instability, poor discipline, and institutional weakness are supposed to be the reasons that incumbents build parties in the first place. Why did members continue to support cross-filing and other buttresses to the nonpartisan system despite all the problems they created? Simply, they made life easier for incumbents. Reelection was virtually guaranteed, and few people were watching over their shoulders. As assemblyman Victor Veysey, who tried unsuccessfully to reinstate cross-filing in 1961, explained, "I felt that cross-filing was very beneficial to an incumbent. . . . It saves an incumbent a lot of trouble and difficulty. He can win reelection in the primary. . . . I would have liked [the resumption of cross-filing] because it would make my political life simpler" (Douglass 1988: 138).

The elections of Democratic governor Culbert Olson and Speaker Paul Peek in the late 1930s stand as the exceptions to nonpartisanship that prove the rule. Pursuing a liberal, New Deal–style agenda, Olson and Peek sought to impose party discipline on the assembly. Even though the assembly was solidly Democratic, their efforts were short-lived. Peek became the only California Speaker removed by his colleagues at mid-session, deposed by a bipartisan, "economy bloc" coalition. And the new Speaker, upon receiving the gavel, symbolically ripped out the telephone that had connected the Speaker's desk to Governor Olson's office (Berinstein 1986; *Los Angeles Times* Staff 1940). Voting returned to its bipartisan patterns soon thereafter.

Furthermore, as Buchanan (1963) observes, a strong rival to the party dimension evolved in the Progressive Era assembly. This was the Speaker's coalition, a bipartisan group that rallied around a candidate for Speaker and was rewarded with committee chairmanships and other perquisites of office. Although the Speaker's coalition usually wasn't the dominant voting dimension in any given legislative session, it held together on key votes relevant to the organization of the chamber and was supported strongly by lobbyist money. Buchanan is able to track rival Speaker coalitions—the lobbyist-friendly team headed by Sam Collins and the more reform-oriented group led by James Silliman and Luther

"Abe" Lincoln—over five consecutive sessions from 1947 to 1955. Buchanan charts these coalitions' influence—which often exceeded that of party—on votes affecting the Speaker's powers, committee organization, lobbying restrictions, and regulation of alcohol, oil, gambling, and other powerful interests. Contrary to the common notion that legislators tend toward partisanship and a single long coalition, rival coalitions could and did form with great frequency. As Chinn (1958: 228) noted, "Once elected to the state legislature as a Democrat, the individual legislator is left almost entirely without party guidance, assistance, or direction. Usually his answer is to join alliances and coalitions, but these may or may not consist of fellow Democrats." Absent activist pressures, the California assembly was awash in short coalitions.

THE ABOLISH CROSS-FILING MOVEMENT OF 1952

Cross-filing was repeatedly attacked from within the legislature during its forty-year reign, but never successfully. A majority of lawmakers liked it and fought to save it. Republicans were eager to defend a system that seemed to be maintaining their party's majority status amid increasing Democratic voter registration since the 1930s. Democrats, however, were of two minds on the issue. On one hand, they wanted to preserve an easy environment for incumbents; on the other, they were obviously interested in inducing a change that could bring their party majority control. Democrats had held a healthy majority of the state's registered voters since the early 1930s, and many believed that ending cross-filing would make it easier for voters to vote their party preferences, giving Democrats a statewide majority. Yet Democratic incumbents were receiving many of the same benefits that their Republican colleagues were, and Democratic committee chairmen appointed by Republican Speakers obviously had much to lose by doing away with the nonpartisan system. Tellingly, a Democratic-controlled special senate committee appointed to study cross-filing in 1951 came out strongly in favor of the practice, suggesting that its repeal would "destroy a harmonious and cooperative spirit now prevailing in the State Senate" (California Legislature 1951: 484). As Wilson (1966: 102) found, "elective officers, both Democratic and Republican, are keenly aware that a strong party would weaken their own authority and place burdensome constraints upon them."

Ironically, cross-filing fell at the hands of another Progressive tool, the initiative process. Liberal union activists had come to believe that cross-filing was sustaining a Republican majority in a Democratic state and preventing coordinated action by prolabor Democrats. (The facts back up labor's concerns: despite the Democrats' overwhelming advantage in voter registration since the early 1930s and the state's support for Democratic presidential candidates between 1932 and 1948, Republicans largely held the legislature throughout that time and even won the governorship through the use of cross-filing in 1946. As a result, a number of antiunion policies had become law or seemed about to do so.) These activists organized with Democratic Party officials and the League of Women Voters to place a measure banning cross-filing on the 1952 ballot.

Members of the legislature, recognizing the threat that this change posed for their reelection prospects, drafted a compromise measure, which would allow cross-filing to continue but would require party labels to appear on the primary ballots next to candidates' names. Their aim was to take the steam out of the anti-cross-filing movement altogether. Taking no chances, the legislature gave their compromise proposition the lucky number 7 on the ballot, while the cross-filing repeal proposition was given the unlucky number 13. Tellingly, the compromise measure won broad bipartisan support in the assembly, with all Republicans and 22 of 31 Democrats voting aye. Within the Democratic Party, opposition came mainly from newer, more liberal legislators who had not yet become accustomed to the benefits of cross-filing.

Although the legislature's vote to place Proposition 7 on the ballot had a bipartisan cast, the public's vote on the two competing measures was strongly partisan. Figure 4 shows that more Democratic assembly districts (as measured by the 1956 presidential vote) supported the repeal of cross-filing (Proposition 13) and that more Republican districts supported the compromise measure (Proposition 7). Clearly, the Abolish Cross-Filing in California Committee, the umbrella organization for the Democratic groups that supported Proposition 13, got its partisan message out to its voters. Likewise, Republican voters seemed well aware that the compromise measure would protect their party's dominance of the legislature. Yet despite the partisan nature of the vote and the Democratic edge among registered voters, Proposition 13 lost by a narrow margin, while Proposition 7 won a majority in every district. Notably, even in the districts in which Proposition 13 won, most assemblymen (including a majority of Democrats) had voted to thwart the cross-filing ban against the wishes of their constituents.

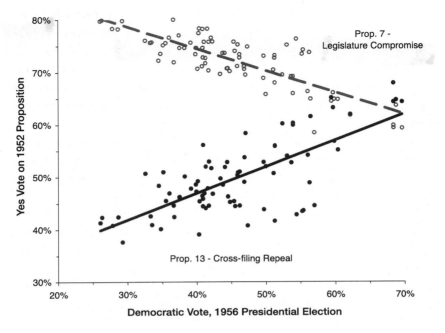

Fig. 4. Partisan voting patterns on cross-filing propositions. Each dot represents one assembly district.

LESSONS FROM CROSS-FILING AND ITS ABOLITION

An examination of the Progressive Era California assembly is highly informative about the importance of the party nomination process to party organizations. With the passage of cross-filing and other Progressive reforms designed to separate incumbents from activists, party discipline in the legislature collapsed, and the influence of the Southern Pacific Railroad machine rapidly waned.

More important, the cross-filing era and its end are highly instructive about sources of legislative partisanship. However appealing the logic of constructing strong parties in a legislature, members of the California assembly did not do so. Indeed, incumbents sought to keep the parties weak and to insulate themselves from pressures to pursue a partisan agenda. Members frequently cross-filed and pursued centrist, bipartisan strategies. Legislative institutions like the caucus existed in name only, and legislative voting on key issues was often dominated by bipartisan coalitions or was chaotic, requiring supporters of bills to construct coalitions on each issue. Of course, this world could only exist through the aid of an artifice: incumbents were shielded from activist pressures by cross-filing and other Progressive reforms. In fact, liberal activists and some conservative activists were trying all along to enforce party discipline but were rebuffed by a legislature that loved party labels when it came to winning their first election but hated real partisanship once they became ensconced in office.

The conditions that led to the demise of cross-filing are perhaps the most revealing. Democratic assemblymen voted to scuttle the cross-filing ban despite the likelihood that the initiative would bring their party majority control and against the clear wishes of liberal activists and their own constituents. What incumbents value, this history teaches us, is a nonpartisan environment with a few superficial and unconstraining trappings of partisanship. Party government was brought to California by activist organizations, specifically labor groups, outside the legislature.

FIRST EFFECTS OF THE DECLINE OF CROSS-FILING

The insertion of party labels on the primary ballot in the 1950s set off a far-reaching sequence of events. Incumbents could no longer easily win the nominations of both parties in low-key primary elections. Instead, they were forced to compete in general elections in which public interest was greater and the party attachments of voters were relevant. Incumbents facing real electoral challenges needed help in fending off these challenges, and local party activists were one likely source of that help. But to secure that help, candidates needed to be more responsive to the opinions of activists than they had been in the past—and to remain responsive even after they had been in office many years. A second development was that out-party primaries, which had formerly been non-events, were now important venues of party choice. In many primaries, candidate-centered organizations prevailed, but the personnel for the candidate organizations were increasingly drawn from stable pools of local activists. Deciding which candidates to support became another point of influence for activists. By assuming the power to nominate, activists had achieved the ability to de-nominate unfaithful incumbents.

Taken together, these developments brought about the revival of partisan politics in California legislative elections. Such revival had, indeed, been the intent of the anti-cross-filing reformers. Yet, the resulting changes did not all occur at the same pace. Some changes were immediate; others took decades to play out. Understanding how this party revival occurred, and the role of activists in it, affords numerous opportunities for understanding the dynamics of party organization.

In this section I show that the insertion of party names on the primary ballot—a result of Proposition 7's passage in 1952—rapidly changed the behavior of voters, activists, and incumbents. As I will demonstrate, voters reacted to the new ballot information by voting more in line with their partisan dispositions; liberal districts became more likely to elect Democrats and less likely to elect Republicans, and vice versa. The increased partisanship of the voters gave activists an opportunity to apply pressure to incumbents by seizing control of the nomination process. Incumbents responded to this new partisan environment in two ways: (1) Representation became based less on district and more on party, with legislators acting less like delegates and more like party trustees; and (2) Floor voting became gradually more partisan.

Effects on Voters

The elimination of party labels from general election ballots made it possible for most incumbents to win the nomination of both parties, as we saw in figure 2. After the insertion of party labels from 1954 on, however, a stark change occurred. The proportion of assembly incumbents who were able to win the nomination of both parties through cross-filing fell from 70 percent in 1952 to 30 percent in 1954 and 20 percent by 1958. Note that this decline in successful cross-filings is not due to any unwillingness by candidates to cross-file. Virtually all candidates tried (it cost only $30 to register as a candidate in a party primary in the 1950s). Indeed, the number of candidates attempting to cross-file actually increased slightly between 1952 and 1954. But the success rate dropped because voters now had access to the information provided by the party label on the primary ballot.

With party labels back on the ballots, voters selected representatives more in tune with their district's general partisan orientation. We can see some evidence of this development on the right side of the chart in figure 2: for the first time, Democrats cross-filed more successfully than Republicans. Democrats were finally taking advantage of the vast voter registration edge they had enjoyed since the early 1930s. Between 1952 and 1958, 23 of the assembly's 80 districts, 20 of which had been held by cross-filers, switched from Republican to Democratic control. Only 2 Democratic seats—both of which were held by cross-filers—switched to Republican control in that same time. Republicans had held 71 percent of the 58 cross-filed seats in 1952; by 1958, only 16 seats were still cross-filed, and Democrats held 14 of them. The partisan breakdown of the chamber went from 54-26 in the Republicans' favor to a Democratic majority of 47-33 in just three elections. Notably, these changes in the Democrats' favor occurred without any real leftward swing by the population: the state's partisan presidential vote remained essentially the same between 1952 and 1956.

If the state's electorate had been largely Democratic for years, and suddenly Democrats were winning the majority of legislative races, this suggests that legislative elections were becoming more responsive to district partisanship. To test this hypothesis, I have employed a logistic regression (logit) equation, measuring the likelihood that a district will elect a Democratic assembly member given the district's liberalism. I use the Democratic share of the vote for president as an indicator of district liberalism. Figure 5 plots the likelihood that districts over a range of ideological persuasions elected a Democratic assembly member in 1952 (the last year of nonpartisan primary ballots) and 1958 (the last year cross-filing was technically legal).

As figure 5 makes clear, the relationship between district ideology and party representation changed dramatically in those few short years after the introduction of party labels on the ballot. What was once basically a linear function had become more like a stepwise one. By 1958, any district that gave a Democratic presidential candidate 55 percent or more of the vote was nearly certain to send a Democrat to Sacramento.

To summarize, once voters had access to the party label, successful cross-filing by incumbents plummeted by more than half, and voters largely stopped voting across party lines in state assembly races. Voters' appetite for partisanship in state politics was neither destroyed nor even noticeably weakened by the Progressive reforms. Californians had merely been starved for information.

Activists after Cross-Filing

The role of local activists under the new partisan primary ballot is harder to document, but there is clear evidence that their efforts were important. As discussed earlier, Jesse Unruh's victory over a cross-filing Repub-

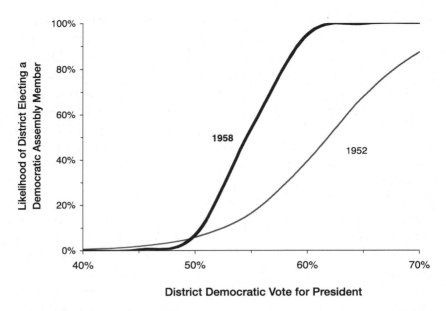

Fig. 5. Relationship of district ideology and partisan representation (1952 and 1958)

lican in 1954 was narrow, and it depended on support from the Guild he had organized and on contributions from organized labor, both in the primary and the general election. The demise of cross-filing was critical to Unruh's victory but hardly sufficient. Help from activists was necessary to clinch the victory. No doubt many of the other new winners in 1954 were likewise able to prevail only because interest groups and activists helped them to run stronger campaigns.

Evidence of such activism is clearest on the Democratic side, which had suffered more under cross-filing. Following the passage of Proposition 7 in 1952, the California Democratic Council (CDC) formed with the mission "to conduct a pre-primary convention every two years to endorse the best possible Democratic candidates for partisan office—and to build party unity behind them" (Fowle 1980: 90). The CDC had Democratic clubs in many assembly districts, but it tended to be strongest in suburban areas that were not natural Democratic strongholds. Yet, by throwing the weight of a statewide convention behind promising, liberal candidates, it hoped to be influential even in districts in which its membership was thin.

The CDC was taken very seriously within Democratic politics

throughout the 1950s, simultaneously lauded for helping the party take over the statehouse in 1958 and lambasted for pulling the party too far to the left. According to former state legislator Dewey Anderson, "Much of the credit [for giving Democrats the majority and putting Pat Brown in the governor's mansion in 1958] must go to the grass-root movement of Democratic clubs, neighborhood groups, and the statewide convention-like endorsement procedure which has resulted in a single slate of candidates representing the Democratic party" (Carney 1958: 16). Political scientist Frank Carney likewise wrote that the "CDC and the Democratic clubs have already made California a two-party state" (16). Yet state Democratic chair Elizabeth Snyder saw a downside to the CDC, accusing it of putting substantial and inappropriate leftward pressure on Democratic incumbents. "The people in the clubs think that it's vicious when one of the big financial contributors to the party has an interest in legislation and expresses the interest to an officeholder," said Snyder, "but I can tell you this, the big contributors . . . never have been as demanding of our incumbents as some of these people in the clubs and councils try to be" (10). State legislator Byron Rumford, while appreciative of the organization that the CDC was bringing to the Democratic Party, also expressed concern that the clubs might be used "to whip legislators into line" (Chinn 1958: 269). Some Democratic incumbents feared that the CDC, with its penchant for issuing resolutions on such matters as the death penalty and recognition of communist China and pressuring elected officials to act on those resolutions (Berinstein 1986), was making the Democratic Party less competitive. Indeed, Republicans regularly attacked their Democratic opponents for the "ultra-liberalism" of their CDC backers. A Democratic state legislator complained that "something has to be done about CDC. I had to run against those damned resolutions my last time up" (Wilson 1966: 148, 151).

It is difficult to state with certainty how effective the CDC was in elections. However, Chinn (1958) provides accounts of CDC activity in several special elections in the 1950s that are revealing. "First," notes Chinn, "the leaders have made a special effort to seek out good candidates and persuade them to run. Then both official and unofficial sources have organized outside support for the selected and endorsed candidate." Through such efforts, CDC-backed state senate candidates were able to defeat incumbent Republicans, and one Democratic assembly candidate was able to beat a former Republican Speaker. In the latter race, "the CDC supplied funds, workers, the professional campaign management of Don Bradley, office staff, and prominent speakers, including Governor Mennen Williams of Michigan." Following several more Democratic victories, Republican governor Goodwin Knight refused to hold any more special elections. Knight's decree was overruled by state courts, and when another special election was held in 1956, a Democrat won an assembly seat in the Republican stronghold of Orange County (Chinn 1958: 263–64).

Although further evidence about the CDC's organizational activity is scant, what evidence does exist depicts these activists as doing exactly what nomination-centered theory claims that activists do—first, working to elect fellow partisans through intervention at the nomination stage, and second, pressuring party officeholders to adhere faithfully to a partisan agenda.

Effects on Legislators

The insertion of party labels on primary ballots in 1954 led not only to the election of more Democrats but also to pressure from activists to stand firm on a partisan agenda. The response of the Democrat-controlled legislature was readily observable. "Now for the first time," a Republican assemblyman complained in 1960, "we have obnoxious and unreasoning party discipline, imposed upon members of the Legislature to the exclusion of the people's interest" (Johnson 1960: 55).

Is this claim reflected in members' actual roll call voting behavior? I analyze this question as follows: If, as argued earlier in this chapter, cross-filing gave legislators an incentive to be responsive to median opinion in a district, their roll call votes should become steadily more liberal as their district becomes more Democratic. In other words, there should be a straight-line relationship between roll call liberalism and the level of support for Democratic candidates in the district. In a weak party system, legislators try to mirror district opinion as closely as possible.

But suppose that legislators are creatures of parties. Under this model, sometimes called the responsible party government model, legislators vote consistently with their party agenda, regardless of district opinion. Liberal districts will still be more likely than conservative districts to elect Democrats to the legislature, but Democrats will support Democratic positions in office and Republicans will support Republican positions regardless of the exact degree of partisanship in their districts.

To see an example of these different types of representation in action, we can compare the cross-filed assembly with the modern one. In figure 6, I present two scatterplots charting district presidential voting against legislators' W-NOMINATE ideal points for the 1945 and 1997 assembly session. The 1945 scatterplot shows evidence of both district and party at work. Republicans are, on average, .9 points more conservative than Democrats on this −1 to +1 scale. But, as the party trend lines illustrate, legislators are clearly willing to adjust their positions to meet the needs of their districts. Several Democrats from conservative districts vote more conservatively than several Republicans from liberal districts.

The difference between this chart and the one from 1997 is profound. In the latter, the majority Democrats are shown to be virtually unresponsive to district sentiment. Democrats from districts in which Bill Clinton barely eked out a victory in 1996 behave virtually the same as those from districts in which Clinton won by a landslide. At least for the majority party, cohesion is extraordinarily high, and the responsible party government model is clearly in effect. The minority Republicans, by contrast, appear somewhat interested in pleasing their districts. Note, however, that the Republican contingent is clustered toward the top of the graph much more tightly than it was in 1945; even if these members are paying attention to their districts, they begin from a much higher degree of party responsiveness. Furthermore, the upward slope in the trend line is driven almost entirely by five relatively moderate Republicans, none of whom serve in the assembly today.

It is my contention that the roots of this change in representational style can be found in the end of cross-filing. If, as I have argued, the demise of cross-filing weakened the incentive to appeal to the median voter and increased the leverage of activist opinion, we should see district representation give way to responsible party government once party labels are inserted on the ballot. Of course, fifty-two years separate the two scatterplots in figure 6, and we should not expect to see this dramatic shift in style occur immediately. However, some change should be detectable.

To test the delegate and party trustee models in a simple regression setup, we can use the following equation:

$$\text{Ideal Point} = \beta_0 + \beta_1 \cdot \text{District Partisanship} + \beta_2 \cdot \text{Party of Member} + \varepsilon$$

District Partisanship is measured as the Democratic percentage of the vote for president in each member's district; and Party is the party of the

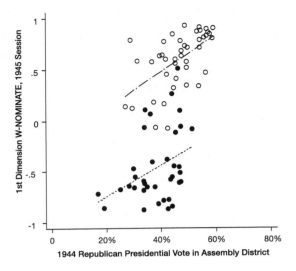

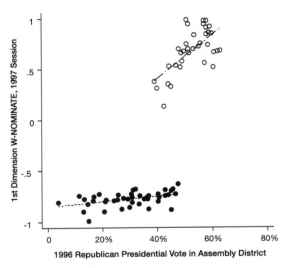

Fig. 6. Representational styles in two assembly sessions. Scatterplots depict the roll call conservatism of members of the California assembly (as measured by W-NOMINATE scores) plotted against the conservatism of their districts (as measured by the percentage voting Republican in the previous presidential election). Hollow dots indicate Republican assembly members; solid dots indicate Democratic assembly members.

assembly member. Given this model, high scores on β_1 indicate a high level of delegate style representation; high values of β_2 indicate support for the responsible party or trustee style. The theoretical expectation is that β_1 will be stronger in the cross-filing period, because members will stick close to the median voter in their district; and that β_2 will become stronger after the demise of cross-filing, because members will then adhere more closely to the party agenda, regardless of district opinion.

I have run this model in every year from 1913 to 2003, with the results shown graphically in figure 7. Two opposing trends are clearly visible in this period: The effect of an assembly member's party on her labor ratings has grown stronger over time, and the effect of district partisanship has grown weaker. In other words, district representation decreased, and party representation increased.

Let us now focus on the effect of the insertion of party labels in the 1954 elections on these trends. To judge from figure 7, the strength of party had approached—if not quite equaled—the strength of district in influencing legislative voting as of the 1930s, thanks to an infusion of Democrats into the chamber. However, party's influence had stalled and begun to retreat in the 1940s and early 1950s. Once party labels appeared on the primary ballot, however, party began to surge in strength, and it continues to rise to this day. What caused this surge in party strength? Did incumbents, alerted to the rising power of ideological activists, suddenly move toward their parties' extreme positions? Or were moderate incumbents simply replaced by more extreme challengers? The evidence available is limited, but it appears both effects were at work. There was a high degree of turnover in the California assembly in the 1950s, and those incumbents who lost or retired were often replaced by more ideologically extreme freshmen. Meanwhile, those who managed to stay in the chamber did experience some polarization, although the number of cases is so few that it is difficult to report this trend with great confidence. The totality of forces at work, however, induced a rise in the role of party determining legislators' votes and a decline in the power of districts.

Party did not immediately overwhelm district's influence, however. Indeed, there was a sudden surge in district's correlation with legislative voting behavior since the demise of cross-filing caused voters to elect people more reflective of their district's own preferences; liberal districts were no longer sending Republicans to Sacramento. But when that sorting-out of districts ended in the early 1960s, the influence of district suddenly and dramatically waned, dropping below that of party and never

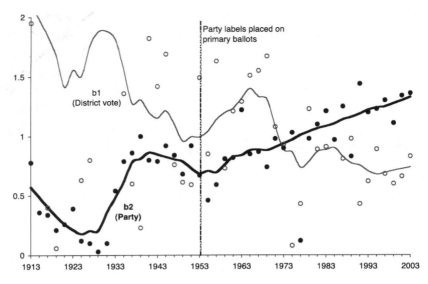

Fig. 7. Regression coefficients for district and party influences on assembly roll call voting, 1913–2003. Dependent variable is W-NOMINATE score in each session.

again rising above it. At that point, party became more important, and delegate style became less important—and the change turned out to be permanent.

What shall we conclude from these data about the effect of the insertion of ballot labels on style of representation? Obviously, these data do not provide definitive evidence that the change from district to party representation was *caused* by the insertion of party labels on the ballot in 1954, since the two lines do not intersect precisely at that point.

The absence of such an intersection at 1954 is not, I think, a problem for the notion that control of nominations is the key to party polarization. After all, who can say how long it should take for activists, empowered by the end of cross-filing after decades of impotence, to actually gain control of the behavior of officeholders? Strong activist organizations are unlikely to spring to life overnight throughout the state, and entrenched incumbents often have some power to resist party pressure even in strong party systems. Yet, as described in the previous section, we have clear evidence that CDC activists were at least *trying* to assert control over officeholders from the earliest moment of their empowerment and that their efforts were credited by close observers as being highly influential. Furthermore, the efforts of the CDC activists to control officeholders were irritating enough to Jesse Unruh that, as I discuss in a subsequent chapter, he proposed a law prohibiting the CDC from making endorsements in primaries. This qualitative evidence constitutes the clearest support for nomination-centered theory. What figure 7 adds is a finding consistent with the trend of theory and evidence but not by itself conclusive: shortly after the empowerment of activists, voting in the assembly became more detached from district opinion and more constrained by party norms, as would be expected if informal party organizations were the source of partisan backbone.

DISCUSSION

While California's political history during the twentieth century is unusual, it holds important lessons for party scholars everywhere. In this chapter, I have taken advantage of some natural experiments in California's history as critical tests of some of the leading theories of parties.

This review of California's political history contains much new information for those who see parties as creatures of politicians. Despite the impressive logic for why strategic politicians would choose to create legislative party institutions, we see in California a four-decade stretch in which legislators chose to avoid such party tools; they enjoyed the nonpartisan environment and sought to protect it from a creeping partisan resurgence from outside. This is particularly relevant to conditional party government scholars, who argue that legislative partisanship is conditioned upon electoral forces outside the legislature. Here, we see a case in which the electoral forces themselves were largely stable, at least from 1932 on (Rogin and Shover 1970), but legislative partisanship was in flux. It took outside ideological activists, and a change in electoral rules that allowed those activists to participate in primaries, to actually instill partisanship in the California legislature.

It is possible to view the events described in this chapter as consistent with cartel theory (Cox and McCubbins 1993, 2005). After all, cartel theory says that legislators will be electorally motivated to create and enhance a party brand name; if, thanks to cross-filing, voters didn't know the party affiliation of their candidates, there was little incentive to worry about the brand. Cartel theory is helpful here, but only to a point. It suggests that the value of party cohesion in the legislature will be contingent upon voter awareness of the brand name in the general election. But cross-filing mainly impacted primary elections. General elections still existed, and candidates there still had party labels attached to their names. Granted, many of them had eliminated their competitors in the primaries, but a good number, particularly those from competitive districts, had not. Thus there was still plenty of electorally induced motivation to protect the party brand names under cross-filing—incumbents just didn't do it.

What this evidence does show us is that control of the nomination is the essence of party discipline. The machines that ran California politics at the turn of the twentieth century did so through manipulation of party nominations. Progressive reformers recognized this fact and reasoned that party discipline could be broken by separating the legislative parties from the activists and benefit seekers that had controlled nominations. The response to these reforms proved the Progressives right.

In short, legislative parties in the California assembly were strong when ideological organizations outside the government could influence or control party nominations, and weak when they could not. As expected by my approach, outside groups sought this control and were resisted by officeholders. Legislators stuck close to the median district voter when informal party organizations were disempowered; once it became possible for IPOs to influence nominations, legislators became more loyal to party agendas.

This chapter has largely focused on legislative behavior during and immediately after the cross-filing era. To better understand legislators' responses to Progressive reforms, it would be helpful to have a baseline estimate of partisanship prior to the imposition of cross-filing. It would also profit us to understand how incumbents responded to a host of institutional conditions during a broader swath of history. It is to these tasks that I turn in the next chapter.

CHAPTER 3

150 Years of Legislative
Party Behavior

The previous chapter largely focused on California's political history in the 1950s, noting changes in voter and legislative behavior in response to the insertion of party labels on the primary ballot and the banning of cross-filing. This analysis painted a picture of politicians as nonideological reelection-seekers. With extralegislative activists excluded from party activity, incumbents moderated and ran the chamber in a way that discouraged partisanship but facilitated their own reelections. The removal of Progressive party-killing reforms cleared the way for local activists to reassert themselves in party nominations, and only then did legislators begin to act like legislative partisans.

The availability of 150 years of legislative roll call data makes it possible to look beyond those crucial years of the 1950s and see how assembly incumbents behaved over a larger time frame. We can observe how they reacted to the imposition of Progressive reforms in the first place, and how they have behaved in recent years.

These data also provide a more general opportunity for researchers to understand how incumbents respond to a vast range of institutional conditions. Using long time-series of roll call data, legislative researchers in recent years have drawn all manner of valuable conclusions about legislative behavior, including the influence of parties on members' votes (see, e.g., Krehbiel 2000; Poole and Rosenthal 1997; Snyder and Groseclose 2000).

Unfortunately, these studies, enlightening as they are, share a common limitation: a focus on the American Congress. Apart from Jenkins's

(2000, 1999) innovative studies of the short-lived, partyless Confederate Congress, all of these studies examine the national legislature, a body that has enjoyed a functional two-party system essentially since the 1820s. The U.S. Congress has experienced remarkably little structural change in the past two centuries.

By contrast, there is a great deal of variance in the legislative structure of statehouses. Several states have highly competitive party systems, while others—notably Rhode Island, Hawaii, and the pre-1970 South—have had essentially one-party rule, and Nebraska has banned parties altogether. Territorial legislatures were often nonpartisan, as well (Espino and Hindman 2007). States offer significant variations on institutional constraints, including term limits, redistricting practices, salaries, and electoral rules, allowing legislative researchers to make inferences about the influence of those constraints on legislative behavior. However, until now, comprehensive roll call data have not existed. One exception is the recent work of Gerald Wright and colleagues (Wright and Osborn 2002; Wright and Schaffner 2002; Wright and Winburn 2002), which utilizes complete roll call datasets from all 99 state legislatures in several recent sessions. But extended time-series for state legislatures have been unavailable, until now.

The vast dataset employed here, the first of its kind for a state legislature, allows us to investigate incumbents' responses to a variety of institutional conditions. California, after all, has gone from being a virtual one-party state in the early twentieth century, to a two-party state with suppressed partisanship during the cross-filing years, and finally to the fiercely polarized state that exists today. Using these data, I am able to quantify the levels of partisan polarization in the assembly at various times in history and to measure the impact of various influences on legislative behavior. The evidence testifies to the strong polarization of the modern assembly, the profound dampening effect that cross-filing had on partisanship, and the tendency for incumbents to follow the wishes of whoever can control their fates.

THE HISTORY OF THE CALIFORNIA ASSEMBLY AT A GLANCE

Before using the roll call data, however, I attempt to sketch out partisan behavior in the California assembly by examining Speaker elections. The election of a Speaker is a party's most important vote in any assembly session—the Speaker exerts a great deal of power over the staffing and leadership of committees, the resources available to individual assembly members, and the fate of legislation (Blair and Flournoy 1967). In a strong party system, the Speaker would be expected to act in a way that benefits his party at the expense of the minority. In the U.S. House of Representatives, for example, Speaker elections have been strictly party-line affairs for over a century, and rare deviations on this key vote are considered punishable offenses. Thus elections for Speaker are a critical indicator of legislative partisanship (Koger 2000).

Figure 8 shows the partisan breakdown of Speaker contests between 1851 and 1999 using a Rice cohesion score. Two moving averages chart the trends in party cohesion on contested Speaker elections and all Speaker elections during this time frame. The first point to notice is the number of uncontested Speaker elections, which appear on the horizontal axis. Prior to the Progressive takeover of the assembly in 1911, all the Speaker votes were contested, mirroring the custom of the U.S. House. Between 1911 and the demise of cross-filing (the Progressives' chief antiparty legacy) in 1959, however, only 44 percent of the Speaker elections were contested. This is uncommon among state legislatures and unheard of in the modern U.S. House. Still, the trend lines tell a clear story: parties fiercely contested the speakership prior to the imposition of cross-filing. In the years following the Progressive reforms, Speaker elections called forth odd coalitions, with the winner occasionally receiving more votes from the minority party than from his own. With the exception of a briefly partisan period in the late 1930s under the leadership of liberal Democrat Paul Peek as Speaker, partisanship remained low from the beginning of the Progressive era until the 1960s. In the years since, partisanship on Speaker votes has obviously become stronger, and steadily fewer of those votes have been uncontested.

Left to police themselves, it appears, legislators ceased to be partisan on the key vote that, in genuinely partisan bodies, is more likely than any other to be decided on partisan lines. Even during the New Deal, when the two major parties proceeded from vastly different worldviews and sought to enact nearly opposite agendas for the state, partisanship could not be maintained. But, of course, these results turn on just one vote per session. Do the same patterns show up if we examine all the legislative roll call votes?

To boil down so much data into a few meaningful statistics, I employed Poole's W-NOMINATE software program. W-NOMINATE pro-

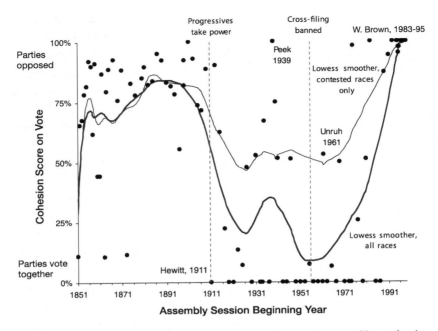

Fig. 8. Assembly Speaker elections, 1851–1999. Data points are Rice cohesion scores for assembly Speaker elections. These scores were calculated by dichotomizing Speaker election results, with the votes for the winner compared with the combined votes for losing candidates and those who simply voted no or refused to vote. The resulting cohesion number is the absolute value of the percentage of Democrats voting for the winning Speaker minus the percentage of Republicans doing so. When all Democrats vote in one direction and all Republicans vote in the other, cohesion is 100 percent; a zero score would result when the parties each split in their support for Speaker or when all members of the chamber vote the same way.

duces a variety of helpful indicators that describe the levels of polarization and the dimensionality of the chamber.

The first statistic I utilize is the aggregate proportion reduction in error (APRE), which simply describes the percentage of the variance in roll call behavior that can be explained by each dimension. In highly partisan chambers, the APRE of the first dimension should be high (the U.S. House of Representatives and Senate had first-dimension APREs of 63.4 and 72.6, respectively, in 1999), and the contribution of rival dimensions should be low. That is, most or all voting behavior should fall along the main liberal-conservative dimension. In weakly polarized chambers, the first dimension will have a relatively low APRE, and other dimensions will occasionally rival party. The danger of using such a statistic to describe partisanship in the California assembly is that it ignores a potentially confounding variable—the size of the majority party. As state legislative scholars have shown (Aldrich and Battista 2002), majority size is an important determinant of legislative partisanship. This is particularly vexing issue for California, since the Democratic Party itself largely vanished from California between 1897 and 1931 (Chinn 1958; Rogin and Shover 1970). At no point in this period did the Democrats ever hold more than 24 of the assembly's 80 seats; in most years they held fewer than ten.

To compensate for this confounding problem, I have calculated the residual APRE of each session after controlling for majority size. This residual plot appears in figure 9. I have added two dotted lines indicating when cross-filing was imposed by the Progressives and when it was eliminated by the Democratic majority in 1959. The trend is such that, in the nineteenth century, APRE, controlling for majority size, stayed relatively flat but began rising in the early twentieth century. Soon after, it began a decline that continued until the end of cross-filing in 1959. Immediately after that, APRE began its sharp upward move that continues to this day. The pattern is about as clear as it could be: the trend on partisan voting turns downward within a few sessions of the imposition of cross-filing and reverses almost immediately upon cross-filing's abolition.

The sharpest break in the data lies at the end of cross-filing in 1959. To demonstrate the sharpness of this break, I have drawn scatterplots of the legislator ideal points for the years 1953 (near the end of the cross-filing era) and 1963 (shortly after cross-filing's demise). These years are indicated in figure 9 with hollow dots. Although these years are somewhat extreme relative to the smoother line, they are far from unique as indicators of partisan behavior in their respective time periods.

The scatterplot for 1953, shown in figure 10, shows that while chamber Democrats are generally to the left of their Republican counterparts, there is essentially no space in between the two parties, and there is considerable overlap, with several Democrats voting more conservatively than some moderate Republicans. Instead of there being an ideological gap between the parties, there is a seamless spectrum from the left to the center to the right. The political center was a legitimate place for politicians to reside, and many chose to reside there.

Just five sessions later, the scatterplot from the 1963 session is strikingly different (fig. 11). The assembly has transformed itself into a

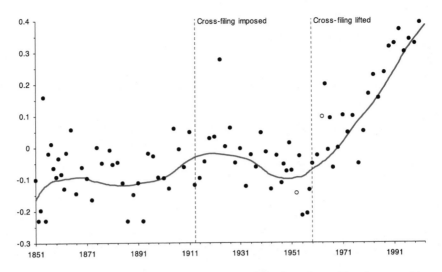

Fig. 9. Aggregate proportion reduction in error (APRE) in the California assembly, 1851–2003, controlling for majority size. Points are residuals from the regression of first-dimension APRE on the percentage of the chamber held by the majority party.

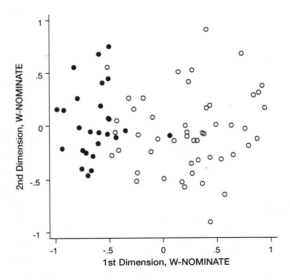

Fig. 10. Legislator ideal points, 1953. Hollow points represent Republicans; solid points are Democrats.

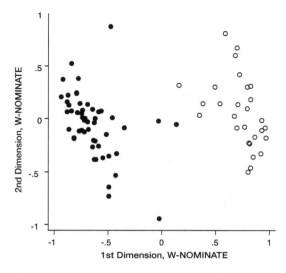

Fig. 11. Legislator ideal points, 1963. Hollow points represent Republicans; solid points are Democrats.

sharply polarized legislature, with virtually all Republicans to the far right, virtually all Democrats to the far left, and only a few legislators in the center. Clearly, the demise of cross-filing had a dramatic effect on legislative behavior in a very short time span. With party activists suddenly able to monitor the behavior of legislators and hold them accountable to a party agenda, incumbents quickly fled the center. Extremism was the far safer course for career-minded legislators.

The change has been quite profound. As figure 9 demonstrated, the polarization of the chamber has increased dramatically since that time. And as party has increased as an influence on legislative voting, district preferences have decreased. Throughout much of the century, the best predictor of legislative behavior was district opinion. Legislators could look out for themselves by voting their districts. Today, however, that is no longer true. Modern legislators look to their party first and to their district second. The continuation of these trends to the present day is what has created modern legislative gridlock, with each party pleasing its activists and neither side much interested in voters.

The extent to which modern assembly members do *not* represent their districts is made clear in figure 12. In each of four time periods, the figure shows the relationship between presidential vote at the district

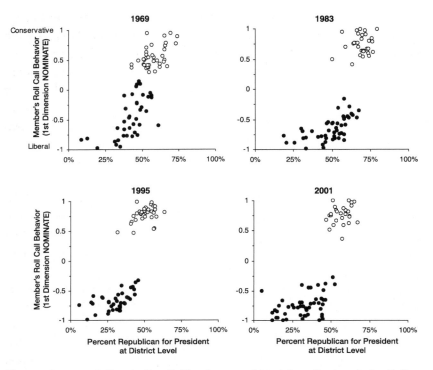

Fig. 12. Representation in the California assembly at four time periods. Hollow points represent Republicans; solid points are Democrats.

level (which is taken as a measure of district partisanship) and the roll call voting of the assembly member from that district. In 1969, there is a healthy relationship between the two variables: as a district becomes more Republican in its presidential voting, its assembly member becomes more conservative in her roll call voting. And, critically, when a district is middle-of-the-road in its presidential voting, it gets a middle-of-the-road legislator to represent it. But now look at the graphs for later years. Middle-of-the-road legislators have virtually disappeared, and districts today get a stark choice: they can vote for a very liberal Democrat or a very conservative Republican, but apparently nothing in between. The party of the legislator determines roll call voting; shades of district opinion matter hardly at all.

It is fair to ask at this point whether the bygone pattern of strong district influence was necessarily a bad thing. I address this normative question in some detail in my concluding chapter. For the moment, however, let me simply observe that, as the qualitative evidence in the next chapter will show, the tendency of legislators to vote their districts was *not* the equivalent of government of the people, by the people, and for the people. The late cross-filing era was one of the most corrupt in the history of the California legislature. This was the era in which famed lobbyist Artie Samish stepped in to fill the role that party would later play—working to nominate and fund candidates, rounding up votes for key measures, and punishing members who were overly independent-minded. He also attended to the personal pleasures of legislators in ways that parties normally do not. As one indication of Samish's power in this period, consider this bit of legislative achievement: the legislature delayed for several years the adoption of daylight saving time in California because one of Samish's clients in the motion picture industry believed that longer summer days would mean fewer customers in theaters. Or so Samish himself claimed (1971).

As the cross-filing period ended, Samish was sent to jail, as was a former assembly Speaker. "District influence" began to subside, and party influence increased. But we should not believe that "district influence" was ever actually high in the cross-filing period. As the qualitative evidence indicates, members took positions on the side of voter opinion without really representing it—an example of what Mayhew later called "position-taking."

RIVAL INFLUENCES ON LEGISLATIVE VOTING BEHAVIOR

At a time when parties were weak in the California assembly, other voting coalitions emerged. A particularly important one was the Speaker's coalition. Buchanan (1963) noted in his study of California politics during the 1940s and 1950s that bipartisan Speaker coalitions would form and maintain discipline on some subset of roll call votes over the course of several legislative sessions.

The importance of the Speaker's coalition explains how the influence of district could apparently be strong even as constituents' wishes were, according to all qualitative accounts, being thwarted. Lobbyists did not need to control every vote, or even most of them, to get what they wanted out of the legislature. Only a few key votes were necessary. One of these was the vote for assembly Speaker. Since the Speaker has the power to appoint committees and to determine whether and when legislation got to the floor, control of the speakership obviated the need for direct control over most other legislative votes. One member reported in the 1950s:

> You're a free agent 99 percent of the time—except on the speakership. They [industry lobbyists] want to control the speaker because they want to control the committees, so they can bottle up their bills. They all three [oil, liquor, and race track advocates] have money, have always given large amounts— twenty times what one man can give. If you go along with them you can make a 99 percent perfect record. (Buchanan 1963: 43)

Because control of the speakership was so vital, coalitions of lobbyists regularly nominated their own candidates for Speaker and tried to assemble support for them among other legislators. In a telling example, Governor Earl Warren personally lobbied assembly Republicans to elect Don Field as Speaker in 1946, while liquor industry lobbyist Artie Samish pushed the GOP to elect Sam Collins to the same post. The chamber ultimately went with Collins (Buchanan 1963: 28). What's more, the lobbyists' oversight of legislators didn't end when the Speaker was selected. They made sure that the coalition stayed together on a subset of votes that were essential to their interests. Unlike the parties of the time, the lobbyists bankrolling the Speaker's coalitions had the means to monitor legislators' behavior and distribute rewards and punishments. California's legislators stood out among their counterparts in other states in their reliance upon lobbyists to guide their roll call votes and assemble voting coalitions (106).

While in most sessions the Speaker's coalition only controlled the outcomes of a few key votes, it could occasionally become the dominant schism in a legislative session. This is what happened in 1925. The previous session had been dominated by conservative Republicans, who passed much of governor Friend William Richardson's "economy" agenda, which drastically reduced funding for education and humanitarian agencies. Interpreting Richardson's agenda as an attack on Hiram Johnson's Progressive legacy, a group of journalists and current and former officeholders created the Progressive Voters' League, tasked with winning enough Republican primaries in 1924 to seize control of the legislature. The League soon boasted a statewide membership of 542 people in 40 counties, financing its work through newsletter subscriptions (Posner 1957).

The 1924 Republican primaries were bitterly fought, with the League hiring a public speaker to trail Governor Richardson around the state and

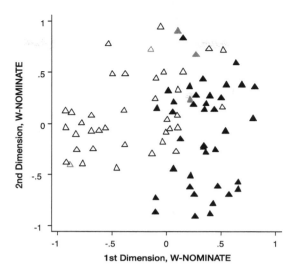

Fig. 13. Legislator ideal points, 1925. Points are labeled by vote for Speaker. Supporters of Frank Merriam appear as hollow triangles; supporters of Isaac Jones appear as solid triangles. Black triangles are Republicans; gray triangles are Democrats. Merriam and Jones were both Republicans.

inform voters of the Progressive cause. The primaries resulted in a near perfect split of the assembly's Republican contingent, and the first battle between the two sides was over the speakership. On this vote, conservative Frank Merriam defeated the Progressive Voters' League challenger Isaac Jones 40-39. This vote set the pattern for legislative voting throughout the legislative term. In figure 13, I have plotted the members' ideal points from 1925, with each legislator depicted by his vote for Speaker: hollow triangles indicate supporters of Merriam and solid triangles indicate Jones's backers. These coalitions split the first dimension, with Merriam's supporters all appearing on the right and Jones's supporters appearing to the left. For at least one session, this extralegislative coalition of Progressive advocates managed to enforce some legislative discipline among the incumbents they supported (Hopper 1975). This was not, incidentally, the only session in which a Speaker's coalition controlled the first dimension of legislative voting. Such splits occurred in 1923 and 1931, as well, and the Speaker's coalition was a significant rival schism in several other sessions.

Another key session for the Speaker's coalition was 1955, a scatterplot of which can be seen in figure 14. Again, all points are depicted by vote for Speaker: solid triangles indicate supporters of Speaker Luther "Abe" Lincoln, while hollow triangles mark supporters of Allen Smith. Both candidates were Republicans, and Lincoln was actually elected despite the majority of Republicans in the chamber having preferred Smith 24-23. This bipartisan coalition had a strong hold over legislative voting, as virtually all of Lincoln's supporters are at the top left of the graph, and all of Smith's are clustered at the bottom right. Thus we see again that absence of party voting is not absence of structured voting. Buchanan (1963: 59) describes this particular Speaker contest as being largely geographical in nature but also driven by water battles and Lincoln's support from the *Los Angeles Times* and the petroleum industry. Both the *Times*, with its highly visible and respected endorsement, and the petroleum industry, with its considerable financial resources, likely had far greater ability to reward or punish legislators for their roll call behavior than did the legislative parties of the day.

Going back further in time, one can see that legislative coalitions could form quickly when groups external to the legislature pressed for them. The Populist revolt of the 1890s, for example, manifested itself most impressively during the 1897 legislative session in California. As can be seen in figure 15, Democrats and People's Party (Populist) assembly members, along with Fusion candidates representing both parties, formed a strong voting bloc and consistently opposed the Republican Party on a wide swath of legislative votes. All the Republicans are well to the right, and the Democrats and People's Party members are to the left, with a yawning gap between them. Clearly, Democrats and People's Party candidates either felt strongly about the Populist agenda on which they were elected or feared the agrarian activists who got them nominated in the first place.

Earlier years under study provide evidence of more traditional party organizations and their influence over elected officials. During much of the 1880s, for example, Democrats from San Francisco owed their elections to Christopher Buckley, the "blind boss" of San Francisco. Buckley's organization was clearly in line with traditional notions of machine politics. He was, for one thing, adept at using patronage to reward regime adherents. The city's school system, in particular, contained roughly half of San Francisco's 1,400 patronage posts, and Buckley brazenly awarded such posts to political allies. Under his leadership, the school system cre-

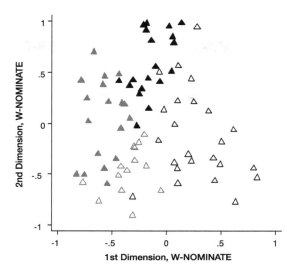

Fig. 14. Legislator ideal points, 1955. Points are labeled by vote for Speaker. Supporters of Luther "Abe" Lincoln appear as solid triangles; supporters of Allen Smith appear as hollow triangles. Black triangles are Republicans; gray triangles are Democrats.

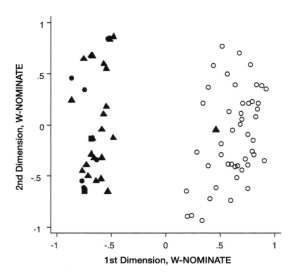

Fig. 15. Legislator ideal points, 1897. Hollow circles are Republicans; solid circles are Democrats; squares are members of the People's Party; and triangles depict those running under the Democrat-People's Party Fusion label.

ated an Inspecting Teacher position, the holder of which would evaluate other teachers and could hire and fire them at will. A classroom at the Mission Grammar School was subsequently staffed by a steady stream of women with either romantic or familial ties to prominent ward leaders (Bullough 1979: 130–31).

Like other urban bosses, Buckley avoided taking ideological stances whenever possible. As one of his critics wrote, "Political principals [*sic*] are to him only a synonym for political pelf, and like the Hessians, he was ready to sell his services to the highest bidder" (Lynch 1889: 9). Buckley also resorted to traditional methods of manipulating election results, including paying voters up to three dollars each for their support at the polls (Bullough 1979: 178). Most important, though, Buckley controlled his delegation to state nominating conventions and used this control to influence legislative behavior. As Lynch (1889: 13) writes, "People who wanted certain measures defeated, or passed, never went to the member of the Legislature direct. All their negotiations were with Buckley." Bullough (1979) adds,

> Buckley exerted a determined effort, from his first experience at a state convention in 1882, to make his presence felt in the California Democracy, and he successfully retained sufficient authority to influence those state governmental and political affairs which directly involved San Francisco. (157)

To see an example of his influence, we can look at a scatterplot of the 1889 session, depicted in figure 16. While party obviously played some significant role in this session—virtually all Republicans appear at the top half of the graph, while all Democrats appear on the bottom—it is only the second dimension of legislative behavior. The first dimension can best be explained as a coalition of San Francisco Democrats (marked with triangles) lined up against the rest of the chamber. Those under Buckley's control demonstrated a level of discipline in voting that any modern legislative caucus would envy. Judging from the roll call data, the boss's poor eyesight didn't prevent him from keeping an eye on those whose nominations he controlled.

A similar dynamic can be detected in the 1905 session. At this time there were essentially no Democrats in the chamber—any attempt at partisan organization would have been futile for the Democrats and unnecessary for the Republicans. Organization on a regional basis, however,

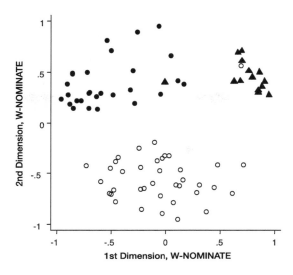

Fig. 16. Legislator ideal points, 1889. Democrats from San Francisco are marked with triangles; non–San Francisco Democrats are marked with solid circles; and Republicans are marked with hollow circles.

was useful, as evidenced by Republican boss Abraham Ruef's influence over San Francisco's delegation. Through shrewd alliances with the city's labor activists and the leaders of the Southern Pacific Railroad, Ruef exerted great control over nominating conventions and the candidates that they produced. Ruef was widely credited, for example, with grooming and installing Eugene Schmitz as San Francisco's mayor in 1901. Their initial meeting, during which Ruef encouraged Schmitz to run, is telling. Schmitz, although considered a handsome and intelligent man, complained that he'd be a poor candidate since he had little political experience, knowledge of local affairs, public speaking skills, or money. Ruef replied,

> You have as much experience and information as many men who have been nominated . . . and more than some who have filled the office. What you lack can easily be supplied. The speeches and the funds we can take care of. (Bean 1952: 21)

With such skills and assets available to him, Ruef was able to influence votes and control the destinies of many San Francisco politicians, as is evidenced by the scatterplot of ideal points of the 1905 legislature, seen in figure 17. The San Francisco delegation clearly held together, occupying the right portion of the graph. So again we have a case in which the primary dimension of roll call voting is determined by a group outside the legislature that is able to hold officeholders accountable for their behavior. The true party leaders were outside the government, exerting control over those inside it.

Another instance of outside forces controlling state legislators can be seen during the Progressive ascendancy in the 1910s. California's Progressive Party began as an alliance of reform-minded journalists, attorneys, and wealthy benefactors who wished to drive the Southern Pacific Railroad from its position of power. They formed organizations in various cities that raised issues, amassed funds, slated candidates, and got them nominated. Those who owed their position of power to the Progressive activists knew they could pay a price for straying from the organization's detailed agenda.

At least part of the Progressives' organizational strength can be attributed to their alliance with labor. Although the Progressive and labor agendas didn't correspond perfectly, many unions strongly backed Hiram Johnson and the Progressives (Mason 1994), and reelection-seeking incumbents knew that disappointed labor unions could impose heavy costs on their careers. In addition, although women were new to the franchise, several women's political organizations began advocating for Progressive causes and candidates, and some observers of the time held these women's clubs responsible for Republican presidential candidate Charles Evan Hughes's narrow statewide loss to President Woodrow Wilson in 1916 (Raftery 1994).

Figure 18 shows a scatterplot of legislators in 1915. In this graph, the Xs indicate members who won the nomination of the Progressive Party. Several of these took advantage of the new cross-filing rules to win other parties' nominations, as well. Republicans appear as hollow dots and Democrats as solid dots. As can be seen, virtually everyone affiliated with the Progressive Party appears to the left, while others are arrayed on the right. The first dimension in this session is essentially a division between Progressive and Standpat Republicans. The alliance of journalists, attorneys, women's clubs, unions, and good-government activists—all losers under the railroad-controlled legislature who were united by various tenets of the Progressive Party—showed itself to be a powerful and con-

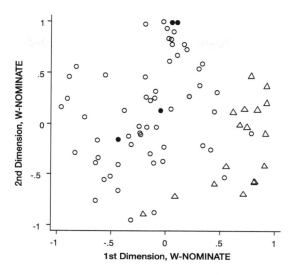

Fig. 17. Legislator ideal points, 1905. Solid dots depict Democrats; triangles depict Republicans from San Francisco; hollow dots depict Republicans from places other than San Francisco.

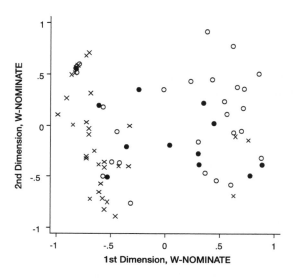

Fig. 18. Legislator ideal points, 1915. Solid dots indicate Democrats; hollow dots indicate Republicans; Xs indicate members who filed as Progressives. Many Progressives cross-filed with other parties, as well.

tinuing influence on behavior within the chamber. Ironically, although the Progressives considered themselves opponents of party organizations, they proved to be one of the more disciplined legislative coalitions that Sacramento chamber had seen.

Given the apparent ease with which groups outside the legislature could structure its voting, one would expect a resurgence of legislative partisanship during the New Deal. And, indeed, some occurred. In the 1920s, Democrats were some 50 percentage points behind the Republicans in voter registration, but in the 1930s they pulled ahead of Republicans by 20 points. Democrats, however, had a difficult time translating that voter registration advantage into electoral success. In part, this was due to cross-filing. Republican incumbents were still able to prevail in many Democratic primary contests, keeping the Democratic candidates off the general election ballot. The Democrats also shot themselves in the foot by nominating author Upton Sinclair for the governorship in 1934. Sinclair's End Poverty in California (EPIC) platform was widely perceived to be outside the political mainstream and embracing of socialism. Democrat Culbert Olson, however, was able to win the governorship in 1938, and the Democrats took the legislature that year, as well.

At this point, conditions appeared to strongly favor a resurgence of legislative partisanship. The Democrats had their first majority of the century, and they had a potent national agenda. Furthermore, unlike the parties in the contemporary U.S. Congress, California's parties were not torn internally on questions of race and civil rights. Yet, as we saw in the last chapter, they accomplished nothing. In a contested partisan vote that stands out as such in figure 8, the Democrats elected New Dealer Paul Peek as Speaker, who began working with the governor to pass a Democratic program. But the stress of party discipline was apparently too much. Peek was removed from the speakership by his colleagues, a new Speaker was elected on a bipartisan vote, and the legislature, despite its "potential partisanship" (Buchanan 1963: 18), returned to its undisciplined ways.

Why were nineteenth-century Populists, San Francisco machine politicians, and Progressive reformers able to impose party discipline on legislative voting while New Deal Democrats were not? My inference is that the former could control nominations to office and that, as a result of cross-filing, New Deal Democrats could not.

DISCUSSION

Many of today's leading legislative scholars proceed from the common as-sumption that parties are the creatures of politicians. Career-minded leg-islators and candidates will build parties if they think they will be useful, and will avoid them if they find them unnecessary or bothersome. The evidence presented in this chapter calls these assumptions into question. When partisan forces were incapable of holding their legislators to a party agenda—due to either insufficient numbers or Progressive an-tiparty devices—legislators did not seek to build up party institutions and enforce discipline. They did sometimes vote in disciplined fashion but only in response to specific external pressures. Urban party bosses, Pop-ulist or Progressive activists, lobbyists, and others have alternately held sway over legislative behavior thanks to their ability to punish or reward legislators, something that the parties either could not or would not do for decades.

It is particularly interesting to see such "islands of accountability" form even at the turn of the twentieth century. This was a time when leg-islators served only a few months out of a two-year session, were paid but a paltry sum for it, and held office in most cases for only a single term. In these conditions, it would not be surprising to find legislators incapable of forming any sort of long coalition for controlling legislative behavior. Yet even under such constraints, partisan control of the legislative seemed to be increasing, as we saw in figure 9, right up until the passage of cross-filing. And throughout this period, a variety of short-lived, exter-nally driven coalitions formed and voted together with considerable dis-cipline.

But cross-filing and the nonpartisan ballot proved devastating to party discipline, since activists could neither nominate officeholders nor hold them accountable. Even during the New Deal, when a revitalized Demo-cratic Party had the numbers to control the assembly, it was unable to sustain party discipline.

Tellingly, as we saw in the previous chapter, the reform that would reintroduce party discipline to California—the banning of cross-filing—was fought by legislators of both parties in 1952. Even the minority Democrats fought against a reform that could bring them control of the legislature. Partisanship, when it finally returned to the assembly, had to be imposed from outside.

With the Progressive rules removed, partisanship shot upward in the late 1950s and has continued to climb ever since. The influence of district, meanwhile, plateaued at that time and ultimately began to wane. By the mid-1980s, party actually became a better predictor of legislative behavior than district. In other words, members are now sticking with their parties, even at the risk of offending the median voter in their districts. This is hardly consistent with the notion of parties as creatures of legislators. Members are actually putting their careers at risk to please their parties. This reflects an increase both in the power of legislative parties and in the influence of the ideologues who control primaries today.

This study of California's assembly offers us a chance to see legislative parties under conditions that the modern U.S. Congress has never experienced. We can see what happens when the link between incumbents and outside activists is severed. We can also see what happens when that link is restored. The results suggest that this link is the linchpin for legislative partisanship. Legislators have no discernible love for parties—what they want is to remain in office.

It may be insufficient, however, to conclude that incumbents never want to create party institutions. There have been instances in California assembly history in which partisanship did actually come from within the chamber, such as during Jesse Unruh's tenure as Speaker in the 1960s and under Sen. Jim Brulte's leadership during the 2003 budget standoff. Perhaps the best way to deal with this matter is to specify that there are two types of politicians who serve in America's legislatures. The first type is not interested in parties—what she wants is to remain in office, to enjoy the benefits of power without needing to do anything more than taking occasional positions. If she sometimes needs to hew the party line to stay in office, that's what she'll do; if she can ignore parties, that's just as well. This is the type of politician famously depicted by Mayhew in *Congress: The Electoral Connection* (1974). The second type of politician is a fierce partisan who wants to enact an agenda and to prevent the opposing party's agenda from becoming law. Such a politician is willing to risk a general election defeat to serve the higher cause of party and ideological fealty.

Conditions *outside* the legislature strongly determine which type of politician will dominate the government. Partisan activists prefer the second type and will work to get such a person nominated and elected. So long as these activists control the nominations process, the latter type of politician will predominate. If these activists, because of institutional rules like cross-filing or crackdowns on traditional party organizations, cannot control the primaries, the first type of politician—neither driven by ideological fervor nor troubled by strong activists—will tend to dominate elections through moderation. Thus, whether strong legislative parties form and persist is a function of which type of legislator dominates the chamber. That, in turn, is a function of whether activists are able to control nominations. The claim that ideologically motivated officeholders create legislative parties is a strong one, but it is incomplete. To judge from the California experience, legislative parties do not form unless extralegislative forces push for them. It therefore makes sense to view these extralegislative forces as the source of legislative parties.

Throughout this chapter and the previous one, I have been able to provide only limited and secondhand accounts of the conduct of informal party organizations external to the legislature and have been forced to infer a great deal about their activity and influence. However, if partisanship is truly dependent upon the efforts of activists and other actors outside the government, then studying the behavior of these actors is critical to understanding how parties function. That is precisely what I do in the next chapter.

CHAPTER 4

A Visit to the Smoke-Filled Room

An old joke tells of a drunk who looks for his lost car keys under a lamppost because that's where the light is best. Political scientists are commonly criticized for this sort of "drunkard's search." They are accused, that is, of using the most convenient forms of data to test their theories, even if such data miss much of the story.

This problem is especially acute in the study of political parties. Much of what parties do—deciding whom and what to support, and what to demand in exchange for it—is highly sensitive. Some of it is barely legal. Almost none of it would party members like to see in a newspaper at election time. Given this, parties normally try to keep the public record of their internal processes as limited as possible. Yet, the decisions that parties make in these low-light conditions are so fundamental to their operation that one cannot neglect them and still provide a full picture of how parties function. I have therefore ventured into the field to speak with members of informal party organizations and to watch them work in several different communities. I inquired into the motives, methods, and effectiveness of informal party organizations. Relying on historical materials, I also describe a partylike system known as the "Speaker's organization," which emerged in Sacramento shortly after the demise of cross-filing. Most of the data, however, come from interviews conducted between 2001 and 2004 in local communities.

The interviews, each lasting roughly an hour, consist of a series of open-ended questions asked of prominent local political figures, including officeholders, donors, activists, and consultants. In designing the interviews, I drew upon the works of Fenno (1978) and Fowler and McClure (1989), in which extensive, open-ended surveys of local elites are used to make general inferences about the behavior of incumbents and candidates in American politics. I offered respondents the opportunity to speak anonymously but was able to develop enough rapport with subjects that most were willing to speak on the record. In many cases, political journalists from local newspapers helped me identify key partisan actors; respondents helped me identify other actors for additional interviews. With the respondents' permission, I recorded all interviews and later transcribed important segments (see the appendix for a list of interviewees).

The chapter begins with overviews of the political systems I found in each region: the assembly Speaker's office in Sacramento, the Republicans of Orange County, the Democrats in the southern, western, and eastern portions of Los Angeles County, and both Democrats and Republicans of Fresno County. I then describe the different roles played by each of the four types of actors in the IPO model (activists, officeholders, donors, and brokers), using evidence from each of the regions under study. I also delve into how candidates are chosen, how discipline is enforced, and the role of extremism.

The information reported in this chapter bears in important ways on theories of party organization. For example, when a major politician reports that benefit seekers recently urged him to become more active in channeling their contributions to other politicians, it helps validate the idea that there is a demand for party organization among benefit seekers. Similarly, a politician's description of how he had to pay his dues before gaining organizational support in a nomination contest sheds light on how the nomination process works. As in any empirical analysis, no single piece of evidence is definitive; but together with the historical and quantitative data from other chapters, the interview data in this chapter contribute to a persuasive theoretical account of how contemporary political parties operate.

INFORMAL PARTY ORGANIZATIONS OPERATING IN CALIFORNIA

The Speaker's Organization

California's Progressive reformers believed that breaking the hold of party insiders over nominations would break parties, and that breaking parties would break the hold of special interests on state government. They were half right. The combination of direct primaries and cross-filing did break parties, but breaking parties did not break the power of special interests. In some ways, it simply gave the special interests freer reign. Well-heeled lobbyists rushed in to provide the legislative leadership that the parties were either unable or unwilling to provide.

Artie Samish, a prominent lobbyist for the liquor industry and several other powerful interests in the 1930s and 1940s, was one individual who sought to fill the power vacuum in the legislature. According to Elmer Rusco, who studied Samish's organization for his doctoral dissertation, Samish "had better financing and a statewide plan of action, and he probably employed more experienced campaigners on a year-in, year-out basis than either of the major parties" (1961: 124). Samish took on the task of "selecting and electing": "I selected the candidates that I thought would be agreeable to my clients, and I saw that they got elected. And if they didn't behave, I saw that they got unelected." His influence in elections and officeholders' dependence on him made his a very powerful voice on the fate of legislation. "On matters that affect his clients," conceded Governor Earl Warren, "Artie unquestionably has more power than the governor" (Samish 1971: 188, 146). Samish, as mentioned earlier, is even credited with delaying California's adoption of daylight saving time by a full decade because the motion picture studios that employed him were concerned that the extra daylight would discourage people from going to the movies.

The key to Samish's power was his mastery of basic principles of political organization. For example, he understood the value of centralizing funds. In return for his lobbying services for the alcoholic beverage industry, Samish levied five cents on every barrel of liquor sold in the state. Between 1945 and 1950, these funds totaled some $160,000 per year, most of which Samish devoted toward political campaigns. Since the average assembly campaign cost only five to ten thousand dollars at that time, Samish could be influential in many races simultaneously. Samish also urged liquor retailers throughout the state not to donate to any candidates but rather to let his organization do the donating for them. In a preelection letter to liquor retailers, Samish wrote:

> We urge you make no contributions, make no commitments, permit no solicitation, financial or otherwise, for your support of any candidate or proposition. An industry-wide committee is now making a careful survey. This committee will report to the industry association of which you are a member. Every advantage you now enjoy in California has been made possible because a united industry stood solidly behind its leaders. (Rusco 1961: 128–29)

Other lobbyists, if not quite so flamboyant as Samish, were eager to fill the role of boss, as well, providing legislators with money, food, liquor, housing, female companionship, and anything else a poorly compensated forty-something male might desire while away from home. In return, the lobbyists asked relatively little. They did not need to control every piece of legislation on the floor—just a few per session that affected their clients. One such crucial vote was the vote for assembly Speaker, since the Speaker could exert so much power over committee staffing and the fate of legislation. Buchanan (1963) charts assembly Speaker votes in the 1940s and 1950s and finds lobbyist-controlled bipartisan cliques vying for control of the office, something that is unheard of in most states and the modern U.S. Congress.

At the end of the day, many industries got what they wanted out of the legislature because incumbents could trade a few key votes for money and other campaign resources and still serve their districts well the rest of the time, virtually ensuring reelection. "It was just unbeliev-able how . . . little money could result in legislation," remarks Stanford Shaw, who served in the assembly in the early 1950s. "Looking back, the most surprising thing is how cheap they could buy these votes" (1988: 209–10). The decades of the 1920s, 1930s, and 1940s in California may not have been worse than the period in which Boss Ruef and the South-ern Pacific Railroad held sway in Sacramento, but they were not much better, either.

The money-driven system broke down in the early 1950s when Samish was jailed on corruption charges, and a former Speaker of the as-sembly and other lobbyists were targeted by prosecutors. The breakdown left business in an awkward and dangerous situation. One member recalls a Southern California lobbyist showing up in Sacramento and asking, "Who do we pay? We have the money" (Reinier 1987: 187).

Into this vacuum stepped Jesse Unruh, a freshman Democrat from Inglewood, first elected in 1954. Confident in his own reelection chances, he asked lobbyists interested in winning his favor to make dona-tions to other candidates whose positions were less secure. Unruh's bene-factors, including business magnate Howard Ahmanson, Richfield Oil, and Prudential Insurance, ended up funneling roughly thirty to forty thousand dollars to candidates at Unruh's behest. Though not an enor-mous amount of money, it was sent early and targeted effectively enough to be useful and memorable to rising candidates. Unruh, a Los Angeles Republican Party leader observed, knew that a relatively small amount of money given to an incumbent or a new candidate at an early time was worth five times that much later down the road. He could assess with a very sharp eye who had a chance to be elected and who was in trouble, so he has been very wise for the most part in doling out those dollars that he had control of. (Cannon 1969: 99–100)

These politicians returned the favor by supporting Unruh in key situations, which Unruh parlayed into still more influence with lobbyists. "Money is the mother's milk of politics," as Unruh famously described his system. Later, Unruh wouldn't wait for the lobbyists to approach him. Instead, he would organize testimonial dinners and charge industry representatives $100 or $1,000 per plate to attend. That money would be channeled to various Democratic campaigns as Unruh saw fit. Unruh's network not only helped Democrats improve their election fortunes, but it also created a contingent of incumbents indebted to him (Boyarsky 2008).

It seems fair to ask why lobbyists were willing to pool donations through Unruh and abandon their individual relationships with legislators. One answer was that the Unruh system was more efficient; he knew better than the lobbyists did who needed help and who would be receptive to donations. Another answer was that Unruh knew he could be more powerful by controlling donations, so he didn't give lobbyists a choice. For example, during the campaign for Proposition 1A, a legislative professionalization measure championed by Unruh, he held "Take a Lobbyist to Lunch Week." According to political scientist and onetime Unruh staffer Sherry Bebitch Jeffe, "He would just sit down over lunch with a lobbyist and say, 'This is how much I expect you to contribute to Prop. 1A.' And they did. I mean, what else are you going to do? . . . They gave because they had to, if they wanted to see their bills move, or kill the bills they wanted killed."

Despite his ties to relatively conservative monetary sources, Unruh nonetheless charted a liberal course as an assemblyman. In 1959, he authored a far-reaching civil rights act that prohibited business leaders from engaging in racial discrimination—legislation that was considerably more progressive than the NAACP leadership had expected from the statehouse (Cannon 1969: 103). He also advanced the Unruh Retail Credit Act, which aimed to drive out loan sharks that had preyed on lower-income Californians, often African Americans. Unruh also distinguished himself through his fights against a state right-to-work law and a proposition that would have taxed parochial schools (Berinstein 1986; Morris 1987; Dvorin and Misner 1966).

It is striking that a neophyte legislator, even one as talented as Unruh, could so quickly become the central player in the Sacramento money game. What Unruh's rapid rise suggests is a point central to the IPO model: benefit seekers need political kingpins as much as kingpins need the campaign resources of benefit seekers. We can infer this from the fact that money did not flow to Unruh because he was powerful; it flowed to him because lobbyists recognized that, if given money, he could become powerful enough to get things done. As a lobbyist of the mid-1950s remarked,

> The guy with real dough respects someone who wants money to accomplish something, not just to have it. If Unruh had used the money to line his own pockets, he wouldn't have accomplished his own purposes as far as power is concerned—and he wouldn't have got the money. (Cannon 1969: 99)

The group that abhors legislative inefficiency and inaction, this suggests, is not the legislature itself, but the actors outside the legislature that want it to accomplish something.

With his strong connections to big money, Unruh rose quickly through the ranks, becoming the chair of the powerful Ways and Means committee in 1959 and Speaker in 1961. As Speaker, Unruh continued to exert great power over his fellow Democrats by informally controlling the flow of lobbyist money to them. He groomed and helped elect numerous candidates to the assembly over the course of his speakership, including Mervyn Dymally, Bill Greene, James Mills, and Leon Ralph (Carr 1997: 107–8). Dymally, for his part, was a schoolteacher who was active with the New Frontiers Democratic Club in South Los Angeles when Unruh noticed him in the early 1960s. According to former *Los Angeles Times* city editor Bill Boyarsky, Unruh was alerted to the fact that Dymally was "raising hell there against Unruh's candidates. And Unruh met him and said, 'You're the guy who's raising all that hell?' 'Yeah.' Well, they just hit it off. Unruh could see this guy was really smart and conniving—his kind of guy." By co-opting a potentially powerful activist, Unruh simultaneously eliminated a threat and created an important ally. "He made Dymally," says Boyarsky. Indeed, Unruh backed Dymally in his first quest for office. "When I ran in the Assembly," says Dymally, "he said to me, 'You can't win . . . but I'm going to support you because you have *chutz-*

pah.' And so I've been in this camp." With Unruh's help, Dymally over-whelmed seven other Democrats in the primary and won an assembly seat.

Unruh also pressured unions to send out slate mailers backing his preferred candidates, and he was active in primaries for many offices, from the county party central committees to the House of Representatives (Cannon 1969: 120). Here, Unruh was clearly playing the role of the broker, in a style quite reminiscent of the old party bosses. He recruited candidates from the activist community and supported their attempts to gain office. He put his anointed candidates in touch with campaign contributors or simply sent them the benefit seekers' money that he'd collected. And he made sure his candidates were aided by labor and expenditures from the activist and benefit-seeker communities.

Although Unruh had gained office with the support of activists in his district, he soon came into conflict with the principal liberal activist organization in the state, the California Democratic Council (CDC). CDC activists were uncomfortable with Unruh's perceived pragmatism and sought to pull the party further to the left by backing particularly liberal candidates in nominations and repeatedly lobbying them when in office (Berinstein 1986). Unruh argued that this pressure would make the party uncompetitive at the state level, and he openly and frequently battled with the CDC within Democratic primaries (Cannon 2003). The perspective from the Unruh camp, according to Jeffe, was that "the CDC was the enemy." To Unruh, a group like the CDC had no place in electoral politics: "The group which is concerned with agitating, with being the gadfly, with being out in left field should not also be the group which makes the selection of men to run with the Democratic party label. This group has no responsibility and dreads responsibility" (Wilson 1966; Mayhew 1986). Unruh provided funding and campaign assistance that enabled assemblyman Charles Wilson to defeat the CDC-endorsed Jerry Pacht in a 1962 congressional primary and later cajoled labor unions into sending out a slate mailer endorsing a slew of Unruh candidates over CDC candidates for the Los Angeles County Democratic Committee (Cannon 1969: 120). Unruh and his supporters also advanced legislation to prohibit unofficial groups from using the Democratic name in endorsements, a move squarely aimed at cutting the CDC out of electoral politics, although this legislation failed to pass. In addition, Unruh worked to eliminate the last vestiges of the patronage system within the state Controller's Office, professionalizing the inheritance tax appraisers that had previously been selected by the Controller. Observers at the time saw this as less a move toward a professional government than an assault on then controller Alan Cranston, an early organizer of the CDC. Unruh's use of amateur clubs during his rise to power and his attempts to stifle them once in power is an example of how officeholders chafe under the constraints of party activists.

Speakers Leo McCarthy (1974–80) and Willie Brown (1981–95) expanded on Unruh's fund-raising system during their speakerships; McCarthy raised $500,000 from lobbyists to help candidates in 1978, and Brown doled out $1.7 million in 1982 and $5.3 million in 1992 (Rood 1978; Rosenthal 1984; Richardson 1996). This system of a Speaker using lobbyist largesse to benefit a party has become standard practice in California—and recently in the U.S. Congress, as well (Cannon 1969; Clucas 1995; Eilperin 2003).

In the heyday of the Speaker system under Unruh and Brown, a Speaker needed only nod toward his preferred candidate; knowing that a candidate has the Speaker's backing causes potential donors to either follow suit or to refrain from backing other candidates. Today, term limits have reduced the tenure of individual Speakers, and the growth of strong IPOs in local communities has further constrained the Speaker's ability to control nominations. In the 2002 primaries, for example, Speaker Herb Wesson and his immediate predecessor, Robert Hertzberg, both offered strong endorsements for Andrei Cherny for an assembly seat from the San Fernando Valley. Cherny ended up losing to Lloyd Levine, an assembly staffer and the son of a prominent local political consultant. Even so, the Unruh system continues to influence partisan politics in California. Speakers are routinely active in local nominations, supporting candidates they believe will serve the majority party best and sending considerable sums of money in their direction.

The reader will note that the Unruh system does not fully exemplify my nomination-centered model. That is, while he was active in nominations and in centralizing money to aid preferred candidates, his system seemed to emerge from within the legislature rather than outside it. Once established, it was centered in Sacramento, not the local communities. This is not a great threat to my model—long coalitions certainly may emerge within the legislature, even if they more often emerge from local communities.

Unruh's system is also interesting because it was powered much more by benefit seekers than by political activists. Most likely, this is because strong local political organizations did not spring into existence at the moment cross-filing expired and were therefore unable to hold their own against benefit seekers. With time, however, strong local organizations did develop and became an effective counterweight to both private benefit seekers and the Speaker's organization itself. I have only rough knowledge of how this growth occurred, but I have a good deal of information about the IPOs that have existed in local communities for the past decade.

In the remainder of this chapter, I lay out this information. The intent is to give the reader a concrete idea of what these IPOs look like in action.

Five Local Party Organizations

The five IPOs whose features I sketch in this section have rich histories in which the same elite leaders have watched—and aided—the rise and fall of numerous candidates. Four of the five organizations find their roots in or just after the time that Jesse Unruh got his start. Conservatives in Orange County organized the Lincoln Club in 1962 following Richard Nixon's failed gubernatorial campaign. Representative Maxine Waters got her start in Los Angeles politics through Mayor Tom Bradley's organization, which he built in the early 1960s on top of a loose structure laid down by California Democratic Council activists. Many of Waters's rivals began work under Mervyn Dymally's organization, which was assembled in the early 1960s with the aid of Unruh. The origins of Latino organizations in LA's Eastside can be traced back to City Councilman Ed Roybal's alliance with community activist Saul Alinsky in the early 1950s. And the leaders of the Waxman-Berman machine in West Los Angeles began their association as members of the Young Democrats in the early 1960s.

The emergence of these disparate organizations at roughly the same moment in history is not a coincidence. As described in the previous chapter, the demise of cross-filing—which had prevented activists and essentially anyone outside the government from influencing party nominations—made it worthwhile beginning in about 1954 for political actors to work together to control politics. Some of the earliest of these organizers were in the CDC, but others soon began building on their model, recruiting and grooming ideologically committed candidates and helping them win nominations.

In this section, I offer quick preliminary sketches of the five regional political systems. The following section then provides detailed descriptions of the roles played by the different actors within an IPO, with a particular emphasis on candidate selection, ideological extremism, and intraparty discipline.

Orange County Republicans

Orange County has long been a breeding ground for modern conservatism, having produced many of the activists that gave Barry Goldwater the Republican presidential nomination in 1964 and put Ronald Reagan in the governor's mansion in 1967 (McGirr 2001). Indeed, by the mid-1990s, Orange County Republicans occupied many of the key positions in the state party and the state government, prompting Sherry Bebitch Jeffe to dub the region the "center of the political universe" (Bailey, Warren, and Filkins 1996). In the county's vast, affluent suburbs, activists generally have the money and time to get involved in politics. The most prominent have been wealthy land developers or former officeholders who have used their political contacts to build successful consulting businesses. Many of these influential conservatives are members of the Lincoln Club, a political organization that collects $3,500 in annual dues from each member and uses the money to recruit conservative candidates at the local level and to back more established Republicans for higher offices.

The Lincoln Club's structure is hierarchical and professionalized. Labor within the Club is apportioned to various committees. For example, a legislative committee tracks local, state, and national issues and ballot measures and recommends positions to members; a membership committee sets standards for admission to the club; a local cities committee will recruit and train candidates. Furthermore, the committee chairs and the club's officers (including a paid executive director) make up an executive committee to oversee day-to-day operations, and a twenty-five-member board of directors sets overall club policy. Although most club members are wealthy business entrepreneurs—people who instinctively "don't herd real good," according to one member—the membership is highly deferential to club leaders and others with considerable political expertise. This enables members to avoid infighting and maximize the benefits of organization.

For most of the past three decades, these conservatives seem to have maintained a united front in Republican Party nominations. Having identified the right candidates, they give them start-up cash and a nod noticed around the county. Donors pay attention to these nods for two reasons. First, it keeps them from wasting their money on noncredible candidates; anyone with the backing of most Lincoln Club members is probably a good bet. Second, pooling resources with other donors through the prominent leaders can help enhance one's influence over elected officials.

Besides just backing their preferred candidates, Orange County's conservative activists have been accused of using unsavory means to discourage moderates, including making threatening phone calls and trying to drive people out of the county. These same activists were also behind the recalls of two assembly members in 1995 for their collaboration with outgoing Democratic Speaker Willie Brown. As moderate political consultant Eileen Padberg reported, "If you don't walk the line in Orange County Republican politics, they punish you by costing you business. . . . They try to hurt you in any way they can, demoralize you, talk about you in the newspapers, whatever." Adds Republican consultant Stu Mollrich, "If you are a friend, they will do anything for you, and if you are an enemy, they will destroy you" (Bailey, Warren, and Filkins 1996).

The influence of these conservatives in elections is decisive, according to both their supporters and detractors. Respondents made a point of noting that just having money is not enough; you still need the backing of some influential elites in the area if you're going to win office. As former assembly Speaker Curt Pringle notes, "If you're a Republican, there's a handful of [elites] you certainly want either neutralized or on your side regardless of how much personal money you're putting into it. . . . You don't want to alienate them so they go out to look for candidates to run against you in a primary or otherwise."

In recent years, the Orange County conservatives have been challenged by a group of wealthy moderates calling themselves the New Majority. This group charges $10,000 annual dues and devotes the money toward electing moderate Republicans, prioritizing the construction of a GOP majority in Sacramento over the maintenance of the minority's ideological purity. As with the Lincoln Club, the members of the New Majority see the value of centralizing resources to maximize the effectiveness of their donations. Their effectiveness thus far, however, is debatable. Although they take credit for electing two moderates to the assembly in 2000, they failed spectacularly in a bid to take over the County Central Committee and threw half a million dollars at former Los Angeles mayor Richard Riordan's disappointing gubernatorial bid in early 2002. Still, as Lincoln Club member Buck Johns notes, "The fact that the

New Majority has more money than the Lincoln Club means it's something to be reckoned with."

South Los Angeles Democrats

Politics is the same only different in nearby South Los Angeles. The differences are most obvious. While Orange County is notably rich, Republican, and white, South LA is overwhelmingly poor, Democratic, and nonwhite. Although Latinos have begun moving into this historically African American area in large numbers over the past decade, its electorate, and the leaders it chooses, remain predominantly black. Another key difference is that the real bosses of Orange County politics are private citizens. In South LA, they tend to be elected officials and their publicly paid staffers.

What's the same in South LA is that nominations are effectively controlled by a small group of individuals whose influence depends on their control over the resources necessary to run for office. Congresswoman Maxine Waters, who has represented this area since 1977 in the assembly and the U.S. House, leads one of the major factions in this region. Several prominent state senators, assembly members, and city council members regularly line up with her when she makes endorsements. She is also closely tied with the New Frontiers Democratic Club, the oldest African American political club in the state. When candidates seek the Democratic nomination in South LA—the equivalent of election in this overwhelmingly Democratic area—they almost invariably seek Waters's support. When she has chosen which candidates she will back, Waters will campaign vigorously for them. As campaign consultant Kerman Maddox, a former Waters employee, explains,

> When you're opposite Maxine Waters, you better be prepared to really fight and work hard, because, unlike many other people, she doesn't just give her name. She gets involved. She knocks on doors, she goes to churches, she visits senior citizen homes, she's walking precincts. She's involved. She's going before Democratic clubs to get them to endorse you. So you want her endorsement because with her endorsement comes a lot of energy, and a lot of activity, and a lot of resources. So when you're against Maxine Waters, you better roll up your sleeves, because it's going to be a battle.

In addition to all that, Waters publicizes her chosen candidates in a sample ballot, managed by her daughter Karen, that she sends out to voters before the primary. In resource-poor South LA, where many church and civic leaders follow Waters's lead, her slate goes a long way toward election.

Local activists speak with reverence about the Waters slate. "Maxine has her sample ballot," says Don Stephenson, a local activist and organizer for the NAACP, "and if you get on her sample ballot, that goes a long way towards you getting elected." Bobbie Anderson adds, "If she puts out a slate, or if she supports a candidate . . . as a rule, they will win. Because that's how strong her influence is in her district." Can a slate mailer live up to such a reputation under careful scrutiny? It appears that it can. In an analysis of Los Angeles County voting patterns in the 1992 general election, Lewis (2003) found roughly 16,000 cast ballots that were identical to the Waters slate, a ballot pattern that involved mostly low-level offices and little-publicized ballot propositions. Another 9,000 ballots were close to the pattern recommended by Waters, with just one or two different choices, as if a mistake or two had been made. Moreover, virtually all of the ballots identical to the Waters mailer were cast in three South LA districts—Waters's and the two immediately adjacent to it. Altogether, Lewis estimates that about 10 percent of ballots cast within Waters's district came from voters following her mailer. These votes were over and above any influence due to mass advertising or party contacting, over which Waters also has influence.

In another example of the slate mailer's influence, Waters was noncommittal in a 1992 county supervisorial primary but chose to make an endorsement anyway. Her slate recommended a vote for either Diane Watson or Yvonne Brathwaite Burke out of a field of 12 candidates. Some 5,000 voters in South LA cast ballots for *both* Watson and Burke— roughly five times the normal incidence of overvoting. The number of votes that Lewis links to the Waters mailers is more than enough to tip a contested primary election for a city council or assembly seat.

The faction opposing Waters's is not as well defined. One of its leaders is Congresswoman Diane Watson, who does not have Waters's popular following but does have the support of several prominent city council members, assembly members, and members of Congress. Mervyn Dymally, a veteran assembly member, also usually joins Watson in opposing Waters, and indeed Dymally used to run his own organization in the 1970s in opposition to Mayor Tom Bradley's group, of which Waters was a member (Sonenshein 1993). County supervisor Yvonne Brathwaite Burke also manages a campaign organization of her own at times, usually lining up against Waters. Former assembly Speaker Herb Wesson, Supervisor Burke's onetime chief of staff, is considered a close ally of hers and usually follows her lead in endorsements.

It seems virtually impossible for a moderate or conservative candidate—or anyone not committed to affirmative action and a few other key liberal issues—to be slated by any of the South LA organizations. The resulting factional candidates are roughly equally liberal and thus separated not by ideology but by personal loyalties; the feuding can be bitter. People lined up on different sides of a primary race may refuse to be in a room with each other ten years later.

Although factional politics can appear petty at times, membership in one of these camps is vital for anyone planning a serious run for office. "If you're not in any of those camps," reports Don Stephenson, "you have no chance. . . . Any of the established politicians who are already plugged into the money can be a source of getting you plugged into the money. But just operating cold, you're spinning your wheels for days, because you don't know who to call."

Candidates who come with their own money aren't necessarily much better off if they're not tied to a local political camp. Indeed, 1998 Democratic gubernatorial candidate Al Checchi spent a small fortune to turn out a sympathetic vote in South LA. Beneficiaries of his largesse, reports Bobbie Anderson, simply took his money and voted for his opponent Gray Davis.

Eastside Los Angeles County Democrats

To the east of Los Angeles' downtown is a region consisting of parts of the city, the unincorporated county area known as East LA, and many small cities that make up the San Gabriel Valley. This region is overwhelmingly Latino and strongly Democratic. Like South LA, the Eastside is divided up into factions that are led by elected officials.

Perhaps the most influential organization in the Eastside over the past three decades has been the Alatorre-Torres machine, most recently under the leadership of Richard Polanco, who was termed out of the state senate in 2002. Organized in the 1970s by assemblyman Walter Karabian and two of his aides—Richard Alatorre (later an assemblyman and state senator) and Art Torres (later the state Democratic chair)—this group has produced dozens of young officeholders from its ranks of public staff members.

Although there is an unofficial pecking order for which staffers get to run for public office next, that order was apparently violated in 1982 when Alatorre moved up to the state senate and his assembly seat opened up. Gloria Molina was passed over as the organization's anointed candidate for that race in favor of Polanco. Angry at this slight, Molina broke with the organization and ran on her own, defeating Polanco, and in 1991 defeated Art Torres to win a newly created county supervisorial seat. She has served in this seat ever since and now runs an organization that rivals the Alatorre-Torres group (Skerry 1993: 242–43). Her endorsement is highly coveted.

As in South LA, these factions are not much divided by ideology as by factional loyalty. Moderates and conservatives have largely been selected out of politics here; candidates and officeholders are generally well to the left of their districts' median voters. Yet the factional divisions are no less sharp for their lack of ideological foundation. For many years, one could see them even on Olvera Street, a popular Mexican "old town" in downtown Los Angeles. "One side of the street was Richard Alatorre's, the other side was Gloria Molina's," explains political broker Matt Klink. On the Eastside, people stick with their camps, and terms like *whore* are applied to consultants and politicians who cross over to other camps for a paycheck.

This factionalism can take its toll on staffers who are more committed to policy than to politics. Dan Farkas, a transportation policy aide to state senator Gil Cedillo (a Polanco affiliate), expressed annoyance that his counterparts in the offices of elected officials aligned with Molina haven't worked with him. "Consequently, projects didn't get followed through on," he explains. Indeed, Farkas reports, policy offices within the city bureaucracy are very leery of political staffers who come to work with them, fearing that they will try to influence public spending decisions in favor of their former factional bosses.

According to respondents, membership in one of these camps is critical for a victory. People who wish to run for office must work their way up within an organization if they're to have a serious chance at winning an election. Mike Hernandez reported that he had some respectable endorsements when he ran for assembly in 1986 but he lost—narrowly—because he wasn't well tied to an established organization. He spent the next four years paying his dues to the Gloria Molina organization by helping to elect people that she supported, and when it was his turn to run for office, the organization helped clear a path for him. "I became very focused on getting people elected to office who ultimately would be able to help me get elected," Hernandez explains, "and that's why when I ran the second time for office, I didn't have any opposition. There [were] four candidates that ran against me, but nobody had the kind of background and support that I had. And so I became the candidate to beat." Here, we see an ambitious politician investing time and effort in a partylike group in order to derive the benefit of organization: a better shot at winning office.

West Los Angeles Democrats

Much of what the world associates with Los Angeles—sunny beaches, Wolfgang Puck restaurants, Beverly Hills mansions—can be found in the western portion of LA County. This area, notably wealthier, whiter, and more Jewish than the southern and eastern portions of the county, has been home to one of the most sophisticated political machines in state history, the Waxman-Berman organization. Henry Waxman and Howard Berman, both currently Democratic members of Congress, became friends as activists in the UCLA Young Democrats in 1960 and worked together over the years on such efforts as drafting Adlai Stevenson to run for president and opposing the Vietnam War. With the aid of the Young Democrats, Waxman was elected to the assembly in 1968, and Berman followed him in 1972.

Soon after winning office, these two and their Westside allies became involved in electing other like-minded people to office. Their first foray into electioneering began as a simple endorsement, and their chosen candidate lost, which proved surprisingly costly to them. As Waxman explains,

> You support a candidate that loses, you get somebody else in there, and then they're angry at you because, presumably, you supported their opponent, and you're already at least on unfriendly terms. We had some other close political friends who wanted to run for offices in this area of West LA, so we said, if we really care about it, let's endorse the candidate and really help the candidate win.

Waxman and Berman proceeded to make serious investments in the candidates they backed. They helped raise money for them. They would recruit and train candidates for offices at various levels, and they could count those candidates among their allies once they won office. Berman's brother Michael, described by a Waxman-Berman candidate as "one of the smartest political strategists in the state, maybe ever in the history of the state," started doing campaign strategy, voter targeting, and direct mail for their candidates. "What they were evolving," reported the *Los Angeles Times* (Meyerson 1994), "was a substitute political party."

Rick Tuttle, who today directs UCLA's International Student Center, claims that the Waxman-Berman organization was instrumental in his getting appointed to the Los Angeles Community College Board in 1975, as it produced support from all over the state:

> Howard [Berman] was an enormous help, and Henry [Waxman] helped out. . . . They made phone calls . . . to the six members [of the board]. . . . Howard made phone calls, and then he would call people to call people. We had . . . Gray Davis calling, the Speaker of the Assembly Leo McCarthy making calls, Howard making calls. I had some of my own relationships, of course. . . . It was just an all-out effort, and a significant part of it was what Howard did, and to some extent Henry.

There are few if any reports of Waxman or Berman directly pressuring any of their allies on a legislative vote. This signals not weakness on the machine's part, but rather its effectiveness in slating an ideologically similar group of candidates. Virtually everyone affiliated with the group is a firm advocate for health care reform, environmental protection, and support for the state of Israel. "Philosophically, we were all fairly closely aligned," reports Burt Margolin, a former assembly member and longtime affiliate of the organization.

Rather than worrying about corralling legislative votes, the organization spent much of its energy trying to win elections. "The real coordination was on politics, on endorsement of candidates, how we could advance our particular political agenda," says Margolin. "That's where there was collaboration." And, indeed, the candidates that the Waxman-Berman organization backed tended to win in district primaries, although the record was not quite so stellar in statewide races. "For a period of many, many years, we had a phenomenal success rate," boasts Margolin. For example, Julian Dixon, a popular African American member of Congress until his death in 2000, was not favored to win in his first run for the seat in 1978, but the help of Waxman-Berman was widely credited for changing the outcome.

The Waxman-Berman machine is notably absent from Westside politics today. Its withdrawal began in the early 1990s, when Waxman simply grew more interested in legislating in Washington than in organizing local politics. There was also likely some ideological disagreement between Waxman and the Berman brothers over the Gulf War, the LA riots, and the best ways for campaigns to address these issues—matters that came to a head during Mel Levine's failed U.S. Senate campaign in 1992. "I think his Senate campaign was a turning point for me, because I thought it was a very poorly run Senate campaign," says Waxman. "So we had some tensions during that period of time that led me to conclude what I had already been thinking, and that was that there was no great demand for a political machine, and that I ought to focus more on activities in Congress." Today, the task of organizing Westside Democratic politics has fallen to the LA County Federation of Labor, which is active throughout the county.

Fresno Democrats and Republicans

Two hundred miles to the north of Los Angeles lies Fresno County, a collection of small cities and vast farmlands in the middle of California's breadbasket, the San Joaquin Valley. There is plenty to distinguish Fresno from the sprawling suburbs of Orange County or the dense urban tracts of Los Angeles, but one of the more interesting differences is that both parties are relatively competitive here: The county's four congressional districts are split between Republicans and Democrats, and Republicans control two of the area's five assembly districts to the Democrats' three. It would still be fair to call the area conservative, though, and Democrats might hold few or no elected seats were it not for state redistricting plans favorable to their party.

Despite these differences, political patterns similar to those found in the other regions can be identified in Fresno. The formal party structures are considered weak on the Republican side and virtually nonexistent on the Democratic side. As with the other areas, loose affiliations between officeholders, activists, and wealthy donors have risen to fill this void with structure, striving to influence the party nomination processes. On the Democratic side, the principal power brokers are generally to be found in the ranks of elected officials. Former Congressman Cal Dooley earned a reputation as a kingmaker due to his practice of hiring people who might be interested in running some day and grooming them for office. Assemblyman Juan Arambula and former assemblywoman Sarah Reyes are also widely considered important voices on the Democratic side. Reyes, for example, "has access to contributors statewide. And she is a good sounding board in terms of what to expect and what's required to get into politics," says Arambula. As Dooley staffer Will Hensley notes, "If you can walk away with an endorsement from Cal, Sarah, and Juan, then you're in great shape."

Labor unions—the Service Employees International Union Local 535, in particular—are credited with having a lot of influence in Democratic politics, particularly within the city of Fresno. The involvement of labor introduces some degree of in-party factionalism, since unions have traditionally not trusted the pro-trade Cal Dooley. Instead, they often side with Reyes and other more liberal Democrats.

The Republican side is marked by a bit of factionalism between moderates and conservatives, although the rivalry between the two sides seems, at least on the surface, less intense than that found in Orange County. The most energetic leader among the conservatives is Michael Der Manouel Jr., a member of the county Republican Central Committee and president of an insurance company. Der Manouel spent several years working in an Indianapolis precinct organization and tried to import some of its structure to Fresno area politics; he's widely credited for recent GOP surges in voter registration and for several of the party's electoral victories. He works closely with many conservative leaders, including congressman George Radanovich and onetime assemblyman Steve Samuelian. Although he represented Bakersfield (some hundred miles south of Fresno), former congressman Bill Thomas has served as a strong moderate leader whose influence extends throughout the lower San Joaquin Valley, and he is credited with getting twenty-eight-year old Devin Nunes elected to the Congress from Fresno County in 2002. The divisions within the party are well understood by local politicians. "If I'm going to run for office," says a Fresno city councilman, "and I go to Devin Nunes for help, well I'm not going to count on Steve Samuelian, or vice versa. . . . That's no secret, either."

Even if locals prefer to downplay ideological rifts within the Republican Party, it is clear that conservatives do not suffer moderates gladly. Although no Republican incumbents have been forcibly removed from office, a few have had their careers cut short for committing the crime of bipartisanship. Two-term Republican assemblyman Mike Briggs attempted to run for Congress in 2002, only to find himself defeated in the primary by a virtual unknown. Briggs's apostasy was being the deciding vote that passed the Democratic majority's 2001–2 state budget. That vote earned Briggs the ire of conservative Republicans across the country, including the leaders of the Washington-based Club for Growth. With Briggs—a well-known officeholder and the leading candidate for the congressional seat—now untouchable because of his vote, Republican donors sought an alternative candidate to back. One option was businessman Jim Patterson, who was well known but had no ties to local party organizations. The other was the unknown Devin Nunes, who had nothing on his side but the mentorship and active endorsement of Rep. Bill Thomas, a local IPO leader. Nunes won.

The story of Mike Briggs doesn't end there. Briggs's district director, Nathan Magsig, briefly considered running for Briggs's vacated assembly seat in 2002 but then bowed out of the race. In interviews, Magsig specifically rejected the notion that a small group of power brokers are controlling Fresno area politics, framing his decision not to run for assembly that year as a largely personal one. Yet he did note that several conservative activists and party officials "approached me discouraging me from running." That nomination ended up going to conservative Steve Samuelian.

Candidates for office traditionally seek the endorsement of firefighter and law enforcement organizations. Candidates across the ideological spectrum appeal for such support, although these organizations seem to get more involved in Republican politics. The endorsements of the Fresno Deputy Sheriffs' Association and the Fresno Police Officers' Association, in particular, are highly coveted, and when these groups unite on a candidate, their backing is considered very powerful.

In working with other officeholders, leaders will frequently cross party lines. There is a recognition among Fresno elites that agriculture and other issues that affect the region are neither Republican nor Democratic issues, and that "a regional issue demands a regional response." To some extent, this bipartisan tone is set by the area's elite donors (many of whom come from the agriculture industry), who will frequently cross party lines to back candidates they believe will help them advance their interests. The Hallowell family, for example, contributed thousands of dollars to both Democrat Cal Dooley and the Bush-Cheney campaign in 2000. James Hallowell, the Republican son of a successful local Chevrolet salesman, his wife Coke, a Democrat, and their children all regularly contribute to city, county, state, and federal candidates. While each claims a certain ideological stance, their contributions appear to be much more pragmatically motivated. Coke Hallowell, for example, is president of a local nonprofit land trust that receives funds from all levels of government, and she wants to remain on good terms with her elected officials. "What we always hoped for is that they would at least respond to phone calls and listen to requests," she explains.

The fact that Democratic and Republican elected officials in Fresno County are willing to work together, and that prominent donors are active across party lines, suggests that, while informal political organizations exist in this area, they do not have the polarizing effect that those in other areas do. Part of this may be due to the recognition, mentioned earlier, that the major issues of interest to rural voters and elites do not map easily onto the left-right spectrum. There is no obvious Republican or Democratic position on water usage or grazing rights. Furthermore, as I have investigated elsewhere (Masket 2007), less populous political communities generally nominate less partisan elected officials and experience less polarization in their deliberative chambers (see also Lee and Oppenheimer 1999). Fresno County, with 900,000 residents, simply has far fewer people than Los Angeles County (10,000,000) or Orange County (3,000,000).

Media coverage may also explain why Fresno seems to be less partisan than other areas. As Cohen, Noel, and Zaller (2004) have shown, higher-quality monitoring of politics by the media tends to induce more centrist behavior among elected officials. Fresno's newspaper of record is the *Bee,* which is owned by the McClatchy Company, whose papers (including Central California dailies like the Sacramento and Modesto *Bees* and the Merced *Sun-Star*) are noted for their unusually high-quality political coverage. Even city councilmembers in small towns can expect to find their name and actions appearing regularly in the paper. The same is not true in larger cities.

Preliminary Discussion

The findings presented thus far strongly challenge the frequent descriptions of California (and national) politics as candidate-centered. In each region, respondents mentioned a similar set of individuals—officeholders, donors, and activists—whose influence they felt was important in nominations. The degree of similarity within regions seems to me remarkable; I believe any researcher could speak to astute political observers in an area and tease out essentially the same small world of influential leaders. Furthermore, the influence of this elite group is widely considered determinative or at least highly influential in party nominations.

Granted, then, that informal party organizations exist and that they regulate nominations for office, the next question is: How do they work? How are IPOs structured, and what key roles do members play? These are the questions I address in the remainder of this chapter.

ACTORS AND THEIR ROLES

The regional organizations I have examined differ greatly in terms of political persuasions, wealth, racial composition, and degree of urbanization. Yet many similarities transcend these differences. In all of these systems, prominent officeholders, activists, and benefit seekers are making up for the relative weakness of the formal party organizations by working together to control party nominations. These informal organizations search for talented candidates who will adhere to a party program, and they will threaten and occasionally punish those who engage in bipartisanship once in office. In no place does one organization maintain absolute control; persistent bifactionalism seems common, although the ideological distinction between intraparty factions is often minimal or nonexistent.

In this section, I investigate the roles of the different actors that make up the IPO: officeholders/candidates, activists, benefit seekers, and brokers. This analysis allows us to address not only the behavior of these actors but, thanks to the nature of the interview data, the motivations behind this behavior. I pay special attention to the process of candidate selection, the role of ideology, and the virtues of forging relationships across multiple levels of government.

Top Leaders and Inner Circles

Officeholders, I have suggested, are often the builders of and top players in IPOs. They provide much of the effort to forge alliances with other officeholders and to get their own protégés elected. But what motivates them to make such efforts, when just taking care of their own legislative work and reelection efforts must surely be time-consuming enough?

Many are motivated simply by their own designs for power. Supporters and detractors of Speaker Jesse Unruh, for example, have noted the sheer pleasure he took in being able to exert control over politics (see Cannon 1969; Vásquez 1987). Others may have more pragmatic motivations, such as a desire to keep potential rivals from turning on them. Former representative Cal Dooley (D-Fresno) made a practice of helping promising protégés at least in part to keep them from challenging him. According to Dooley aide Sarah Woolf, "I think he truly believes that all these people that he's helped . . . are talented and qualified and deserving of the positions they've won. But he's not going to sit back and not support them, because at some point in time they're going to say, 'You know, you haven't been that helpful to me' [and run against him]." Dooley also tended to hire those who eventually planned to run for office, believing that such career-minded staffers would do a better job of representing him to his constituents.

Others may try to get people elected in order to effect some change in policy or representation. As Henry Waxman explains, "I'm better able to get things done in Congress, or the state legislature, or wherever, if I have people serving with me who have the same views that I have, the same interests, the same passions, and we're going to work as allies to get things done." Burt Margolin, a Waxman ally, agrees. "Anyone who's skillful at the legislative process and gets bills made into law—which all of us had done in our own realm—needs allies. We need people who think the same way, who are smart, and who are willing to work with you. And you're much more powerful at the lawmaking job if you're politically potent, and politically active." In eastside LA County, both Gloria Molina and Richard Polanco have sought to get Latinos elected to improve the representation for the ethnic group that comprises roughly a third of the state. Polanco, in particular, gets credit for having dramatically increased the number of Latinos serving in the California legislature over the course of his tenure. According to lobbyist Keith Parker, many of the members of the Latino Legislative Caucus owe their success to Polanco:

> There wouldn't be a Latino Caucus with 26 or so members had it not been for Richard Polanco. He is more successful than Alatorre or Torres at identifying, fund-raising, developing, and then getting candidates elected. If you look at people that are there, there are a lot of direct connections that come right back to Polanco.

Although acknowledged as leaders of their organization, most of the key elected officials I studied rely heavily on the advice and guidance of others. A few get this advice mainly from their own staff members and those of close allies, keeping their own counsel about who should run for which office and when. (Staffers themselves seem particularly well equipped as potential candidates, and many elected officials today started as employees of other elected officials.) Most, however, seem to rely on some inner circle of advisers, representing all elements of the IPO, in slating candidates. Such inner circles may only be collegial on the surface: the principal officeholder may make the final decisions, but she will get a sense of which candidates have support among which constituencies within the organization. Once candidates are slated, members of the inner circle will usually play important advisory roles in their campaigns. Often, the inner circle members will be the most powerful players on a campaign team, determining the campaign's message and staff membership.

The inner circle technique is probably best exemplified by Rep. Maxine Waters in South LA. Prior to each election season, Waters organizes a core group of fifteen to twenty influential people, including local officeholders, benefit seekers, and activists. Bobbie Anderson, the president of the New Frontiers Democratic Club, is a member of this circle, as is David Gould, Waters's campaign treasurer and a close ally since she first won office in 1976. Although the membership is not fixed from election to election, there are invariably representatives from prominent black churches, labor unions, and Democratic clubs, comprising, according to Anderson, a "small group of individuals who can always be trusted to be there for her." Waters's inner circle meets regularly in the precampaign season to hear out potential candidates and decide which to support. Although the group is close and collegial, Waters maintains the final say on matters and is influential over others in the group. As Anderson explains, "I have been influenced by [Waters] to change my mind to go for another candidate that she was supporting and I really initially didn't want to."

Waters has been at the center of her own inner circle since her days as a community outreach staffer for Mayor Tom Bradley in the 1970s. Dispatched by Bradley to aid some of his allies in 1975 and 1976, Waters assembled a small team of advisers that effectively ran two city council campaigns and two assembly campaigns, including her own. "Bradley's candidates," writes Sonenshein (1984: 131), "had the aid of a sort of

Bradley sub-organization available to help his endorsed candidates in the black community." Indeed, Sonenshein tells of his own experiences as a press secretary for assembly hopeful Kenneth Washington, a Bradley candidate. Waters hired Sonenshein directly for the post "with no apparent input from the candidate" (131).

The inner circle approach to slating and campaigning is common in LA's Eastside, too. In 1990, city council candidate Mike Hernandez fired his campaign manager, Tom Griego, for trying to exert too much control. Henry Lozano, a member of Hernandez's inner circle and a veteran member of the Gloria Molina organization, describes his experience in confronting Hernandez and forcing him to take back the campaign manager:

> I said, "Look, here . . . all these guys, they all want this seat, and you're this close to getting it. That's going from high school to the major leagues. . . . You're this goddamned close to getting it and you're gonna blow it. You know how many people would give their right nut to be in the place where you're at? [Tom] is doing a damned good job for you. He listened to the folks in our inner circle. And if we don't control you, who the hell is? That was, is his job . . . to make sure you do the right thing. . . . You've got to apologize to Tom and take him back."

Hernandez did take Tom Griego back, won the election, and hired Griego as his chief of staff.

The informal party systems sketched in this section do not exhibit the firm command-and-control hierarchy associated with Richard Daley's machine in Chicago, Boss Ruef's organization in San Francisco, and other traditional party organizations. But they lack neither structure nor authority. Orange County's Lincoln Club, as described in a previous section, has a formal mechanism for screening candidates and a top leadership group capable of making and enforcing decisions. In South LA, Maxine Waters is the unquestioned leader of an organization that, according to Lewis's (2003) estimates, directly controls about 10 percent of the vote in her area and influences another sizable fraction of the vote through advertising. I report similar statistical evidence in the next chapter for East Los Angeles County, where, as my interview data show, a succession of "inner circles" can be traced back continuously to the 1950s. Only the Fresno area seems to lack well-defined party groups, although even here, important partylike organizations exist. The bottom line, then, is that California's thriving informal party organizations are in many ways the functional equivalents of traditional party organizations.

Benefit Seekers

Much of the demand for IPOs comes from benefit seekers. In one sense, they desire these organizations because they reduce wasted money and effort. Henry Waxman says that benefit seekers have approached him asking him to rebuild the fabled Waxman-Berman machine. "Some people argue that we should [start up the organization again]," says Waxman, "because it saves a lot of money. Our campaign contributors are solicited by so many different candidates running against each other. They would like to have the avoidance of all the waste of money in primaries."

Beyond reducing unnecessary expenses, benefit seekers also desire IPOs because they enable them to participate in politics without having to know everything about the candidates. Gathering information about politics is expensive and time-consuming, and it is far easier to rely on a cue—such as the backing of a prominent officeholder or trusted community leader—in deciding whom to support. Dooley staffer Sarah Woolf explains, "I think [donors] feel by and large they don't follow [politics] closely enough, and they entrust it to the people who do." Assembly member Arambula believes there is "kind of a herd mentality. If the prevailing wind says 'You go with Joe Schmoe,' that's what you do." Westside LA's Burt Margolin says that those who donated to the Waxman-Berman organization "didn't necessarily want to or have the time or interest in following political trends in other parts of the state or the nation, but knew that if they gave money to Henry [Waxman] and Howard [Berman], that Henry and Howard . . . would exercise judgment rooted in the philosophy and values that these people had in terms of impacting races elsewhere."

Finally, operating within an IPO helps benefit seekers compensate for a major problem of theirs: politicians who cash their checks but quickly forget their concerns. Benefit seekers and others frequently complain about this. "When they're running, they'll all listen to you, man. Once they get elected, all of a sudden they know it all," argues Eastside LA consultant Henry Lozano. Fresno consultant Mike Der Manouel says, "After candidates run and win, I normally lose contact with them for a long time." Lobbyist Ken Spiker agrees, "The only thing that you can hope for is to be able to tell your story. . . . That we would have the ability to go in and explain our side. That's all I can ask for." Lincoln Club member Buck Johns agrees that it is hard to control politicians once they're elected: "The best time to have a candidate listen to you is when they're running for reelection and need money. Oftentimes, after they get elected, they can't find your phone number and can't get back to you."

So how can a benefit seeker be sure that her needs will be addressed by the politicians she supports? Organization provides a remedy. By centralizing donations through prominent community leaders, donors can help ensure that they will be remembered. As Johns explains:

> When I'm supporting a candidate, I'll tend to give money to someone who's raising funds for that candidate. . . . And the reason we do that is, when I need a favor out of a successful candidate, I don't know the guy. I call him, and I gave him a hundred bucks. He got ten thousand. The guy remembers the ten thousand; he doesn't remember the hundred. . . . So I'm going to give it to the guy who's the fund-raiser who gave him the ten thousand.

This way, Johns can place his request via the fund-raiser, who will have access to the officeholder and will be remembered. Through this intermediary, says Johns, the officeholder "will do my bidding."

Politicians, adds Johns, are more responsive to the leaders of the Lincoln Club and other prominent community leaders than to the average donor, making it worthwhile to run a request through the leaders: "You always consider your source." Being able to spot good candidates early also gives influence-seekers the opportunity to ingratiate themselves to future elected officials. As Orange County lobbyist Roger Faubel explains, "The first one hundred dollars is more important that the second one thousand. . . . I want them to know we were there in the beginning, to remember that we were there."

One way to make sure that leaders remember they were there is to give not just to the leaders' campaign, but to those campaigns endorsed by the leader. Rep. Waters, for example, is quite secure in her congressional seat, and while she might appreciate a campaign contribution, it wouldn't make a huge difference in her career prospects. Such a donation might, however, make a huge difference in the fortunes of a candidate she's backing. Donors wishing access to Maxine Waters in 2002 would have been wise to follow her suggestion and donate to Mike Davis's assembly campaign—even though Davis lost. "If you were really shrewd," says Keith Parker, "you'd send the check to Maxine for Mike Davis. You wouldn't send it directly to Mike Davis. Or you'd find a way to make sure Maxine knew . . . you were at a public event and you make sure she saw you give Mike Davis a check. Because that's the audience you were trying to reach." When deciding on a donation, explains Parker, "People will make those decisions not about the race itself, but who the endorsers are and what you really want to be able to do there."

Suggestions for donations are usually offered by prominent office-holders. Waters is known to do this frequently. According to Bobbie Anderson, Waters "raises this money so that she can let the next person know, 'If I endorse this person, I'm putting my resources behind him.' It's like a signal. . . . She can go to [Southern California grocery magnate] Ron Burkle, and tell him, 'I don't care if you support any candidate, I want you to give my candidate money.'" Indeed, donors often seek out these hints from officeholders. Jorge Morales, a staffer for Eastside LA's former assemblyman Marco Antonio Firebaugh, reports, "We'll receive calls here, 'Hey, has the Assemblyman endorsed anyone yet?' And we'll go, 'Not yet.' And they'll say, 'Whoever he endorses, we're going to put all our support for him. . . . I'm not endorsing anyone until Marco does.'" Kerman Maddox agrees:

> You'll see someone at a reception, you'll see someone at a cocktail party, you'll see someone there, they'll come up to you. Because donors want to know, "So where are you at on the Tenth [city council district]? Where are you at on the Eighth?" They want to know. "OK, cool, now that I know that you're there, I'll write a check." Because they like the relationship, and they like to stay on the good side of certain people. So invariably, it's the donors who come to the electeds and say, "Who's your candidate?" We hear that all the time. And once they find out, then the donors will know what to do.

Oftentimes, however, it is prominent local donors who set the example for other donors to follow. For example, cattle rancher John Harris, whose endorsement and largesse are sought across party lines in Fresno County, was considered instrumental in Secretary of State Bill Jones's defeat in the 2002 Republican gubernatorial primary. Harris caught the attention of other donors by refusing to donate to Jones, despite their former business partnership. As Dooley staffer Sarah Woolf explains, "John [Harris] is just very firm in his commitments in politics that 'You go with the winning horse.' And it was clear Bill [Jones] was not going to be able to beat [Governor] Davis at that point in time. And I think everyone in turn followed, and Bill was not able to raise the money that he needed." Harris is also credited for being a key early supporter of Democratic assemblywoman Nicole Parra, encouraging other donors to back her in the

2002 primary contest. Judging from her performance in the general election, in which Parra beat her Republican opponent by a mere 187 votes despite a six-to-one spending advantage and a 13-point Democratic registration edge, she was not a particularly strong candidate (*California Journal* Editors 2002). Yet, with Harris's help, she was able to dominate the Democratic primary, garnering 55 percent of the vote in a field of four candidates.

Benefit seekers are decidedly pragmatic in their choices of candidates to back. While they may have some ideological preferences of their own, they recognize that it does them little good to back a loser (unless they're doing it at the behest of a factional leader). For benefit seekers who went into politics at a young age with noble intentions, the pragmatism comes at a personal cost. It means that they cannot always support the candidate who would be best for the job or who resonates with them personally in some way. "The bigger, more philosophical question of whether good government's a good thing, it is a good thing," says Chris Hammond. "But there's also the realities of trying to get things done. . . . Actions in the community, to the extent you can provide good actions that improve the community, you have to have some relationship with whoever's sitting in that seat." Benefit seekers are often willing to put ideology aside to use government to obtain some benefit for an interest.

A good example of this pragmatism winning out over ideology among benefit seekers comes from the Lincoln Club of Orange County. Many of its members are wealthy real estate developers and businesspeople who stand to make or lose substantial sums of money depending on the whims of lawmakers locally and in Sacramento. The club was founded in 1962 by people who, in the words of executive director Beth Holder, "felt that if they got together . . . to really support candidates that they felt would support their interests the best, that would be more impactual than dealing on an individual level." In other words, they saw the benefits of aggregating and realized they could accomplish more through organization than by acting alone.

The effectiveness of the Lincoln Club stems chiefly from its ability to centralize campaign donations. Members' annual dues are redistributed to candidates based on the decisions of the club's board of directors. Although the club's rules discourage (though do not explicitly prohibit) siding with candidates in a contested party primary, says member Buck Johns, "that does not mean that our membership does not get involved in contested primaries. I'm involved in a bunch of 'em. Members can do what the hell they want to." Indeed, given the confluence of wealthy, highly knowledgeable, highly opinionated activists and donors at club events, it is not hard for a key leader to influence others to help out a preferred primary candidate. Members are reportedly very deferential to the club's leaders, which include former County Central Committee chair Tom Fuentes. In addition to centralizing and redistributing money, the club also helps groom and encourage new candidates for local office, co-sponsoring an annual candidate training event with the conservative Claremont Institute.

Members of the Lincoln Club strike a fiercely ideological tone on the issues of taxes, government regulation, abortion, and gun control. But, when push comes to shove, ideology may occasionally take a back seat to pragmatism. Tom Rogers, who chaired the Republican County Central Committee from 1969 through 1973, complains that land developers within the group were willing to abandon their conservative ideals in 1984 to back a $5 billion county sales tax increase to pay for roads and infrastructure in undeveloped county lands. Many of the same members supported local sales tax increases to pay for jails and to cover the county's financial bailout in 1995. According to *Los Angeles Times* journalist Jean Pasco, although the Orange County activists are avowedly against raising taxes, "they support it when government provides something they need that they don't want to have to pay for themselves." The Lincoln Club also struck a pragmatic posture during the 2003 gubernatorial recall election when they endorsed Arnold Schwarzenegger over his more conservative challengers.

The evidence presented in this section suggests that benefit seekers do more than just tolerate a system of informal party organization—they advocate for it and help to create it. The West LA donors who have appealed to Rep. Waxman to restart the Waxman-Berman organization are hardly chafing under a party system imposed by legislators or candidates. They're literally begging to be hit up for money. What's more, donors often play vital roles in building these party structures. Orange County's Lincoln Club, an autonomous, hierarchical organization with a long history of involvement in nominations at various levels of government, comes very close to meeting Mayhew's (1986) definition of a traditional party organization (TPO), even though it was essentially constructed by benefit seekers. Why do benefit seekers desire and assemble such structure? From the benefit seeker's perspective, the informal party organization model is a more efficient method of doing business than going it alone. It allows them to avoid wasting money and to increase their impact on politics. Simply, they can get more bang for their political buck. The IPOs also afford plausible deniability for potential charges of illegal influence peddling. Handing out wads of cash to legislators ahead of key votes is a corrupt practice; giving money to party organizations during a campaign is, in Jesse Unruh's words, "the mother's milk of politics."

Activists

Political activists may use tactics similar to those of the benefit seekers, but their motives are decidedly different. For one thing, they are not animated by money. Their incentives are often purposive—committed in principle to some sort of change in the way the world works—or solidary—enjoying the interaction with their fellow activists. The evidence gathered suggests that the motivation is often the former. For example, Earl Smittcamp, a prominent peach industry lobbyist in Fresno, has donated generously to Republicans over the years, often following the suggestions of a Sacramento-based professional Republican fund-raiser. His reasons for giving seem purely ideological. "I expect nothing," he says. "In fact, it pisses me off when I read the *Fresno Bee* when I see someone . . . who contributed wanted something in return. . . . I sure as hell don't need a job from them, and they don't have any money to give me." What Smittcamp does want are policies that reflect his notion of good public policy.

An activist's notion of good policy is often experienced by officeholders as ideological pressure—and it may be resented. According to a Fresno-area staffer who visits organizations of both parties, most activists are simply extremists: "I don't know why that is, if they're the only ones willing to go to the meetings or what it is. But you go to those meetings, and you wonder, 'Who let the insane asylum out?' I mean, these people are crazy. They're certifiable."

But crazy does not necessarily mean irrational. When ideological activists dispense campaign resources, they take care to dispense them to candidates who share—or at least seem to share—their preferences. Many activists work within the formal county party central committees. Although state laws preclude these committees from endorsing candidates in the primary, individual members can work for or endorse primary candidates on their own time. County committees are permitted to make endorsements in nonpartisan elections for city and county offices.

Those endorsements can come with slate mailers and considerable campaign contributions. In light of the Progressives' desire to take the party out of local elections, the activity of county party organizations in municipal races is a rather ironic twist.

Other activists typically get involved through the club movement. The clubs are not as feared or revered as they were during the 1950s and early 1960s, when the California Democratic Council sought to control their party by making preprimary endorsements and threatening centrist Democrats with primary challengers (see Wilson 1966). Yet the clubs still exist today, affiliated with local party organizations. In South LA, for example, the venerable New Frontiers Democratic Club is closely tied to Rep. Waters. Bobbie Anderson, the club's president, boasts,

> We provide everything that a candidate would have need of . . . money, strategy, GOTV, voter registration drives. . . . We were able to . . . deliver the vote for [2001 mayoral candidate James Hahn] through just dogged campaigning in the streets, and we gave him thousands of dollars in campaign funds, and gave him volunteers, you know, just delivered the vote to him in every way. We met with him, strategized, told him how to combat certain things with his opponent . . . just told him from our point of view as a people what appeal he had to make to get our vote.

Activist groups also help train the next generation of political candidates and organizers. The United States Junior Chamber (Jaycees), for example, has given many Los Angeles area political figures their first taste of organization. According to consultant Victor Griego, "We were very progressive, we were young Latinos, but we saw with the Jaycees the structure. Because they taught about fund-raising, they taught about community development, they talked about recruiting other young people." In rural Fresno County, the California Agricultural Leadership Program (CALP) provides a similar base for training leaders. Reps. Radanovich, Nunes, and Dooley are all CALP graduates, as are state senator Mike Machado, former assembly member Rusty Areias, and former secretary of state Bill Jones.

Although the formal party organizations in most parts of the state are considered quite weak, some of the more effective activists can be found on Orange County's Republican Central Committee. These activists maintain ties to the benefit-seeking Lincoln Club, although the Central Committee activists fall much more into the "true believer" camp, according to the *Times*'s Jean Pasco. These activists are committed to electing conservatives and keeping the Republican Party from straying into moderate territory. That means backing very conservative candidates who could win locally, thanks to heavily skewed party registration in state and federal legislative districts, but might not win statewide. Likewise, it means thwarting the campaigns of those Republicans who are pro-choice, favor restrictions on gun ownership, or have ever supported a tax increase.

As explained in chapter 1, activists are likely to be extreme because (1) they have been exposed to partisan information and have sought to reinforce that information with similar messages (Zaller 1992); and (2) they perceive important differences between the parties and a substantial ideological payoff if their chosen party wins (Aldrich 1983). The activists within an IPO who are involved in candidate recruitment will tend to be ideologically motivated and polarized for the same reasons. For these reasons, liberals and conservatives will tend to do better in the nominations process than moderates.

Respondents in the Democratic areas tended to agree that only those candidates espousing liberal views would have much chance of winning the activist support necessary to win a nomination fight. "Most of these candidates running in an area like this, they're basically center to liberal," says Eastside LA consultant Henry Lozano. "Most of them are almost identical in ideology. . . . A right-to-life candidate couldn't win in this area. Same with gun control." Victor Griego agrees, "If somebody is talking about an issue that is close to the heart of the Democratic Party at that time; let's say it's same-sex marriages. The Central Committee is for it . . . then you've got this moderate who says, 'Well, you know, I'm not really sure.' So we're going to go with [the supporter of same-sex marriages], because we know he's going to [follow through]."

Others agree that, given their purposive motivations and their relatively extreme views, activists are highly demanding of ideological purity on the part of the candidates they back. In the 2002 primaries, for example, San Diego city councilmember George Stevens, an African American, ran for a Democratic assembly seat nomination and expected black activists to back him. They did not, and he lost the primary. Mervyn Dymally explains what went wrong for Stevens:

> Guess why they didn't support him. He was anti-abortion and pro-vouchers. So he took two very unpopular positions. . . . He felt that the party should have supported him and labor should have supported him to increase minor-

ity representation, and that's a good position to take. But [you lose support] when your views are counter to the party and to the activists.

Fernando Guerra, who has spent his academic career studying Los Angeles politics, feels that moderates are simply selected out of the political environment. "In South Central LA," Guerra says, "you know that the candidate's going to have a very strong pursuit of affirmative action type issues, equity issues, inclusion, etc. You don't even run—you don't stand a chance unless you believe and will pursue a whole group of issues."

I noted earlier that the New Majority, one of the IPOs in conservative Orange County, has a reputation for being somewhat more moderate than the Lincoln Club. Yet, to judge from the records of the candidates backed by the two IPOs, their ideological differences are often subtle. Assembly members Lynn Daucher and Tom Harman, who won seats in 2000 with the backing of the New Majority, appear to be no more moderate than the area's conservative officeholders on many issues. For example, in the 2001–2 legislative session, the California Federation of Labor (AFL-CIO) gave Harman and Daucher average ratings of 6.5 and 3, respectively, out of a possible 100. Orange County's other Republican assembly members had an average rating of 4.75 over the same period. The main issue splitting the Republican Party in Orange County is the one that often divides it at the national level: abortion. On that issue, Planned Parenthood of California gave Harman and Daucher ratings of 43.5 and 78.5, respectively, out of 100; the other area Republicans averaged a 7. Yet abortion comes up rarely on the floor of the statehouse. On the bulk of issues, the moderates would appear to be not much more centrist than the conservatives. The IPOs running Republican politics in Orange County clearly deserve some credit for the relative extremism of the Republicans serving in Sacramento.

A similar trend can be spotted in Fresno. There, conservative Republicans are frequently distrustful of the candidates backed by Rep. Bill Thomas of Bakersfield; Thomas has a reputation as a moderate in Fresno circles. Yet Thomas received a score of 0 from the AFL-CIO and 100 from the U.S. Chamber of Commerce for the 2002 session, although he earned a 64 score from Planned Parenthood that same year. Again, leaving aside the abortion issue, there appears to be little difference between Republican moderates and conservatives in California. Even the moderates are helping to polarize the state.

Where are the real moderates in California? For the most part, they're not in Republican Party politics—those who run nominations have made sure that true centrists do not win primaries. One rare example of a prominent moderate is former Los Angeles Mayor Richard Riordan, a Republican so centrist that he often endorsed Democratic senator Dianne Feinstein in her reelection campaigns. To capture conservative activist attitudes toward such a moderate, one need look no further than the 2002 Republican gubernatorial primary. Four months prior to Election Day, Riordan, then by far the leading candidate in the primary and widely considered a serious threat to incumbent Governor Gray Davis, discussed his political philosophy in a press conference:

> My basic conviction is what is in the best interest of the poor. We need to have successful businesses so there will be quality jobs. . . . We should fire bureaucrats in school districts who fail poor children. . . . And the poor should have the same option on abortion that the rich have. Government should supply the resources so poor people have a choice. I just lost the Republican nomination. (Skelton 2001)

Riordan's last sentence was meant as a joke. It turned out to be quite serious. Riordan lost the primary to Bill Simon, an unknown who was nonetheless more doctrinaire in his conservative principles. Simon went on to lose to Davis in the general election.

Looking back on this outcome, the Lincoln Club's Buck Johns expressed few regrets over his failure to back Riordan in the primaries.

> Riordan comes out of the box, starts talking about this abortion issue, and he says that the way we are going to be able to expand the Republican Party is that we need to change our position on the abortion issue. And he's nutty as a goddamned fruitcake. . . . I'm not interested in trying to convince somebody that [abortion] is nuts. If they want to believe that, or to do that kind of stuff, don't use taxpayer dollars, okay? Don't take my money to subsidize that activity. And then, you know, the incest, the rape, and this kind of stuff, that's the position. That's the position Reagan outlined, and lived with it. George W. was elected president of the United States on that very position. People beat him up and said that women will never vote for you. It's bullshit. So, Riordan is a Republican and he spent too much time on that issue. I think he also spent too much time on the gun control issue. . . . Those are issues that have been the backbone of the Republican Party for too long. It's, you have the right to do what the hell you want to. We're not going to have government mandate these things. So when the Republican Party starts doing that, I think that we start hurting ourselves.

A more obvious example of a successful moderate Republican in California is Governor Arnold Schwarzenegger. However, he is the exception that proves the rule; Schwarzenegger gained office in the 2003 gubernatorial recall election, a contest that had no primary. A ballot with 135 candidates is ripe for candidate-centered politics—the person with the most money and name recognition can win—and is brutal for those who rely upon party primaries to control access to office.

Activists are an obvious answer to the question of why politics is so partisan. With their insistence on ideological purity, their disdain for pragmatism, and their considerable influence over the resources necessary to win nomination, they tend to freeze moderate candidates out of politics and to encourage the politics of partisan extremism.

Brokers

The final group of actors in the IPO is the brokers. Brokers act as liaisons between the different actors, putting donors in touch with candidates, offering advice to key officeholders, and providing money and guidance to candidates. A Tammany-style party boss could be thought of as a broker, although such individuals are a rarity in politics today.

Typically, the broker is an experienced lobbyist or political consultant. Being a broker is not a main source of income—it may not pay off at all, at least directly. Through her lobbying or consulting business, however, such an individual has worked with many of the key players in an IPO over the years and is usually trusted and respected for her expertise. Often, brokers are aligned with particular factions, and they assist these factions by putting influence-seeking clients in contact with the candidates favored by the factional leaders.

The broker's modus operandi is to host a series of "intimate" fundraisers, in which ten to twenty business clients meet at the broker's office with a candidate. By centralizing money in this fashion, brokers aid donors, recipients, and factional leaders. Donors, always fearful that the politician will ignore them once elected, get valuable face time with the candidate. As Matt Klink, a vice president with the venerable Los Angeles political consulting firm Cerrell and Associates, explains, "Over time, you begin to establish a personal relationship so that it's not just the XYZ Company, it's Joe at the XYZ Company; Joe has two kids and likes to play golf."

Furthermore, explains Klink, candidates receive a decent-sized contribution with little effort and get to know the issues they will face in office: "We do the candidate a real advantage, because they don't have to sit around and talk to six hundred of their closest friends. They get an on-the-ground feel for what the newest streetlight technology is, or what the latest science says about this type of product versus another type of product." Chris Hammond, who works as a broker in South LA, similarly describes his work as a favor to the candidate: "We have a three- to four-hundred-dollar buffet type of thing—kind of cheap—and then we spend maybe twenty or thirty minutes mingling and letting them speak, and they'll be on their way within an hour, which they appreciate, because they don't have to work that hard for the money."

Through the aid of these brokers, donors can stay in contact with their elected officials throughout the year. From retiring campaign debts to enhancing officeholder accounts to supporting nonprofit corporations or ballot initiatives, politicians nearly always need some kind of additional money from supporters. And brokers are happy to centralize the money and put the politicians in touch with their benefactors. "We've got a politician in here once a week," claims broker Ken Spiker of Spiker and Associates.

Brokers aid the factional leaders by doing a good deal of financial and political work for them. In backing candidates, the brokers tend to defer to the leaders of the factions with which they are aligned. Then they put the leaders' anointed candidates in touch with the people who can provide campaign resources. Cerrell, for example, was closely aligned with veteran city councilmember Nate Holden. "Usually," explains Matt Klink, "Nate will know the district so well, he'll have a candidate. He'll want us to help his person by moving him around to meet the right people, things of that nature."

Brokers are, to borrow a description of famed California lobbyist Artie Samish, guys who get things done. Samish got things done by working directly with individual legislators, and he eventually went to jail for it. In the current period, brokers get things done by working through and helping to create local party organizations. For this reason, they are a direct challenge to scholarship that views parties as emerging from a legislature. The guys who get things done apparently don't need to hold office to do it. Indeed, as I demonstrated in chapter 2, the history of legislators during the cross-filing era suggests that people in office don't necessarily even want to get much done, short of securing their own reelections. The desire to get things done, and the ability to do so, reside outside the capitol.

Candidate Selection

What sorts of candidates do informal party organizations back? They are not looking for an obscure candidate who would require a great deal of grooming. Rather, they look for indications of credibility, usually in the form of money (or fund-raising potential) and endorsements. Candidates need to do a considerable amount of organizing before the party selects them. It is extremely rare for party organizations to pluck citizens from obscurity and make viable candidates of them. It is far easier to find people with connections of their own to the voters or to resource providers, people who have demonstrated that they can win.

Waxman-Berman ally Burt Margolin largely endorsed these sentiments:

> Running for office is tough. Running for office requires a thick skin. Running for office requires a tremendous commitment of energy and resources and time. And the best candidates are candidates who are self-motivated, who have come to the point in their lives where they want to run for office. And the best candidates are candidates who have an independent rationale for their candidacy.

Other respondents agreed that candidates must do a lot on their own, typically raising funds or seeking endorsements to impress factional leaders. Consultant Victor Griego described this process as a precampaign campaign: candidates try to look like they have the most money and backing so they will be slated by an organization that will provide them with more money and support. As Griego describes it, the factional leaders say, "It will be better for us. We're not going to have to work as hard, so we're going to support you. Because you've got your own business, or you come from a union that would support you. . . . But then we'll throw all our support behind you." Assemblyman Juan Arambula agrees, saying he looks for "somebody who has been successful in their field, somebody who has established themselves. . . . I may observe from a distance that somebody has access to money." Such an arrangement works out well for both parties: the organization gets a likely officeholder at a low cost, while the candidate gets a better chance at election and a team of allies for getting things done in government.

IPO members tend to be instinctively pragmatic in the candidate selection process. Brokers, for example, have little incentive to back a loser. If a broker makes her living as a lobbyist, it really only helps her to back winners; you can't make money by lobbying the loser of an election. Similarly, if a broker makes her living as a campaign consultant, she wants a high win-loss ratio. With their experience in politics and their ties to factional leaders, they develop a good sense of which candidates are credible. "We make smart decisions based on our experience," explains Klink. "We make a difference in the margin. If someone wins by one or two points, I think we can help them squeeze a point or two. If someone loses by thirty, I'm hoping that we wouldn't have gone with that candidate."

Similarly, benefit seekers get involved in campaigns because they want to have access to officeholders, and candidates who do not become officeholders have little to offer. As Chris Hammond explains, "I'm unfortunately a business guy. It really doesn't help me to back somebody on the losing side. I'd rather stay out of the election and come in after the fact. Backing a candidate who loses, it's a terrible thing." Even activists have their pragmatic side when it comes to candidate selection. Bobbie Anderson notes, "People say, 'You should support the best candidate.' Not necessarily. You have to look out for who's going to get you access to stuff that's going to help your constituency or your group."

Between fund-raising and endorsements, most local leaders seem to consider the former the most important indication of candidate credibility, at least initially. "You have to prove that you have the ability to raise money before anyone will notice you," claims Bill Boyarsky, who has observed California politics as a journalist since the 1960s. Orange County political consultant Eileen Padberg agrees. "If I have a great . . . candidate that has no ability to raise money, there's no sense in trying to run her."

But although fund-raising ability is chief among several leaders' lists of criteria, there are other tests of candidate credibility. According to Chris Hammond, a onetime member of Waters's inner circle, the list of candidate assets proceeds as follows: "First and foremost, [the candidate's] ability to raise money. Second, what kind of skeletons that person's got, although that's usually less of an issue in terms of ranking. And then, what kind of ground support and resources, other than money, that that person can bring to the table. . . . And then, people's political alliances." An extensive network of insider support for a candidate can sometimes be considered a substitute for money. "When I talk to candidates," says Mike Hernandez, "I always ask them how large their Christmas card list is. . . . If they tell me 60, they don't have a shot. If they tell me 600, they've got a very good shot. Because those are the people you know will give you money." Assembly member Mervyn Dymally, who once ran a powerful organization that opposed Mayor Tom Bradley's in the 1970s, simply says to candidates, "One, give me a checkbook with $50,000; two, give me a poll; three, let me see your endorsements; and what's your campaign structure? Those are tough criteria." In his 1991 campaign for the Los Angeles City Council, Mike Hernandez followed this advice to help him win the support of the Molina organization. "Before I'd even announced," Hernandez explains, "I'd raised $50,000. I'd already had 50 local community endorsements, before I even went after one elected official's endorsement. And I'd already supported all these elected officials for office that were going to support me, but I didn't ask them for endorsements until I had the $50,000."

Several points about this $50,000 entry fee deserve comment here. First, raising $50,000 on one's own is not easy, and it generally can't be done through mass mailings to the general public requesting $25 donations. There are very few people in a given community who will make significant contributions to an unknown candidate a year or more prior to an election. The candidates who have the respect of these few donors are greatly advantaged over those who don't. Thus, the $50,000 benchmark is not only a test of a candidate's willingness to make phone calls, it also measures what political insiders think of her.

Second, it is curious that several politicians from different regions came up with the $50,000 figure. This quantity is, interestingly, usually insufficient for winning an election. Between 1998 and 2002, the typical assembly race in these areas cost about $260,000 and an average Los Angeles City Council race cost roughly $125,000. Most candidates, it seems, do not raise sufficient funds to run an entire campaign on their own, but some amass enough for an IPO to take them seriously. Through this effort, the candidate demonstrates credibility, but she still needs the organization to get her into office.

A good example of the relationship between initial financial support and network support comes from the 2001 LA City Council elections. In the Fifth District, attorney Jack Weiss ran against Tom Hayden, a former state senator and prominent anti–Vietnam War activist. As Bill Boyarsky explains, Weiss had to do a lot of organizing on his own before foes of Hayden (of which there were no shortage) would coordinate their efforts on Weiss and provide him with the help he needed to win:

> Jack comes from sort of an affluent family, I think, so he had a bit of money there. He had a credential that looks good on a ballot—he was a U.S. attor-

ney. He went everywhere. Every time I'd go somewhere, there was Jack. He put all this together, and he showed people that he was willing to raise money, he was willing to work his ass off, he was willing to not stay home with his family at night. He'd go out and do all that shit that you have to do. . . . He had the fighting heart. Then, he started getting money from people who had a lot of money and didn't want Hayden to be on the City Council.

Weiss was only able to garner 22 percent of the vote in a crowded field, but that was enough to put him in a runoff election with Hayden. The funds and assistance Weiss received in that race allowed him to edge out Hayden by fewer than 400 votes.

This is not to imply that any candidate that shows some initiative will be rewarded with money and endorsements. Sometimes a candidate just doesn't appear credible. In that case, factional leaders will usually try to dissuade her from running. This is usually done in a diplomatic manner, at least on the Democratic side. As Dymally explains, "You don't want to [discourage people]. Because when you get ready to run, you don't want anybody to talk you out of it." To dissuade a potential candidate, says California Democratic Party secretary Reggie Jones-Sawyer, elected officials will meet with the candidate and say:

"Let's run through what you've got. Have you really thought this thing through?" And they listen to your ideas, and run through your whole campaign, how you plan to get from point A to point Z. And they give some helpful advice. . . . I always tell people to do milestones . . . "If you haven't raised this amount by this time, if you haven't got this amount of endorsements . . . by this time, maybe you need to reevaluate what you want to do." And I kind of leave it open-ended.

Victor Griego uses a similar method to dissuade candidates he doesn't think are worthy of support:

What I do is I explain the pitfalls. Recently, two guys came to me, asking my support, to help them, you know. And I just said, "You can run if you want, but understand that my role will be limited, because I think so-and-so has got a better chance, and so-and-so has been there, and so-and-so is probably going to win. But you're my friend, and I'm going to encourage you to do what you think is right. But understand, my role's going to be limited, because I'm not going to waste my time." . . . You can't say, "You're not going to win, you're lousy, you're this, you're that." Ten years from now, the person's the state senator from the region, and you're saying, "Oh, shit, I told this person not to run." You don't do that. You become very subtle in how you communicate to people.

Sometimes leaders use an even softer sell, accruing so much money and support for their preferred candidate that the other candidates see no alternative to dropping out. "What we try to do," says Dymally, "is to get so many endorsements that the other guy looks at it. . . . If they see you have both endorsements and money, that influences."

The Republican style of dissuading candidates may be a bit harsher. Fresno Republican consultant Mike Der Manouel is blunt with candidates he doesn't think are ready to run: "I usually ask them, 'Why are you doing this? What do you want to accomplish?' And then I hammer 'em with some hard questions, and if they're not prepared, I give 'em an earful. . . . I've had several people come in here hell bent on running, and based on our conversation, decided not to run."

Orange County leaders report similarly blunt tactics for getting candidates to withdraw from primaries. When moderate Republican Judy Ryan ran against Rep. Bob Dornan (R-Garden Grove) in 1992, the conservative county leaders came out swinging in the incumbent's defense. Tom Fuentes, the one-time chairman of the county's Republican Central Committee, even left menacing phone messages on Ryan's answering machine and threatened to get her husband fired from the Heinz Corporation. As Buck Johns of the conservative Lincoln Club explains:

We didn't hit her, but we threatened her a lot. We basically said that it would cost us a lot of money in defeating her and she doesn't have a chance. This is not her turn to run. She can put in as much money as she wants to. We will raise a lot of money and we will pummel her. She will come out of this candidacy all bruised up. And if you want to get into the political process, that's a bad place to start.

Such candidate dissuasion techniques have a long and proud history among Orange County conservatives. Tom Rogers, who chaired the county's Republican Central Committee between 1969 and 1973, claims during his tenure to have sent some aides to the office of the Registrar of Voters on the day of the candidate filing deadline to make sure that no challengers to an incumbent filed. When one potential candidate showed up, Rogers's men promptly escorted him to a car and drove him around until after the filing deadline had passed. Rogers also dispatched an assistant to ram into the car of a potential primary challenger in a U.S. Senate race to prevent him from filing before the deadline. Rogers learned too late, however, that the challenger had traveled by helicopter.

To summarize, IPO leaders look for candidates who have some money (or access to it), support from prominent backers, or maybe even just a good set of values. This initial backing is not easy to come by; generally, only candidates who are known and respected and have paid some dues within the small world of the IPO can develop the initial support that will lead the IPO leaders to consider an official endorsement. The backing of top IPO leaders, when given, can take various forms, including intense pressure on competitors to get out of the race. What IPOs do for a candidate, or to her potential opponents, varies from race to race even within the same IPO. The Republicans of Orange County seem to deal in nods that make fund-raising easy or hard; the Waters organization offers a mailer that can add 10 percent to a candidate's vote total, plus help on fund-raising, networking, and canvassing. What is important to realize, though, is that the leaders are virtually always active in open-seat primaries. Even in the face of a self-starting candidate with substantial money and name recognition, leaders are not passive. They seek to shape the field, perhaps by clearing it of lesser challengers. For example, in an unusual show of unity, Reps. Waters and Watson joined Speaker Wesson and Supervisor Burke in backing former LA Police Chief Bernard Parks's 2003 run for city council. Parks was popular among the district's African American voters and surely would have won anyway, but the backing of so many IPO leaders helped clear the field of all but the least significant rival candidates. Parks won in a field of five candidates with 78 percent of the vote.

At a minimum, IPO leaders may earn the gratitude of the candidate who was likely to win anyway. At the other extreme, leaders may select a virtual nobody (albeit one deemed to have the skills to run a competitive race) and elevate her above the field of seemingly better qualified candidates. Between these two extremes, IPO leaders are always doing something.

An example I consider especially instructive comes from the 2002 primary race for Fresno's Twenty-ninth Assembly District. Five candidates initially expressed interest in the Republican nomination for that open seat. Many prominent conservative leaders clearly preferred Steve Samuelian, the district director for Rep. George Radanovich (R-Fresno), but would have had a hard time coordinating money and support on one candidate in such a crowded field. For various reasons, however, other candidates began dropping out. Debbie Poochigian, the wife of a state senator, planned to run but then withdrew to deal with a family illness. Nathan Magsig, whom I discussed previously, had the misfortune of being the district director for assemblyman Mike Briggs, who had won the hatred of his fellow Republicans by voting for the Democratic state budget. For a number of reasons, including the urging of some party members and activists, Magsig dropped out of the race. Veteran newscaster John Wallace also considered the race, but withdrew after receiving what he described as a series of anonymous faxes and phone calls "of a personal nature and a family nature. . . . Not physical threats, just comments, missives, indicating to me that the next four months of the campaign would be the most uncomfortable four months of my life." Through a variety of events both accidental and orchestrated, an unmanageable field of five candidates was winnowed to a much more manageable field of two. This left only Samuelian and Larry Willey, a businessman with few ties to established local Republican officeholders. Samuelian received the lion's share of campaign contributions and endorsements in the primary and edged out Willey, 56-44.

Disciplining Slackards and Apostates

IPO leaders must constantly worry whether the people they get elected will stay faithful to them and their ideological agenda, as noted previously. Maintaining a coterie of loyal followers is one of the motivations for forming IPOs in the first place. By picking the right sorts of candidates and maintaining control over their campaign resources, IPOs can usually keep an incumbent voting as they wish, at least on critical matters. But breakdowns do occur, and when they do, more drastic remedies can be brought to bear. These remedies include de-nomination and recall.

An interesting case of an incumbent who lost favor with an IPO is Congressman Matthew "Marty" Martinez (D-El Monte), who was denied renomination in 2000. Martinez had slowly drifted away from the West LA Waxman-Berman organization that helped him get elected in 1982, and his personality and conservative stances on guns, abortion, and free trade prevented him from building effective alliances with either local activists or within the Democratic or Hispanic caucuses in Congress. By the late 1990s, the Los Angeles County Federation of Labor, considered a powerhouse in Eastside elections, was seeking to raise the bar for Democratic officeholders who sought its support. Backing Hilda Solis, a young second-term state senator, against Martinez seemed like an excellent place to start.

Solis began her campaign for the party's nomination in early 1999 by conducting and distributing a poll that suggested that area residents weren't very familiar with Rep. Martinez even after eighteen years of service and that she had a chance of winning. She also aggressively raised funds from within the district, surpassing the incumbent's fund-raising tally and proving herself to be a viable competitor. That summer (by which point Solis's fund-raising had crossed the $50,000 rubicon), a coalition of state and local officeholders—including Gloria Molina, state senator John Burton, state party chair Art Torres, congresswoman Loretta Sanchez, and Speaker Antonio Villaraigosa—rallied behind Solis and provided cover for others who wished to dump the incumbent. Following the lead of these endorsers, the Labor Federation and EMILY's List came through with substantial funding for Solis. With the support of this coalition, Solis unseated a nine-term member of Congress in the primary by a 69-31 vote. (Solis would later be President Obama's choice for Secretary of Labor.)

Sometimes an incumbent has committed such an apostasy that IPO leaders can't wait until the next election to remove her. Such was the case in Orange County in 1995. In perhaps their most public display of control, county conservatives mounted recalls of two incumbent assembly members. Having just won a narrow 41-39 majority in the assembly, Republicans were eager to depose liberal Speaker Willie Brown (D-San Francisco). Yet their plans were thwarted when Orange County assemblywoman Dorris Allen, angry with her fellow Republicans over a perceived slight in the previous election, ran as the Democrats' candidate for Speaker; she won with all the Democratic votes and exactly one Republican vote—her own. Furious, Orange County conservatives organized a recall and sent a sitting Speaker of their own party back to private life. As Buck Johns explains, such transgressions cannot be tolerated: "You've got to shoot the son of a bitch. . . . She had to go over the side." The same leaders also successfully recalled another Republican who had crossed party lines to keep Willie Brown in power, and they backed a stealth primary opponent to the moderate, Democrat-backed Speaker who succeeded Allen. They finally installed one of their own, Garden Grove's Curt Pringle, as Speaker for the remainder of the GOP's control of the assembly in 1996.

Virtually every IPO has a bullpen of ambitious young officeholders and aides hungry for higher office. Virtually every incumbent office-holder worth her salt knows this and knows better than to earn a record that a challenger could attack or that would irritate her sponsors. For those who might forget, the cases of Marty Martinez and Dorris Allen are rare but sharp wake-up calls.

For officeholders who stray only slightly, IPOs can employ a number of responses short of the nuclear options of de-nomination and recall. For one thing, IPOs can simply make life harder for an incumbent who seeks renomination. They can make noises about finding a new candidate, even if they don't follow through with it. They can demand overt or secret pledges of loyalty from the incumbent in exchange for continued support. These sorts of things occur more often than de-nominations and are likely at the forefront of incumbents' minds when casting votes on issues of importance to their backers.

As an example of such pressure, one respondent related a story to me about a northern California county supervisor who was being pressured by an environmental interest group to support a particular bill. The supervisor had been receiving financial assistance from the group through many election cycles. Although she felt that the particular bill was a bad one, she nonetheless voted for it. She didn't think the environmental lobby would try to dump her in the next election if she crossed them, but they'd probably withhold campaign donations, and she felt she was too old and tired to go out looking for new donors.

The Benefits of Cross-Government Coordination

Several IPO members openly discussed the importance of working across levels and government and the value of having allies at various levels. Officeholders, for example, believe that having allies at multiple levels of government enables them to serve their constituents better. Fresno city councilman Henry Perea has assigned each of his staffers specific officeholders with whom to act as liaisons. As Perea explains,

> You have to stay in contact with every level of government to really know what's going on, because if you don't, things can get pushed right past you. Yesterday, when I was in Sacramento, I learned that Fresno was number eight on the list of a program to be cut from the state budget. Now, had I not gone, I wouldn't have been able to bring that information back here. When I

was calling people on the way back here, they said, "What are you talking about? What do you mean we're going to have X amount of million dollars cut?" So now that gives us the opportunity to work with our lobbyists and start calling our state legislators and saying, "Hey, you got to get us off this list."

But interoffice cooperation is about more than just retaining funding; it's also about securing new funds. Perea continues:

[Most interoffice work consists of] grant-type issues, helping us to identify what funds are available out there. And, of course, when we do apply as a city, it's [state and federal officeholders'] job politically to start getting involved in maneuvering to help us get the money. Because, of course, every city is applying for the same pot of money. So we need to rely on them and their contacts so they're going to work the political end for us, and making sure that we get our fair share.

The value of such cross-governmental alliances was demonstrated in the late 1980s, when Occidental Petroleum expressed its interest in drilling for oil off the coast of scenic Pacific Palisades. Although Los Angeles' then mayor Tom Bradley championed the drilling plan, many Westside voters were angered by it, and the issue came to a head in 1988 when antidrilling advocates placed Proposition O, which would prevent offshore drilling, on the ballot (Reinhold 1988). Members of the Waxman-Berman organization, including then city councilmember Zev Yaroslavsky, constructed an alliance among state, federal, county, and city officials in support of the proposition, and Michael Berman developed a political strategy to guide them in their efforts. The alliance succeeded; Proposition O won—narrowly—despite Occidental's $10 million campaign to defeat it (Roderick 1988).

This Westside alliance also proved helpful when LA Community College Board member Rick Tuttle faced colleagues who were panicked over the passage of Proposition 13 in 1978. This proposition drastically reduced property taxes, upon which local public agencies depended. State lawmakers then had to decide on a new formula to allocate funds to local agencies, and Tuttle, through his ties to the Waxman-Berman group, had access to these state lawmakers:

I went up and talked to Howard [Berman] about it. In fact, we stayed at . . . Howard's place. . . . Howard helped see to it that community colleges were treated fairly. I have a hunch if you go to Howard and ask if he could re-member this, it was probably one of a million things he was dealing with at the time. It was important to us, though, and to lots of community colleges.

In general, says Tuttle, it is extremely advantageous for a local office-holder to have ties to powerful lawmakers at other governmental levels. People who dealt with him, Tuttle explains, would say, "Here's someone who . . . on Tuesday night says, 'A, B, and C will happen,' by Wednesday afternoon, A, B, and C have happened. That's nice. That's awfully nice."

Even when not involved in such high-stakes battles, cross-govern-mental relationships can just make work a lot easier. Kelly Hart, a case-worker for former Orange County Rep. Christopher Cox, maintains reg-ular contact with her counterparts in local congressional and state legislative offices. "When you build a personal relationship with these people," she explains, "it makes it easier to pick up the phone." Cox's office found such relationships advantageous when the congressman be-came involved with an effort to address noise and traffic issues associated with John Wayne Airport in Orange County. According to press secretary Amy Inaba Freyder, Cox was able to work at the federal level with the Federal Aviation Administration, while his allies on the Newport Beach City Council addressed the problems from the local level.

Recently, some IPO members have sought to institutionalize cross-governmental relationships. For example, Jorge Morales, a district aide to former Eastside LA assemblyman Marco Antonio Firebaugh, has helped to organize the Latino Staff Coalition. This coalition consists of a few dozen area staffers who meet regularly in both social and business settings so that they can more easily contact each other should their jobs necessitate it. As Morales explains, "If you need something, you know where to call." Morales, for example, has personal ties to the Southgate Chamber of Commerce, and he has helped introduce staffers from other offices to the chamber's membership.

Such cross-governmental work helps more than constituents. Accord-ing to Kerman Maddox, a former employee of Rep. Waters, it can make the IPO a much more effective organization, one that is increasingly likely to prevail in campaigns and legislative matters. Says Maddox,

If you can hook up from DC to Sacramento, to the Board [of Supervisors], to the City Council, you can do a lot of good things, *especially if you've got your people in place.* . . . If you can get people in all those different positions, one, you can deliver a lot, and two, politically, you can be pretty potent, because you have your local people with their support, your legislative people with their support, and then your congressional people. If those come together behind a candidate or behind a cause, your chances of winning are pretty good.

Unsurprisingly, these cross-governmental relationships do not occur between all offices. They are usually done within parties and, more important, within factional alliances. One Eastside LA staffer in an office aligned with Richard Polanco reports that when he needs to do work with other area political offices, he'll tend to avoid rival leader Gloria Molina's office:

> We're trying to do an urban cleanup. A lot of the unincorporated areas are really neglected. . . . But we know that if we get Molina's office, they'll want to take credit, be on the fliers, but won't put in the resources. It has nothing to do with Molina's policies or anything, but the reputation.

Cross-governmental alliances are maintained and nurtured by IPO leaders. It is common for leaders to encourage donors to contribute to campaigns that have little to do with their own narrow interests but a lot to do with larger factional alliances. Keith Parker cites several examples in which a large donor organization got involved in city elections because they wanted to influence foes or allies at the state level:

> Indian gaming put an awful lot of money into the [2001 Los Angeles] mayor's race. Well, there are no Indian casinos in Los Angeles. What, if anything, do they have to get out of that? Well, they wanted to punish [mayoral candidate Antonio] Villaraigosa, because Villaraigosa had hurt them in Sacramento. They wanted to punish him. They put a lot of money into Tony Cardenas's [2002] City Council race against Wendy Greuel. They're not getting any new casinos in the San Fernando Valley, but Tony Cardenas had helped them. And they wanted him to continue to help them. Even though he was [running for] the City Council, he has friends in Sacramento.

By getting involved in local races, even ones about which she knows or cares little, a donor can ingratiate herself to a prominent officeholder who can return favors. "When [Congressman] Henry Waxman's son [Michael] ran for LA Community College District Board," says Parker, "well, there's not a whole lot that Michael Waxman can do for anybody, but there's a lot that Henry potentially can do. So you want to make sure that Henry knew you were supporting his son."

Cross-governmental cooperation, it would seem, is not just helpful for an IPO, it is essential. Officeholders rely on such alliances because they enable them to better deliver for constituencies, benefit seekers, and activists. Resource donors, moreover, need such intergovernmental relationships because it gives them an opportunity to ingratiate themselves to an IPO leader who might not otherwise need assistance. Cross-governmental cooperation thus creates both needs and opportunities for exchanges of favors, reinforcing the bonds that allow IPOs to cohere.

DISCUSSION

My aim in this chapter has been to venture onto political terrain where the light is bad in order to learn about aspects of party behavior that cannot be detected with more conventional data. The trip has yielded a vivid view of informal party organizations in action—a view that will, I hope, be valuable to political observers who rarely have access to such information. More to the point, the evidence I have collected is useful for understanding just how political parties function today and how we can best think of them. Describing parties in terms of the machines of yore is not necessarily a bad way to go. Influence over a wide range of offices tends to be concentrated in the hands of just a few individuals operating at the local level. Control is maintained through manipulation of the nomination process. Yet the qualitative evidence suggests some important deviations from the old party machine model. For example, the arrangements at work today are clearly less formal; while traditional machines worked through the formal party organizations, these informal associations I have examined treat the official organizations as just part of a system or else ignore them altogether. Another difference is that patronage clearly does not exist in the way it did in the age of the machines. Today's informal organizations appear to have enough jobs, ceremonial titles, and government benefits to keep their constituent members loyal, but they can't employ every precinct organizer or pay off every voter. Still, that doesn't appear to be a liability. Today's organizations manage to keep themselves afloat in California's relatively patronage-free environment.

The notion that parties are the creatures of politicians fares much less well in my interview data. If anything, the politicians would appear to be the creatures of the parties. The Unruh organization, which began from within the legislature, may seem to be an exception. However, the source of Unruh's power derived at least as much from his control over party nominations as from his manipulation of internal legislative machinery. Furthermore, once Unruh and his cohort became more firmly established in power, they faced continued party pressures from CDC ideologues outside the legislature and considered this pressure a threat to their party's viability. Unruh even made efforts to limit the CDC's power over politics to keep it from fracturing his coalition. In the long run, the Speaker's organization may have lost this struggle. It began to share power with local organizations in the 1980s and seems more recently to have been superseded by them.

The political systems I found are decidedly not organized by the candidates, nor are they lying in service to them. The vast majority of successful candidates enter politics through an established political organization and work their way up within it. Moreover, in both open-and closed-ended interview data, the people closest to local politics strongly rejected the popular academic view that nomination politics is candidate-centered. The same small groups of key officeholders, benefit seekers, and activists keep showing up in campaign after campaign, influencing races for positions on school boards and city councils on up to senatorial and gubernatorial seats. While the practices of these IPO leaders may be somewhat secretive, their identities typically are not: the respondents to whom I spoke reliably mentioned a very similar set of key players in local politics.

There are important differences between regions that should be noted. Politics within South and East Los Angeles County seems to most closely match the informal party organization model I originally postulated. There, prominent elected officials provide the leadership, forming alliances with churches, clubs, and unions that can provide Election Day labor and with other officeholders and benefit seekers that can provide money to fuel the organization. Judging from the descriptions of both adherents and detractors, Orange County conservatives have a very strong organization, but one of a somewhat different form. Business leaders and land developers—not officeholders—do a lot of the coordination, fundraising, and hard work on behalf of candidates, and often manage to keep their names off the campaign literature. The Fresno style is more of a blend: many candidates rise through the ranks as protégés of local officeholders, although organizations like labor and law enforcement are the ones that seem to have the resources and name recognition to mobilize voters on Election Day. Given that Los Angeles—with its large concentrations of poor, modestly assimilated voters dependent on government largesse—most closely matches the conditions in which the traditional party machines once thrived, it is unsurprising that we would find the strongest evidence of organizational activity there.

Despite these regional differences, however, there is a recognizable common model operating in all five communities. Candidates and would-be candidates recognize the difficulties of running for office—the time commitment, the money, the expertise required, and so on—and seek to reduce the costs by working within an organization. By working for or otherwise becoming attached to a local party organization, candidates gain entry to a group of resource donors and other backers who would otherwise be inaccessible. There is a trade-off, though. These organizations exert considerable influence over the would-be candidate's career, deciding when she is ready to run and what she will say and do on the campaign trail. In addition, officeholders are expected to cooperate with a partisan agenda and with colleagues across different levels of government.

For most, this trade-off is acceptable. The party may occasionally ask much, but it provides enough in return to make the arrangement worthwhile. Exactly how much it provides is a difficult question to answer, though. Determining what the party can offer to a campaign, and how we can distinguish that from the candidate's own assets, is the task of the next chapter.

CHAPTER 5

Measuring the Power of Informal
Party Organizations

The qualitative evidence presented in the last chapter suggested that various political actors bond together to form informal party organizations, controlling nominations and exerting influence over the governing process. Ultimately, however, that conclusion is based upon the statements of individuals with their own agendas. It is one thing to show that these organizations exist; proving that they influence elections is quite another matter.

That is precisely what I seek to do in this chapter. I begin with a discussion of the serious endogeneity problem inherent in this line of research: How does one measure the influence of party organizations when they make an effort to pick the candidates likely to win anyway? I then propose several tests that address this problem and seek to distinguish between a party-centered and a candidate-centered political system. From there, I examine the paths that elected officials from city councilmembers to members of Congress took to enter politics. This analysis finds that current incumbents overwhelmingly entered politics via informal party organizations. I also use the results of primary elections to determine whether IPO-affiliated candidates do better than those with other "private" advantages, such as ties to the business or legal community. Again, I find strong support for the IPO model. In the final section, I attempt to characterize each of the political systems I have studied by use of a multivariate regression that measures the impact of IPO leader endorsements while controlling for campaign expenditures and candidate quality. I conclude with a discussion of how each system measures up against the party/candidate tests and what this means for the IPO model.

PARTY-CENTERED VERSUS CANDIDATE-CENTERED: HOW CAN WE TELL?

I have argued that the IPO model is best for understanding modern party politics and that California is a much more party-dominated state than it is generally reported to be. There are various challenges, however, to demonstrating empirically the influence of informal party organizations on politics. It is not always obvious who is running politics in an age when large, urban, patronage-driven machines like Tammany Hall no longer exist. The problem is partly one of visibility: candidates operate in the open, and IPOs stay behind the scenes. Moreover, even when parties have been historically strong, they have invariably funded and controlled campaigns in such a way as to make them appear candidate-centered, promoting the candidate's message over that of the party (Krasno 2007). Thus even observers who are sensitive to the possibility that party organizations are at the center of politics may find it hard to make the case.

The main problem arises from the fact that parties try, whenever possible, to choose candidates who have demonstrated popular appeal and private support. Selecting such candidates means much less work and less chance of embarrassment for the party organization. In addition, depending on the political culture in a given state, machine politics may be very unpopular among the public, even if it is widely practiced (Patterson 1968; Wolfinger 1972; Sonenshein 1984; Coleman 1996). In such states, both organizational leaders and candidates recognize the political unpopularity of machines and bosses and try to avoid being associated with them in voters' minds. It rarely does a candidate much good to boast of running for office because some local leader said she could win; nor do organizational leaders like to brag that they are limiting the public's choice of candidates for office by clearing a path for their own anointed candidate. Kent (1924) effectively depicts the approach of a candidate seeking a machine's support, which he describes as

> the easiest, least expensive, and surest road to the nomination, and there is
> not the slightest thing discreditable in trying to get that support, so long as he

neither truckles to the boss nor makes pledges inconsistent with the public interest or his own self-respect.

On the contrary, it would be a stupid thing not to try. But, whether he is successful in getting the machine back of him or not, does the candidate make public his efforts in that direction? Does he tell the voters when the campaign begins that he sought the support of the bosses and got it, or that he sought their support and did not get it? He does not.

What he does is to conceal the fact, so far as he can, of any touch at all between himself and the boss. If he gets the support, he assumes the attitude of having had it come to him wholly unsolicited and, if he does not get it, he assumes an attitude of uncompromising hostility to the machine and becomes an anti-machine candidate. (219–20)

The lesson here is that we should not let public officials' attempts to downplay organizations blind us to the power of these party organizations to influence politics.

An even bigger methodological problem, however, is the difficulty of demonstrating party influence in situations in which parties back candidates who have some independent strength to begin with. Perhaps the best—and certainly the most entertaining—description of the importance of candidate ambition in a strong party system comes from George Washington Plunkitt. As Plunkitt (Riordan 1963) describes in his lecture on becoming a statesman, a candidate proves his value to an organization by cultivating "marketable commodities," such as pledged votes:

I had a cousin, a young man who didn't take any particular interest in politics. I went to him and said: "Tommy, I'm goin' to be a politician, and I want to get a followin'; can I count on you?" He said: "Sure, George." That's how I started in business. I got a marketable commodity—one vote. Then I went to the district leader and told him I could command two votes on election day, Tommy's and my own. He smiled on me and told me to go ahead.

Plunkitt enjoys the respect the district leader pays to him, and he continues to build up his "organization," asking for pledged votes from friends and neighbors. Soon his organization reaches a critical size that demands that local elites take notice:

Before long I had sixty men back of me, and formed the George Washington Plunkitt Association.

What did the district leader say then when I called at headquarters? I didn't have to call at headquarters. He came after me and said: "George, what do you want? If you don't see what you want, ask for it. Wouldn't you like to have a job or two in the departments for your friends?" I said: "I'll think it over; I haven't yet decided what the George Washington Plunkitt Association will do in the next campaign." You ought to have seen how I was courted and petted then by the leaders of the rival organizations. I had marketable goods and there was bids for them from all sides, and I was a risin' man in politics. As time went on, and my association grew, I thought I would like to go to the Assembly. I just had to hint at what I wanted, and three different organizations offered me the nomination. Afterwards, I went to the Board of Aldermen, then to the State Senate, then became leader of the district, and so on up and up till I became a statesman.

Tammany Hall is, of course, the epitome of strong party organization in the United States. Yet here we see evidence, albeit anecdotal, that candidates needed to do a considerable amount of organizing on their own before the party came calling for them. Rare indeed is the party organization that will pluck citizens from obscurity and make viable candidates of them. It is far better to find people with connections of their own to the voters or to resource providers—people who have demonstrated that they can win.

In a nationwide application of Plunkitt's method, John F. Kennedy entered the 1960 West Virginia Democratic presidential primary to prove to party elites that a Catholic could win in an overwhelmingly Protestant state. His tactful public discussion of the religion issue and his victory in that state gave Democratic delegates some comfort in nominating him. Similarly, Adlai Stevenson entered a number of primaries in 1956 to prove to party elites that he still had some cachet among rank-and-file Democrats despite his loss in 1952. Both Kennedy and Stevenson provide examples of some candidate-initiated activity that made it easier for large party organizations to gauge popular appeal. But the choice of nominee clearly remained in the hands of party leaders, as was apparent in 1968 when Democratic elites nominated Hubert Humphrey over Eugene McCarthy despite the latter's demonstrated success in the primaries and the former's failure to enter even one contest.

But by choosing candidates as they do, parties make it hard for political scientists to discern their actual political importance. Let us assume, for example, that three main factors contribute to a candidate's success: popular appeal, campaign spending, and the backing of a party organization. If parties slate candidates who have already demonstrated their ability to raise campaign funds and win some votes, and if their slating opens the way for more funds and more votes, how can we determine the effect of the party organization? There is a serious endogeneity problem here. Statistical techniques exist that could, in principle, isolate the independent effect of party support, but the quantitative data necessary to use them are not available in this case. Hence, I must proceed by other means.

The study of party influence must address the following question: If candidates must commit themselves to building networks, raising money, and impressing voters before an organization will notice them, is it fair to call politics party-centered at all? If not, then there has never been a strong party system in the United States. But we cannot, as my previous examples have shown, dismiss the role of party because candidates are proactive. Rather, we must acknowledge that many candidates in a given race will be proactive, but only one will get the nomination. The early stages of a primary race are, in a sense, a competition for the resources necessary to win the nomination—endorsements, funding, staff, and volunteers. The one in command of these resources will likely win, but obtaining those resources is not really up to the candidate. Indeed, the providers of those resources make them available to the candidate of their choosing.

Cohen et al. (2008) face much the same conundrum in their study of presidential nominations. From a large field of candidates, party elites choose a strong one who can prevail with the resources those elites provide. Bill Clinton, the authors note, had impressed a number of party insiders in 1991 and 1992 through his work with the Democratic Leadership Council and his fierce campaigning in the New Hampshire primary, convincing them that he was strong and moderate enough to unseat President George H. W. Bush. By providing their endorsements and donations and encouraging others to do the same, those party insiders made it possible for Clinton to win the required primaries to secure the party's nomination. But how can one know whether this is a party-centered or a candidate-centered process?

To decide, Cohen and colleagues establish three critical tests to determine whether the political system is party-centered. First, do the political personnel and campaign backers make up a small world, requiring all potential candidates to compete among a limited group? Second, do the party leaders form a united front, coordinating on candidates that can unite the party and win in November? Third, is support from this small world of party leaders a decisive influence on nominations? An affirmative result for these three tests suggests the presence of a thriving political party. If these conditions are met, political activists, candidates, and donors will find that being part of a party organization is preferable to going it alone in politics.

Passing this test is crucial for IPO theory. If it cannot be shown that the system is party-centered, then the political world is really no different from that described by Mayhew (1974). Party organizations may form, but they have no real determinative impact in elections except to back up candidates' own efforts. Candidates could provide all the resources themselves—anyone with enough money or name recognition could enter a contest at any level of government. On the other hand, if IPO theory is correct, candidates would be dependent upon the backing of loose party structures to win. Candidates who chose to bypass party organizations would tend to lose.

ANALYSIS

The most important pattern to emerge from my interview data is that informal party organizations operate in each of the communities I examined and appear to be highly influential. These organizations are invisible in much political science literature and theory because they are hard to detect with the kind of data that is usually available to researchers. Yet qualitative descriptions of the kind I have provided possess their own limitations. They could, in particular, reflect an overly aggressive interpretation of what I was told. Hence, before proceeding with my analysis, I have sought to buttress my account with two sets of more systematic evidence.

The first involves a small closed-ended survey. After my initial open-ended interviews began to yield what seemed clear patterns of organized party activity, I created a short questionnaire to confirm that my respondents accepted my understanding of what they were telling me. Only 25 respondents—most of whom were respondents in the open-ended survey—replied to this questionnaire, but the results are clear enough to be worth reporting. Exact question wording is shown in table 3.

Asked who controlled local political nominations, 17 of 25 (68 percent) said it was a network of donors, officeholders, and activists. Three

(12 percent) said that just one or two people ran nominations, and only five (20 percent) described politics as candidate-centered. In the same vein, I asked whether prominent officeholders, fund-raisers, or candidates' own "skills and energy" determine nomination. Sixteen respondents (69 percent) felt that either fund-raisers or prominent officeholders have the most influence on nominations, with only five (22 percent) saying that the qualities of candidates are most important. Interestingly, one respondent with a master's degree in political science volunteered a C. Wright Mills term—"elite compacting"—to explain Eastside LA poli-

TABLE 3. Questions and Responses to Closed-Ended Questionnaire

1. *Which of the following statements do you think is the most accurate description of political nominations in this area?*
   A. One or two people largely control nominations for office in this community, determining which candidates can raise money, attract the most skilled campaign workers, and get the votes to win.   12
   B. Nobody controls nominations for office in this area. Successful candidates raise their own funds, assemble their own teams, and run their own campaigns.   20
   C. Candidates for nomination need the help of local officeholders, donors, and activists in order to be successful. These networks largely determine who can raise money, attract the most skilled campaign workers, and get the votes to win.   68

2. *When important elective offices come open in this community, who has the most influence on who gets the party nominations?*
   A. Leading local politicians have the most influence on nomination contests, because they give cues and nods that determine which candidates can raise money and attract staff.   17
   B. Leading fund-raisers have the most influence, because they are the key to whether candidates for nominations can raise money and pay staff or not.   0
   C. Big fund-raisers and leading local politicians have roughly equal influence on the nominations.   52
   D. Neither leading local politicians nor big fund-raisers have much influence at the nomination stage. Nominations are determined by the skills and energy of individual candidates.   22
   E. Decline to state/other.   8

3. *Which of the following statements best describes the effect of ideology in nomination campaigns?*
   A. A candidate for nomination who was politically moderate would have the *same chance* to raise money and attract campaign workers as a candidate who was politically liberal.   33
   B. A candidate for nomination who was politically moderate would have *a harder time* than a liberal raising money and attracting campaign workers, but could usually manage to do it.   46
   C. A candidate for nomination who was politically moderate would have *a tough time* raising money and attracting campaign workers to campaign for office and often wouldn't be able to succeed at it.   21

Note: Questions were asked of 25 respondents. Right column lists percentage of respondents who chose that response.

tics: "Opinion leaders coalesce and they determine things. Well, the unions are part of the opinion leaders. And fund-raisers are there, and politicians are there, and corporations are there. So there's largely a loose coalition."

Respondents also supported the finding from the previous chapter that IPO leaders tend to advantage ideologically extreme candidates. Sixteen of the 24 people who responded (67 percent) said that a moderate would have a harder time than an ideologically extreme candidate in mustering the resources for a nomination or would not be able to do it at all. At least in this small sample, respondents seem very comfortable describing politics in terms consistent with the IPO model.

Probing further into the data at a quantitative level is challenging. As discussed earlier, since party organizations prefer high-quality candidates with access to money, it is difficult to measure what aid the party organization is providing. More generally, it can be challenging to determine who an organization's chosen candidate even is. Despite the influence of these informal organizations, their memberships are not inscribed in stone and are rarely even recorded in newspapers. Much of this information, however, can be teased out of interviews and campaign documents, although these sources have some liabilities. A candidate, for example, may be reluctant to admit being backed by an elite or having worked for a key officeholder, depending on the political sentiments of the time and region. I have sought to corroborate my findings as much as possible through multiple sources, including elite interviews, newspaper articles, and individual campaign statements.

My first test of the power of informal party organizations is simply to look at current incumbents to see where they came from. Weak party areas and strong party areas, we may assume, will see different types of candidates winning office. Money is vital to election in both places, but how one gets the money will be determinative. In a weak party system, candidates with their own easy access to money will tend to prevail. Business leaders, in particular, have experience in borrowing, managing, and making money, and these people should tend to do well in a weak party system. Similarly, attorneys, with their deep knowledge of the legal and political system and their familiarity with the wealthier members of a community, should tend to do better than candidates without a legal background.

In a strong party area, however, candidates will tend to rise from existing political structures. Elected officials tend to know whom to ask for money and how to ask them, and they can make introductions for their protégés. These protégés may include employees and relatives of the elected official or other closely allied politicians. Given their public career paths, few incumbents or protégés are likely to have acquired a great deal of personal wealth over the years. Yet in a system of strong party networks, their access to campaign donors will give them an advantage over those with substantial personal wealth yet little political experience.

As a first attempt to assess the pervasiveness of IPOs, I simply look at all the incumbent legislators in my areas of study who were in office as of the beginning of 2003. My expectation is that they mostly came from political backgrounds. That is, they will mostly have been recruited by local IPO leaders because of their qualities or work within an organization, rather than entering politics on their own without the support of an informal group. This dataset consists of 125 officeholders, including all members of Congress, state senators, assembly members, and county supervisors within Fresno, Los Angeles, and Orange counties. I have also included the city councilmembers of each county's largest city (Fresno, Los Angeles, and Santa Ana, respectively). For this approach, I look at what job each officeholder held just prior to winning her first elected office. I group the results into two categories. The first is organizational routes to office, which includes holding lower office, serving as a political appointee or an aide to an officeholder, working as an activist (such as a union representative or a Chamber of Commerce leader), or being related to a current officeholder. The second category is individual routes to office, which includes being an attorney, a business leader, or simply pursuing any professional nonpolitical career. The results, shown in figure 19, display some clear regional variations. Los Angeles and Fresno incumbents are somewhat more likely to come from organizational positions than individual ones, while Orange County's incumbents are overwhelmingly from the private sector. Overall, half of all current incumbents made their start in politics as staffers, appointees, activists, or relatives of politicians.

This estimate of incumbent reliance on IPOs, however, is quite likely an understatement. This is so, I argue, for several reasons. First, some elected positions may be so low in stature as to require no organizational affiliation, yet a candidate may need an organization's help to rise through the ranks. For example, assemblywoman Lynn Daucher of Orange County was first elected to the Brea Olinda Unified School District. She could have been well tied to an informal party organization but simply

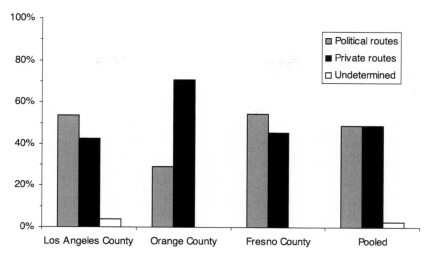

Fig. 19. Positions held by current officeholders immediately prior to taking first elected position. Political routes include activist, political appointee, relative of officeholder, staff of officeholder, and holder of another elected office. Private routes include business experience, professional experience, and working as an attorney. (Data from the League of Women Voters' Smart Voter web site [www .smartvoter.org/], UCLA's Online Campaign Literature Archive [www.library.ucla .edu/libraries/mgi/campaign/], and Project Vote Smart [www.vote-smart.org]).

not needed their support for such an election. However, moving from the school district to a position on the Brea City Council and then to an assembly seat may well have required the assistance of others. Yet my measure would list her as an incumbent who rose through an individual route.

A second difficulty with this method is that it does not account for IPOs that are not closely affiliated with officeholders. As the qualitative descriptions in chapter 4 suggest, Orange County, in particular, has alliances of realtors, club activists, and party officials who do not necessarily hire people as staffers or make formal endorsements. To continue the Lynn Daucher example, she may be supported by an IPO but not the sort of IPO that could hire her for a public staff position or political appointment. In Los Angeles, former city councilman Nick Pacheco was widely known as a close ally of Supervisor Gloria Molina's organization before his first run for office. However, he never worked on her staff, and his years of working on the campaigns of Molina candidates do not show up in the dataset. Homemakers or businesspeople who host campaign fund-raisers and confer regularly with local political elites would also not show up as political people in figure 19.

Finally, this method does not account for candidates who are strongly affiliated with informal party organizations and have even worked within them, but whose most recent work prior to running for office was in the private sector. Assemblyman Keith Richman, for example, is classified as one who took an individual route to office because he was working as a physician immediately prior to running for office. Richman, however, was no stranger to politics. He had previously testified before the U.S. Congress about Medicare, and he had been an appointee of Mayor Riordan to the Los Angeles Redevelopment Agency. Similarly, LA city councilmember Wendy Greuel, who was a corporate affairs director for Dreamworks SKG prior to running for office, worked for Mayor Tom Bradley previously and was also a local representative for the U.S. Department of Housing and Urban Development. And Fresno City Councilman Jerry Duncan, who ran a printing company prior to running for office, was earlier a member of the Fresno County Republican Central Committee, as well as a local activist with the Republican National Committee and the National Rifle Association. Surely he had some ties to local elite political associations, although it doesn't appear that way in the dataset.

Generally speaking, it is difficult to account for those candidates who have been loyal IPO members for years and gained political cachet through the organization but nonetheless pull down a paycheck from a private sector source. To further examine this issue, I randomly selected 20 of the officeholders listed in my dataset as having jumped into politics from a private career path. I spoke with these officeholders or with staff members who were familiar with their bosses' pasts. The results of this inquiry can be seen in table 4. Sixteen out of 20 of these "private" politicians in fact emerged from a political organization. LA City Councilmember Hal Bernson, for example, owned and managed a clothing store in the San Fernando Valley prior to running for office in the late 1970s but was heavily involved with a political business leader association, with the Chamber of Commerce, and with an early Valley secession movement. Indeed, community leaders closely tied with the secession movement urged him to run to represent the Valley's concerns. Similarly, Republican congressman Ken Calvert of Orange County is listed as having gone into politics as a businessman. This simple biography neglects the fact that he had previously been on the staff of Congressman Victor

Veysey (R-El Centro), or that he had chaired the Riverside County Republican Central Committee. Only four politicians on this list are properly described as having entered politics through individualistic routes. Of those four, three entered politics as members of city councils for small cities—the lowest political level possible.

As this sample suggests, perhaps as few as two out of ten "private" individuals entered politics without the help of standing political organizations. And since these "private" individuals made up roughly half of the entire dataset of incumbents, that implies that roughly nine out of ten politicians rose to power under the auspices of informal party organizations.

To get a better sense of how determinative these IPOs are in local elections, I have assembled a dataset consisting of every local election within Fresno County, Orange County, and the southern and eastern portions of Los Angeles County between 1998 and 2004. This dataset spans 94 different elections and contains 366 different candidates. The elections include primary contests for congressional, assembly, and state senate nominations, and both primary and general races in nonpartisan contests, including races for mayor, city council, county supervisor, and other county offices. While I have excluded partisan general elections, I do include several special elections (usually called after the death or retirement of an elected official), since multiple candidates within the same party can run against each other. I have excluded uncontested races and most races with an incumbent, except those in which the incumbent received less than 70 percent of the vote.

Here I am grouping candidates into two main categories with five subcategories. *Individual route* candidates may be attorneys or businesspeople. *Organizational route* candidates may be staffers, relatives of officeholders, or officeholders themselves. Candidates may appear in more than one category; this analysis simply seeks to determine how successful one group is compared to another. If strong party structures are present, we would expect to see organizational candidates do better than those who follow the individual route. On the other hand, individual route candidates, with healthy sums of money or access to them, should prevail if parties are weak.

Table 5 uses the percentage of candidates who won their election as its dependent variable. In the upper left entry of the table, for example, we can see that 36.4 percent of candidates with business experience won their races, while 39.4 percent of those with no business experience won

TABLE 4. Political Backgrounds of Twenty Randomly Selected "Private Route" Incumbents

INCUMBENT NAME	POSITION AS OF 2003	FIRST ELECTED POSITION	ENTRÉE TO POLITICS	PRIVATE OR POLITICAL?
Hal Bernson	LA City Council	LA City Council	Urged to run by San Fernando Valley secessionists and business leaders.	Political
James Silva	Orange County Board of Supervisors	Huntington Beach City Council	As a teacher, was encouraged to run by many students.	Private
Chuck Smith	Orange County Board of Supervisors	Westminster City Council	Westminster mayor and other community leaders urged him to run for city council.	Political
Carol Liu (D-La Cañada-Flintridge)	State Assembly	La Cañada-Flintridge City Council	Union leader; fund-raiser for Sen. Barbara Boxer and Gov. Gray Davis; husband worked for Gov. Jerry Brown.	Political
George Nakano (D-Torrance)	State Assembly	Torrance City Council	Urged to run by local activists to deal with senior residence issue.	Political
Jack Scott (D-Pasadena)	State Senate	State Assembly	Encouraged by friends to run.	Private
William "Pete" Knight (R-Palmdale)	State Senate	Palmdale City Council	As vice commander at Edwards Air Force Base, was urged to run by a land developer who has recruited and promoted candidates for decades.	Political
Judy Case	Fresno County Board of Supervisors	Sanger City Council	Active with Rotary. Unhappy with Sanger City Council and decided to run.	Private
Ken Calvert (R-Riverside)	Member of Congress	Congress	Former aide to Rep. Victor Veysey; chair of Riverside County Republican Central Committee.	Political
Gary Miller (R-Diamond Bar)	Member of Congress	Diamond Bar City Council	Got involved in early cityhood battle to improve business climate.	Private
Loretta Sanchez (D-Santa Ana)	Member of Congress	Congress	Urged to run by Wiley Aitken and other members of Orange County Democratic Foundation.	Political
Bob Waterston	Fresno County Board of Supervisors	Clovis City Council	Urged to run by the chair of the Firefighters Union, which found campaign managers for him.	Political
Juan Arambula	Fresno County Board of Supervisors	Fresno Unified School District	Recruited by activist Virginia Sanchez, who recruited 300 volunteers for his first run. Sanchez has run numerous campaigns.	Political
Howard Berman (D-Los Angeles)	U.S. Congress	State Assembly	Activist with UCLA Bruin Democrats and LA Young Democrats. Also an Assembly fellow and a VISTA volunteer.	Political

TABLE 4.—*Continued*

INCUMBENT NAME	POSITION AS OF 2003	FIRST ELECTED POSITION	ENTRÉE TO POLITICS	PRIVATE OR POLITICAL?
Debra Bowen (D-Los Angeles)	State Senate	State Assembly	As a public interest attorney, was recruited by "The Breakfast Club," a loose campaign organization in West LA involved in local races.	Political
Thomas Wilson	Orange County Board of Supervisors	Laguna Niguel City Council	While working for Rockwell, was on Supervisor Tom Riley's Community Advisory Committee. Recruited by Laguna Niguel Citizens for Cityhood.	Political
Gloria McLeod (D-Los Angeles)	State Assembly	Chaffey Community College Board	While working at college, became president of local state employees' union. Also worked as field rep. for Assemblyman Joe Baca.	Political
Jane Harman (D-Los Angeles)	U.S. Congress	U.S. Congress	Worked as legislative director for U.S. Sen. John Tunney, then as counsel for a U.S. Senate subcommittee, then as a White House deputy cabinet secretary.	Political
Marco Firebaugh (D-Los Angeles)	State Assembly	State Assembly	Former staff member for state Sen. Richard Polanco.	Political
Ken Maddox (R-Garden Grove)	State Assembly	Garden Grove City Council	After losing first run, worked on an Assembly campaign to learn how they worked. Next race was successful.	Political

TABLE 5. Percent of Candidates in Each Category Who Won Election

	FRESNO		ORANGE COUNTY		LA (SOUTH AND EASTSIDE)		POOLED	
	YES	NO	YES	NO	YES	NO	YES	NO
Candidate has . . .								
experience in business	36.4	39.4	20.8	39.2	16.7	31.6	27.2	34.9
experience as an attorney	45.5	37.4	28.6	33.8	43.5	27.7	40.5	32.1
previously held elective office	34.5	39.5	48.5°°	21.4	44.6°°	23.0	43.7°°°	27.8
worked for an elected officeholder	69.2°°	34.0	28.6	33.8	36.6	27.7	42.6°	31.0
a relative who is an elected officeholder	80.0°°	36.2	0.0	33.8	60.0	28.8	63.6°°	32.0

Note: Asterisks indicate the difference between the "yes" and "no" positions is statistically significant.
°$p \leq .10$, °°$p \leq .05$, °°°$p \leq .01$

their races. Where the difference between the two success rates is statistically significant (using a simple difference of means test), I have indicated that with asterisks.

As the table shows, candidates with business experience appear no more successful than those without. Indeed, they are disadvantaged as a group, although the gap between business and nonbusiness candidates' success rates does not reach statistical significance. This business disadvantage spans all the regions under study. Surprisingly, strongly Republican Orange County, with its adulation for private sector experience, appears to be one of the worst regions for business candidates, who have a victory rate 18.4 points lower than those with no business experience. In all regions, business candidates win at a rate 7.7 points below the rate of nonbusiness candidates.

Attorneys appear to do slightly better than businesspeople. In Fresno and LA counties, attorneys' success rates exceed those of nonattorneys by 8.1 and 15.8 points, respectively, although these differences never achieve statistical significance. Lawyers appear to be at a disadvantage in Orange County, although the pooled results show a respectable—if statistically insignificant—8.4 percent advantage for them overall.

The indicators of strong parties, however, show much higher success rates for organizational candidates. Those who have previously held office apparently were able to take advantage of their name identification and previously established ties to donors and activists—they prevailed over inexperienced candidates by statistically significant margins in every region except Fresno. Having worked for an officeholder was also a useful exercise for those considering a public career. Fresno staffers won nearly 70 percent of the time, and LA staffers had an 8.9-point margin over those who hadn't worked on a political staff. In Orange County, where elections often turn on disparagement of government service, it is not surprising to find that staff work is unhelpful. It is possible that some successful candidates declined to mention their public service experience in this region. Nonetheless, in the pooled results, staffers won 42.6 percent of the time, a statistically significant advantage over the nonstaffers' 31 percent success rate.

Finally, candidates who are immediate relatives of officeholders tended to do rather well in elections. Eighty percent of such candidates won in Fresno, as did 60 percent in Los Angeles. Although the one instance of an immediate family member running for office in Orange County (an attempt by Representative Bob Dornan's son Mark to win a congressional seat in 2000) was unsuccessful, the pooled results still show a statistically significant 31.6-point advantage for relatives of politicians seeking to win office.

Table 6 uses the share of the popular vote as its dependent variable, and its findings echo those of table 5. Again, candidates with business experience and legal training did no better than those without such backgrounds. Business candidates from Los Angeles actually received 11.4 percent fewer votes than nonbusiness candidates, a statistically significant figure. When pooled, the vote shares for businesspeople and attorneys were statistically indistinguishable from those without such experience.

Those who had previously held elective office appeared to be at a substantial advantage, receiving a statistically significant additional 11.2 percent of the vote overall and healthy margins in all regions except Fresno. Working for an officeholder also proved to be good way to strengthen one's electoral margin, as staffers from Fresno and LA received statistically significant advantages in the popular vote. Staffers won a significant 8.4 additional points in the pooled results. Finally, family connections were also helpful, particularly for Fresno candidates. LA candidates received a healthy, though statistically nonsignificant, 11.2-point bump for having relatives in office. Again, the one Orange County case went against the trend, although candidates with political relatives overall received a significant 11.8-point bump over those without family connections.

In both tables 5 and 6, the pooled results showed that all groups of organizational candidates received significant advantages from their affiliations, while neither group of individual route candidates did significantly better than other candidates. Membership in an informal party organization, it would seem, is of great value to candidates, while those who choose to go it alone in politics tend to be at a significant comparative dis-

TABLE 6. Average Popular Vote Advantage for Candidates in Each Category

	FRESNO	ORANGE COUNTY	LA (SOUTH AND EASTSIDE)	POOLED
Candidate has . . .				
experience in business	0.1	−4.7	−11.4°°	−2.7
experience as an attorney	6.1	−12.6	3.0	2.0
previously held elective office	2.3	13.8°°°	15.4°°°	11.2°°°
worked for an elected officeholder	15.9°°°	2.3	9.0°°	8.4°°°
a relative who is an				
elected officeholder	19.3°°	−23.1	11.2	11.8°

Note: Asterisks indicate the vote difference is statistically significant.
°$p \leq .10$, °°$p \leq .05$, °°°$p \leq .01$

advantage. These results are inconsistent with the descriptions of California as a weak-party, candidate-centered state. Rather, they imply that there are strong party organizations whose influence candidates ignore at their peril.

But what exactly can one of these IPOs do for a candidate? As suggested by the qualitative evidence, a great deal, including introducing her to prospective donors, producing precinct walkers, providing office space, and so on. But first and foremost, a candidate affiliated with a network should tend to do better than one unaffiliated, all else being equal. Tables 5 and 6 demonstrated this. Yet a fair test of IPO effectiveness requires something more sophisticated than a simple difference-of-means test. After all, as discussed earlier, party groups will tend to recruit candidates who have already made names for themselves or raised money on their own. How can we determine what IPOs provide on top of that?

First, there is a widely held assumption that a party organization, once selecting a candidate, will bestow upon that candidate additional funding by connecting her with wealthy donors or by contributing directly to her campaign. This assumption is empirically testable. For this test, I simply regress each candidate's proportion of expenditures in a given race (measured 0 to 1) on the number of major elite endorsements and a candidate-quality variable (major elites consist of those key influential people named by multiple respondents in each of my regions of study). The more major endorsements a candidate has, the greater support she has within a party organization. Most candidates have no major endorsements, although many have between one and three, and a few have up to five. The candidate-quality variable is a simple dummy that equals one if the candidate has held elective office previously and zero otherwise (Jacobson and Kernell 1983).

The results, depicted in table 7, are broken down by region. There is remarkable consistency across regions: controlling for candidate quality, being slated by a party organization gives one greater access to campaign funding. Each major endorsement brings with it, on average, an additional 9 percent of the campaign expenditures in that race. What's more, in both Orange County and Fresno, the candidate-quality variable is reduced to insignificance in the presence of the endorsement variable (candidate quality is statistically significant in the bivariate model), suggesting that even the better-known candidates need the backing of an established organization to gain access to campaign funds.

Having established the importance of endorsements to campaign funding, we can now attempt to measure the impact of elite backing on the actual vote. The basic test is an ordinary least squares equation:

$$\text{Vote share} = \beta_0 + \beta_1 \cdot \text{Share of expenditures} + \beta_2 \cdot \text{Candidate quality} + \beta_3 \cdot \text{Elite endorsement} + \varepsilon$$

Using this specification, I can measure the influence of an elite's endorsement independent of other dominant factors, such as campaign spending and name recognition, which can affect a local election. The key limitation of this specification, however, is the considerable endogeneity problem. As mentioned previously, elites choose candidates that look very promising, and a good way to look promising is to have a lot of money or be well known. So my elite-endorsement variable may, if anything, have inflated standard errors as a result of conflation with other variables. The endorsement variable may therefore appear statistically insignificant at times even when it is large and important.

Although the regression model is straightforward, the causal interpretation of the elite-endorsement coefficient is not. What this regression approach does is allow us to examine the style and motivations of IPO leaders in the different areas I have examined and to see whether the patterns described by respondents in the qualitative section can be picked up quantitatively.

Table 8 displays the various scenarios that could bring rise to different elite-endorsement coefficients. I simplify the universe of scenarios

TABLE 7. Variables Predicting Candidate's Share of Expenditures in Campaign

VARIABLE	FRESNO	ORANGE COUNTY	LOS ANGELES (SOUTH AND EASTSIDE)	POOLED
Constant	.22°°°	.17°°°	.13°°°	.17°°°
	(.03)	(.04)	(.02)	(.02)
Number of elite endorsements	.10°°°	.07°°°	.10°°°	.09°°°
	(.02)	(.01)	(.01)	(.01)
High quality candidate	.03	.08	.10°°	.07°°
	(.06)	(.05)	(.03)	(.03)
Adjusted R^2	.182	.235	.333	.265
N	87	92	187	366

Note: The dependent variable is each candidate's expenditures as a proportion of all the candidate expenditures in that race, ranging between 0 and 1. Cell entries are ordinary least squares coefficients. Standard errors appear in parentheses beneath coefficients.

Asterisks indicate statistical significance: °$p \leq .05$; °°$p \leq .01$; °°°$p \leq .001$.

greatly by breaking down elite endorsements into two types of styles and two types of motivations. The endorsement style, first of all, may be active or passive. In an active endorsement, elites do not just lend their name but also assertively campaign for a candidate, using their contacts with activist clubs or unions to deploy precinct walkers on Election Day, cajoling newspapers to print positive news stories and make endorsements, and calling donors to ask them to contribute to the candidate. Such active endorsers may also have high name recognition and respect among the voters, and their backing can cause some of their popularity to rub off on the endorsee. Active endorsers will, on balance, aid a candidate even controlling for candidate quality and fund-raising—the endorsement has some additional vote value.

The other style of endorsement is passive. In this case, elites simply lend their name to a campaign. This is usually not an irrelevant act; the endorsement may add to the candidate's credibility in the eyes of prospective donors, boosting the candidate's fund-raising abilities. However, the effect of such an endorsement is likely to be felt only through campaign spending. Controlling for spending, the endorsement is not likely to add much vote value on its own.

The motivation for making an endorsement may also come in two flavors. The first is ideological. In this case, an elite will back the candidate whom she earnestly believes in, regardless of that candidate's likelihood of winning. Such candidates may be ideologically extreme, inarticulate, unattractive, abrasive, or otherwise likely to be found undesirable by many voters. Regardless of the candidate's particular shortcomings, she has been chosen by the elite for her ideological agenda. The endorser wants to shake up the status quo, electing a person who is unlikely to win without her heavy support but who will induce important changes in the way the government functions once elected.

A strategic endorsement, however, reflects the thinking of a savvy

TABLE 8. Expected Value of Elite Endorsement Coefficient Based on Style and Motivation of Endorser

| | | Endorsement Style | |
		Active	Passive
Endorsement Motivation	Ideological	0 or −	−
	Strategic	+	0 or +

elite who wants to back the candidates who are likely to win anyway. This is not to suggest that such an elite wouldn't have some ideological motivations to her choices. Indeed, in an ideologically extreme district, a strategic endorser doesn't have to compromise her ideological fervor to back a successful candidate. Nonetheless, for strategic endorsers, the ability to win will be the paramount concern. The two types of motivations can be boiled down as follows: an ideological elite would rather be right than be in power, while a strategic elite would accept ideological impurity in order to govern.

These two types of styles and motivations produce the two-by-two grid in table 8. The top left box (active-ideological) consists of active endorsers who are energetically trying to elect an imperfect candidate for purposive ends. Such a candidate, even if well-funded, is not likely to win without serious help. On average, these candidates will do poorly when controlling for other variables, but the active role of the endorser will help the candidate at least slightly. Thus we would expect the elite-endorsement variable to be negative or zero, at best. The passive-ideological elite, on the top right, provides only nominal help to a candidate who is unlikely to win. This may aid the candidate's fund-raising efforts, although any positive effect of the endorsement would be captured by the spending variable. The elite-endorsement coefficient is likely to be negative here, since the candidate should do poorly holding other variables constant.

The bottom left box (active-strategic) concerns elites who select a candidate for her likelihood of winning and provide active support for her. Such an endorsement would take a good thing and make it better, producing an electoral boost for the candidate that would enable her to outperform what her résumé and money would lead us to expect. In this case, the elite-endorsement coefficient will be positive. Finally, on the bottom right is the passive-strategic endorser, who provides only nominal support for a good candidate. Here, most of the effect of the endorsement is likely captured in the spending variable. However, because of the candidate's fitness for the district, she may do somewhat better than expected. Her elite-endorsement variable will thus be zero or slightly positive.

Vote share, once again, is measured as the percentage of the vote received by the candidate, measured from 0 to 100. Share of expenditures is the candidate's proportion of the expenditures made by all candidates in the race, running from 0 to 1. Candidate quality equals one if the candidate has held elective office before and zero otherwise. The elite-en-

dorsement variable equals one when the particular elite has publicly supported the candidate and zero if the elite has chosen to endorse one of
the candidate's opponents. Within each region, I have run this regression
equation for each key elite who was named by multiple respondents in
my surveys. Those who were considered important to elections but did
not make enough formal endorsements to include in this equation were
omitted. Campaign finance data was collected from the Federal Elections Commission, the California Secretary of State, the Los Angeles City
Ethics Commission, the Los Angeles County Registrar-Recorder/County
Clerk, the Orange County Clerk-Recorder, the Fresno County Clerk/
Registrar of Voters, and the Fresno City Clerk.

Table 9 shows the regression results for 37 contests held within Los
Angeles County between 1998 and 2004, including South LA and the
Eastside. I have also included the Speaker's organization in this table
since every Speaker during this time period hailed from a Los Angeles
district. The first thing one may notice is that campaign spending explains
the overwhelming amount of variance in election results. (A bivariate regression of vote share on spending yields an R^2-value of .71.)

The endorsement variable tends to support many of the claims made
by interview respondents about the relative power of various elites. The
backing of Maxine Waters, for example, makes a real difference in the
fortunes of her chosen candidates, who received a statistically significant
additional 7 percent of the vote. Although she only lent her endorsement
in a few races during this period, Diane Watson seems to be a very important backer, giving candidates a statistically significant 19.6-point
boost. Supervisor Burke's backing, on the other hand, provided only a
small and statistically insignificant bump. Over in LA's Eastside, meanwhile, all three elites I examined provided statistically significant boosts
for their chosen candidates. Supervisor Molina's endorsement provided
9 additional percentage points, and former state senator Polanco's endorsement, backed by the legendary Alatorre-Torres machine, gave
anointed candidates an extra 6.7 percent of the vote. The Election Day
work provided by its affiliated union members allowed the County Federation of Labor to give its candidates an extra 12.6 percent of the vote.

The results from South LA and the Eastside suggest an elite structure
run by strategic principals. The endorsement variables are all positive
and, with the marginal exception of Supervisor Burke's, statistically
significant. This suggests a pragmatic motivation by elites; they are picking the sorts of candidates who are likely to win. And given the large pres-

TABLE 9. Variables Predicting Candidate Vote Share by Elite Endorser, Los Angeles County

ELITE ENDORSER	SOUTH LA			EASTSIDE LA			SPEAKER'S ORGANIZATION		
	MAXINE WATERS[a]	DIANE WATSON[b]	YVONNE B. BURKE[c]	GLORIA MOLINA[d]	RICHARD POLANCO[e]	LA COUNTY FEDERATION OF LABOR[f]	ROBERT HERTZBERG[g]	ANTONIO VILLARAIGOSA[h]	HERB WESSON[i]
Constant	5.13**	1.99	2.48	2.85	3.08**	6.63***	8.42**	8.58***	7.04***
	(1.72)	(2.53)	(1.46)	(1.47)	(1.16)	(1.38)	(2.43)	(2.28)	(2.03)
Share of expenditures	64.37***	59.16***	81.45***	70.70***	78.33***	57.47***	69.55***	56.73***	70.21***
	(6.07)	(8.91)	(5.72)	(5.83)	(3.96)	(4.58)	(7.07)	(7.86)	(7.82)
High-quality candidate	3.14	8.85*	3.29	4.04	0.02	1.68	2.83	7.15	-0.36
	(2.97)	(4.28)	(2.23)	(2.74)	(1.99)	(2.04)	(3.37)	(4.67)	(3.13)
Elite endorsement	6.98*	19.56***	3.32	8.96**	6.69**	12.64***	-2.64	8.13†	0.09
	(3.50)	(4.78)	(2.89)	(3.21)	(2.13)	(2.79)	(3.90)	(4.62)	(4.39)
Adjusted R^2	.739	.769	.849	.786	.899	.797	.760	.789	.727
N	73	34	60	81	64	108	41	39	60

Notes: Cell entries are ordinary least squares coefficients. Standard errors appear in parentheses beneath coefficients. Asterisks indicate statistical significance: *$p \leq .05$; **$p \leq .01$; ***$p \leq .001$. † indicates $p = .087$.

[a]Member of Congress, 35th district. Coefficients based on 16 elections between 1998 and 2003.

[b]Member of Congress, 32nd district. Coefficients based on 7 elections from 2001 and 2004.

[c]LA County Supervisor, 2nd district. Coefficients based on 13 elections between 2000 and 2004.

[d]LA County Supervisor, 1st district. Coefficients based on 16 elections between 1999 and 2004.

[e]Former state Senator, 22nd district. Coefficients based on 12 elections between 1998 and 2003.

[f]Coefficients based on 26 elections between 1999 and 2004.

[g]Former Assembly Speaker (2000–02). Coefficients based on 12 elections between 2000 and 2004.

[h]Former Assembly Speaker (1998–2000). Coefficients based on 11 elections between 1998 and 2004.

[i]Former Assembly Speaker (2002–04). Coefficients based on 14 elections between 2000 and 2004.

ence of unions, Democratic clubs, and churches in politics in these areas, it would not be surprising to find that the coefficients are consistent with an active endorsement style. Elites do not merely lend their names. They provide the labor necessary to produce a respectable Election Day showing for their chosen candidates. The results from these regions thus seem most consistent with an active-strategic elite system.

The results for the Speaker's Organization, seen on the right of table 9, suggest a very different form of elite organization. Two Speakers—Robert Hertzberg and Herb Wesson—each have endorsement coefficients statistically indistinguishable from zero. Antonio Villaraigosa's endorsement is associated with an 8.1 point bonus for candidates, although this coefficient fails the test of statistical significance (p = .087). These results suggest a Speaker with either a passive or ideological pattern of endorsements, which is surprising, given the history of the office. Speakers Jesse Unruh and Willie Brown, for example, were well known for their pragmatic and energetic approaches to electioneering. Today's Speakers, by contrast, are possibly reduced to a passive role in elections by the amount of legislative work they must do in Sacramento. In addition, term limits may have had a detrimental effect on the Speaker's power in elections. With assembly members limited to six years in office and leaders rarely serving more than two years, Speakers may simply not have enough time to learn who the important players and credible candidates are. With a paucity of information, Speakers may draw upon ideological predilections to make their decisions about candidates.

The findings for the 27 election contests held in Orange County, depicted in table 10, reveal low endorsement coefficients that are statistically indistinguishable from zero. Although conservatives Dick Ackerman, Buck Johns, and Ross Johnson all seem to provide respectable 5- to 8-point boosts for the candidates they support, none of these figures is statistically significant. And Tom Fuentes, widely feared and revered in county Republican circles, actually seems to have a negative impact on the candidates he backs, although this figure is not statistically significant and is based on very few observations. No positive vote value associated with the backing of Senator Lewis or former Speaker Pringle can be demonstrated, either.

These findings are not surprising. Many of the key elites named by respondents are business leaders, not public officeholders, and thus aren't well known by rank-and-file primary voters. These elites often work behind the scenes to help their candidates without even making a formal endorsement. Tom Fuentes, for example, is widely known to work this way (Pringle 2002). And unlike the Los Angeles groups, Orange County organizations do not seem particularly focused on labor-intensive activities like voter turnout or registration efforts. Rather, conservative elites in this county, judging from the qualitative data, are focused on channeling money toward some candidates and away from others. Endorsements certainly translate into funding here, as table 7 indicated, but the IPO leaders do not seem to provide much beyond that. The elite style here is best described as passive; the funding advantage they provide may be enough.

In terms of elite incentives, the qualitative evidence strongly suggested that most of the area's elites are ideologically motivated. To be sure, given the voter party registration of Orange County districts, far right candidates are not necessarily out of step with their constituencies. Yet, at least among the county's conservatives, it seems fair to say that they would prefer to maintain an elected contingent that "stands for something" than to moderate their leaders in the struggle for a majority. This observation, combined with the low or negative values of the endorsement coefficients, strongly suggests that the elites of Orange County should be categorized as passive-ideological.

Finally, we turn to the 27 election results for Fresno, seen in table 11.

TABLE 10. Variables Predicting Candidate Vote Share by Elite Endorser, Orange County

ELITE ENDORSER	DICK ACKERMAN[a]	TOM FUENTES[b]	BUCK JOHNS[c]	ROSS JOHNSON[d]	JOHN LEWIS[e]	CURT PRINGLE[f]
Constant	13.28°°°	17.48°	6.28°	9.04°°°	7.73°°	7.37°°
	(3.29)	(5.25)	(2.62)	(2.50)	(2.60)	(2.45)
Share of expenditures	48.58°°°	66.50°°	56.54°°°	55.49°°°	52.80°°°	60.49°°°
	(8.46)	(13.91)	(7.85)	(6.36)	(6.85)	(7.69)
High-quality candidate	1.27	−10.48	2.82	5.04	5.54	6.43
	(3.59)	(6.20)	(3.81)	(2.95)	(3.38)	(3.09)
Elite endorsement	5.58	−9.87	7.52	5.55	3.81	−3.53
	(4.90)	(9.15)	(5.33)	(3.81)	(4.13)	(4.94)
Adjusted R^2	.652	.752	.801	.775	.740	.714
N	39	11	24	43	36	48

Note: Cell entries are ordinary least squares coefficients. Standard errors appear in parentheses beneath coefficients. Asterisks indicate statistical significance: °$p \leq .05$; °°$p \leq .01$; °°°$p \leq .001$.
[a]State Senator, 33rd district. Coefficients based on 12 races between 1998 and 2004.
[b]President of the Lincoln Club and Chairman of the County Republican Central Committee. Coefficients based on 3 races between 1998 and 2000.
[c]Land developer. Coefficients based on 5 races between 1998 and 2004.
[d]State Senator, 35th district. Coefficients based on 13 races between 1998 and 2004.
[e]Former State Senator. Coefficients based on 9 races between 1998 and 2004.
[f]Former Speaker of the State Assembly (1996). Coefficients based on 12 races between 1998 and 2004.

Interestingly, the only positive and statistically significant endorsement coefficients in this area come from organizations rather than individuals. The Fresno Police Officers' Association aids its chosen candidates with an average of 12.3 additional percentage points, and the local chapter of the Service Employees International Union offers a whopping 19.5 percentage points with its backing. These results indicate the presence of at least one active-strategic organization on each side of the partisan divide capable of turning out Election Day volunteers who can mobilize voters. None of the other endorsement coefficients are distinguishable from zero. Congressman Dooley's backing appears conspicuously negative, associated with a (statistically insignificant) 22.7-point penalty, but given the small number of observations in this and several other regressions, the results are highly questionable. Supervisor Arambula (now an assembly member) and assemblywoman Reyes, for example, had only begun their involvement in local politics during the election cycles under study here. As they cement their power bases and make more endorsements, perhaps we will find that their endorsement comes with considerable activity on the part of the principals. On the other hand, perhaps the rural setting is not well suited to the labor-intensive style of an active endorser, but is tailor-made for a passive endorser who can help raise money. For

TABLE 11. Variables Predicting Candidate Vote Share by Elite Endorser, Fresno

ELITE ENDORSER	DEMOCRATIC-LEANING ELITES				REPUBLICAN-LEANING ELITES		
	SEIU LOCAL 535[a]	JUAN ARAMBULA[b]	SARAH REYES[c]	CAL DOOLEY[d]	FRESNO DEPUTY SHERIFFS' ASSN.[e]	FRESNO POLICE OFFICERS' ASSN.[f]	EARL SMITTCAMP[g]
Constant	5.56	10.65°	38.09	9.19	9.53°°	7.91°	2.51
	(4.05)	(4.39)	(27.65)	(7.48)	(3.21)	(2.94)	(2.30)
Share of expenditures	50.53°°	69.25°°°	21.15	95.97°°	66.47°°°	61.40°°°	92.95°°°
	(11.33)	(10.43)	(56.26)	(15.64)	(8.99)	(8.43)	(7.98)
High-quality candidate	8.36	−1.50	−25.49	2.21	3.41	.10	4.62
	(4.78)	(8.59)	(28.35)	(8.42)	(4.98)	(4.18)	(3.31)
Elite endorsement	19.48°	−2.40	−3.78	−22.68	1.52	12.33°°	−7.71
	(6.38)	(5.00)	(6.47)	(10.53)	(4.48)	(4.47)	(4.22)
Adjusted R^2	.860	.713	.842	.855	.666	.766	.944
N	14	22	5	8	38	33	12

[a]Service Employees International Union, Local 535. Coefficients based on 6 elections between 1998 and 2002.
[b]Fresno County Supervisor, 3rd district. Coefficients based on 8 elections between 1998 and 2002.
[c]Member of the State Assembly, 31st district. Coefficients based on 2 elections from 2002.
[d]Member of Congress, 20th district. Coefficients based on 3 elections from 1998 and 2004.
[e]Coefficients based on 14 elections between 1998 and 2002.
[f]Coefficients based on 13 elections between 1998 and 2002.
[g]Peach grower and industry lobbyist. Coefficients based on 3 elections between 1998 and 2002.

the present, we can only describe the Fresno informal party organizations as strategic in their motivations and either active or passive in style.

DISCUSSION

At the outset of this chapter, I suggested three critical tests to determine whether the political system was party-centered: Do the key political leaders form a small world among which all potential candidates must compete? Do these leaders form a united front, aiding candidates that can unite the party and win in a general election? Finally, is support from this small world of leaders decisive in nomination battles? Mindful of Einstein's warning that "not everything that counts can be counted, and not everything that can be counted counts," I have pursued a variety of methodological approaches to address these questions. In using these various methods, I have attempted to compensate for the endogeneity problem inherent to this line of research: the fact that party organizations recruit the candidates most likely to win, which makes it difficult to determine the organization's impact. Each of the methods employed in this chapter obviously has its advantages and limitations. However, there is a marked degree of consistency across methods, providing strong support for a party-centered conclusion and for the IPO model.

As seen in the previous chapter, respondents in each region mentioned a similar set of individuals—officeholders, donors, and activists—whose influence they felt was important in nominations. These groups of individuals are decisive in nominations: candidates coming from one of these groups do much better in elections than unaffiliated candidates, even those with substantial funds. Furthermore, I showed that more elite support brings more funding, which is highly correlated with vote share. A regression analysis also showed many of these elites to have a significant impact in contested elections, even controlling for funding and candidate quality. Finally, some four-fifths of today's incumbents at all levels of government can be shown to have reached their current jobs through such organizations.

The united front test, however, requires some revision. I have said elsewhere that IPOs typically seek to nominate as extreme a candidate as they feel they can get away with. In most districts, they can get away with quite a bit. The winner of a Democratic assembly primary in South Los Angeles and the winner of a Republican assembly primary in Newport

Beach, Orange County, are going to Sacramento; the general election is little more than a polite ritual. As a result, party organizations do not need to unite around a candidate who can prevail in the general election. They simply need to be unified enough to win in the primary. Almost invariably, one of two major factions will prevail in the nomination battle.

The evidence in this chapter also supports some of the conclusions from the qualitative study about the differences between regions. Again, it is Los Angeles politics that seems to adhere most closely to the original IPO model I postulated. There, prominent elected officials—allied with activist groups that provide Election Day labor and with other office-holders and benefit seekers that can provide money—have the most measurable impact on elections. Even controlling for campaign spending, IPO leaders in LA regularly boost their chosen candidates' vote shares by 10 points or more. Orange County IPOs, while clearly important for those seeking office, seem to expend most of their efforts by giving their candidates access to campaign money. The relatively low public salience of those leaders and their lack of access to public office makes it difficult for them to produce much of a turnout boost beyond what their money can buy. Finally, the Fresno system appears to be a bit of a blend. Although there are too few observations to be very confident about the value of officeholders to those elections, the impact of benefit-seeking groups affiliated with the local parties is significant.

Beyond the regional differences, however, the evidence from this and the previous chapter make certain conclusions about party dynamics all too obvious:

1. Parties are not created or maintained by those within the legislature, at least not solely. They consist of a variety of actors both inside and outside the government with a host of different agendas, all of which are advanced through cooperation.

2. Parties are not benign candidate-service organizations that ambitious politicians can hire or discard with impunity. Candidates *need* these organizations to win election. My research finds numerous examples of organizations finding and grooming candidates for office, and other examples of unaffiliated politicians trying to buy their way into office and failing miserably. Candidates (reluctantly) accept the control over their careers that comes with organizational support. Those who do not are occasionally threatened, disciplined, or even removed.

3. Although they bear some similarities to the urban machines of yesteryear, today's parties lack the formality, hierarchy, and patronage basis of the traditional party organizations. They also seem to have avoided some of the worst aspects of corruption for which the TPOs were famous. Today's party organizations do not control every aspect of the electorate, nor do they win in every race. But they control enough of the political process to win most of the time, and anyone who plans to beat the party has to have no small amount of luck on her side.

Conclusion: The Price
and Payoff of Parties

The preceding chapters have covered more than 150 years of political history utilizing a variety of research methods, from qualitative interviews to complex statistical analyses. Before concluding, it is worth asking what exactly we have learned from this multifaceted view of California's political past.

Perhaps the most important lesson we can draw is that rational, career-minded politicians don't necessarily build or sustain parties. California's legislators in the early twentieth century were presented with just the sort of chaotic, unproductive environment that should demand party building. Yet they did not seek to create strong legislative parties. Instead, they enjoyed and protected the chaos, which, while making legislating difficult, made reelection easy.

As it turns out, the creation of disciplined parties inside the legislature requires the presence and engagement of activist groups outside it. When Progressive reforms in the 1910s made it virtually impossible for activists to participate in primary elections or influence elected officials, the incumbents charted moderate paths, raising the reelection goal above all others. Conversely, when those restrictions on activists were relaxed, and when activists began to form alliances to control primary elections, incumbents responded by behaving as partisans. They began to pay attention to the groups that controlled primaries, working more along party lines in the legislature, fearful that the activists, if displeased, would de-nominate them by running more disciplined challengers against them in the next primary. The reelection goal and the desire to converge on the median voter never vanished, but, for most, the partisan agendas of the activist alliances simply demanded more attention. Thus did the California legislature, along with the U.S. Congress, embrace the strict partisanship for which it is now both famous and infamous.

It is fair to ask at this point whether the California case is generalizable to the rest of the United States. California's experiences with cross-filing, and indeed its whole brand of early-twentieth-century Progressivism, were atypical (Ware 2002). Shouldn't we expect the state to continue to stand apart from the rest of the nation?

Perhaps. At a minimum, we can conclude that the notion that parties are the creatures of politicians isn't true in this particular state during this particular time. However, many other states have had similar experiences. Roughly half the states—mostly in the West and Midwest—experienced some form of Progressive takeover in the early twentieth century. Although strains of Progressivism varied from state to state, there was a widespread belief among Progressive reformers that the political parties were corrupt and that their control over governing institutions had to be curbed. In such states, it would not be surprising to find that interested political actors have found extralegal ways to form and influence government. Colorado, a Progressive state, is rife with informal party organizations, although, as in California, the IPOs from less populated areas appear to have less of a commitment to party purity (Masket 2007). Wisconsin, the home of Progressive hero Robert "Fighting Bob" La Follette, certainly has some history of partylike alliances among political actors (Epstein 1958). It may very well be that in states without such a Progressive legacy, those interested in controlling government could do so within the formal parties and thus never needed to develop an informal apparatus. But control of nominations—regardless of how they are controlled—should still be key to influencing government.

Beyond that, the Golden State offers us more general lessons about parties. California's unusual experience with cross-filing made for a convenient natural experiment, helping us understand the relationship between legislators and their partisan backers. This example shows us that politicians are content with partyless politics. And it shows us that political actors outside the government are usually not content with such politics and will use what means they have at their disposal to force officeholders and candidates to adhere to a program. Politicians, if anything, are the creatures of parties.

ADDRESSING RIVAL HYPOTHESES: WHY IS PARTISANSHIP INCREASING?

This book has made the case that the dramatic increase in legislative partisanship in California is due to the rise of political activists. The reader may legitimately note that the rise of activists is not the only thing to happen in California in the past half century. Could the increase in legislative partisanship in this state and across the country be the result of some other phenomenon? A few rival theories offer themselves here.

It is possible that much of recent polarization is voter driven. As mentioned previously, state and federal legislative districts have been growing safer in recent decades, making most general elections virtually uncontestable. Today, better than 90 percent of congressional districts are "owned" by either the Democratic or Republican parties; the general election there is a formality. The same is true at the state level—typically, only one or two of the California assembly's eighty districts are considered toss-ups in elections; the rest are safely in the hands of one party or another. If districts are so lopsided in favor of one party or the other, then there is no need for elected officials to moderate. Indeed, they would be wise not to, since the median voters in their districts are committed partisans and would likely punish moderate behavior.

The polarization of districts has surely had a substantial effect on the polarization of legislatures (Jacobson 2004)—but not enough. If district polarization were sufficient to generate the sort of polarization we've seen in the California assembly, we wouldn't see informal party organizations threatening or punishing incumbents who have gone moderate on them. We wouldn't see Eastside Los Angeles leaders de-nominating Rep. Marty Martinez for straying rightward on trade and social issues. We wouldn't see Orange County Lincoln Club members recalling Speaker Dorris Allen for her collaboration with Willie Brown. And we wouldn't see Sen. Jim Brulte threatening Republican legislators who were considering voting for Governor Davis's tax-increasing budget, reminding them of the four Republican assembly members from 2001 who lost their jobs over a similar apostasy. We wouldn't see these things because they would be unnecessary—incumbents would toe the party line because it would be in their general reelection interests to do so. Instead, we see informal party organizations threatening apostates and occasionally removing them.

The case for district-induced polarization must also be overstated since, as we saw in earlier chapters, there are still plenty of moderate congressional and state assembly districts that are nonetheless represented by extremists. There is, in other words, no middle ground in today's legislatures—members are either hyper-Democrats or hyper-Republicans—even while there *is* a middle ground among voters and districts.

The polarization of districts, in my model, actually has the effect of empowering informal party organizations. That is, the tension between satisfying the moderate voters of the general election and pleasing the ideological activists who run the primary election has largely been resolved in favor of the latter. If an incumbent is going to be taken down, it is more likely to happen in a primary now, and that makes the IPO all the more important. Today, the IPO, rather than the average voter, is the instrument of accountability in the electoral system.

Another criticism of my claims could begin by noting that California's polarization has been mirrored by similar trends nationwide. After all, the legislatures were weakly partisan at midcentury and have become strongly polarized today. Couldn't state legislators simply be following the lead of their federal colleagues?

In response, it should be noted that the state has not followed national trends perfectly. Indeed, the partisan resurgence in California began in the 1950s, which was the nadir for partisanship in the U.S. Congress. If anything, it would appear that California's parties moved first. However, to be sure, over the broad swath of the twentieth century, the trends have been similar.

This hardly means IPO theory is wrong. In fact, it strongly suggests that the same trends have been occurring within the U.S. Congress, as well. The same sorts of liberal activists who formed the California Democratic Council in California were also taking over governments in Chicago, New York, and other areas of the country in the 1950s and 1960s (Wilson 1966). And the conservative activists who helped polarize California's Republican Party included many of the same people who took over the national Republican Party in the 1960s, giving Barry Goldwater the 1964 presidential nomination and setting the stage for the Reagan revolution. As the traditional party organizations have fallen over the years to civil service and good government reforms (Mayhew 1986), it would seem that ideological activists and informal party organizations have risen to take their place, both in California and elsewhere. People outside the government are still controlling primaries, but those who control them are much more driven by purposive incentives.

One need only look at a few examples from outside California to see that these IPOs are having a profound effect on politics. During the Clinton impeachment, the 1995–96 budget standoff, and the 2001 tax reduction bill, there were reports that activists were pressuring moderate Republican members of Congress to ignore median opinion in their districts, threatening them with primary challengers unless they voted with their party. More systematically, Ansolabehere, Snyder, and Stewart (2001) have shown that, at least since the mid-1800s, candidates for Congress have been regularly diverging more from the median voter in their district than is optimal in a general election. And Canes-Wrone, Brady, and Cogan (2002) have shown that such divergence has cost candidates votes, and occasionally an election. What's more, incumbents know these risks, but diverge anyway, more fearful of those who are organizing primaries. This systematic nonmedian behavior can, I maintain, be linked to activist control of nominations. In the nineteenth and early twentieth centuries, such ideologues generally worked through traditional party organizations. Today, I contend, they function within informal party organizations. The difference is that IPOs can't offer the material incentives that the TPOs had at their disposal; thus ideology becomes a more salient tool for inducing party discipline. In the 1920s, Kent (1924) warned his readers about the dangers of ideologues rising to power if the old TPOs fell apart:

> If the machines did not work and pull and haul to get enough voters out in the primaries to put over the machine candidates, the present state of indifference and ignorance of the average citizen would permit our candidates to be chosen for us by the freaks and fanatics who abound in every community, and are constantly and zealously stirred to political activity in behalf of their half-baked schemes for saving the world. (181)

Arguably, this is precisely what happened. Wilson's *The Amateur Democrat* (1966) is a description of the ideological amateurs who were creeping into urban and suburban political circles in the 1960s. With the demise of the old machines, it was these activists who were providing the time and labor to keep some kind of party organization going. One can easily imagine such amateurs getting involved, but what made them a party? That is, if there was no patronage readily available, what kept these activists in line, pursuing a common partisan agenda across different neighborhoods, legislative districts, and states?

The answer is ideology. Ideology creates coalitions of people who believe in particular policies, even among those personally unaffected by those policies (Bawn 1999). It binds people across geographical distances and allows them to coordinate actions without a formal central coordinator. The utility of ideology as a binding agent for party groups was somewhat compromised in the mid–twentieth century since ideology was only moderately correlated with party—both parties contained significant liberal and conservative elements. In recent decades, however, the parties have sorted themselves out along ideological lines (Noel 2001), making it easier to guide a party organization on ideology alone.

If ideologues have been in control of the parties in California and in the United States generally since the mid–twentieth century, it makes sense that the parties would have become more polarized since then as those parties sorted themselves out ideologically. Their primary tool for organization—ideology—simply became a more potent one as it began to correlate better with party. However, the polarization process has been more intense in California, since activists were uniquely disempowered by Progressive Era reforms until the 1950s. The trends I have described in the preceding chapters are thus national ones; the California example brings the importance of ideological activists to the process into sharper relief.

TORN BETWEEN TWO EXTREMES

As this review of California's political history has shown, strong parties are not inevitable. Institutional rules like cross-filing can suppress them for decades. This means that we have a choice as to whether or not parties will rule our politics. Citizens and policymakers must determine which is the better political universe: one in which ideological activists are prominent and enforce strict party discipline upon government or another in which activists are neutered, parties are weak or nonexistent, and incumbents regularly compromise legislative agendas in the name of re-election. Both these regimes, taken very close to their logical extremes, have existed in California's recent history, so this state gives us a rare opportunity to compare them and weight their respective costs and benefits.

I first turn to the weak party system of Progressive Era California (1910–59). As we saw in chapter 2, the cross-filing system and the accompanying absence of ideological activists from politics had a profound effect on the behavior of officeholders. Able to win reelection at the primary stage and to thwart any attempt to de-nominate them, incumbents had little need to appease activists. They stuck with their districts.

In some sense, this was the ideal of democratic representation. Progressive reformers had complained that some intervening force, such as parties, was coming between the people and their elected officials. By creating cross-filing, they removed the interloper. Legislators were, on average, voting their districts. So what was the problem?

The problem was one of accountability. With activists and other partisan figures out of the picture, the only actors left to police elected officials and ensure that they were legislating responsibly were the voters. What's more, thanks to the confusion of cross-filing and the nonpartisan primary ballot, legislators didn't have reliable party labels with which voters could hold them accountable. As we know from a wealth of research beginning with *The American Voter* (Campbell et al. 1960) and culminating in recent work by Achen and Bartels (2002), voters are notoriously bad at monitoring their elected officials, particularly if they do not have party labels to fall back on. Even today, when roll call voting records are easily and cheaply accessible in newspapers or on the Internet, the overwhelming majority of voters never look to see how their elected officials voted on particular pieces of legislation. The more attentive among them will draw inferences based on media coverage; the rest will follow simple cues—endorsements, advertisements, stereotypes, hearsay—during an election season.

California's experiences during the cross-filing era teach us that this relative lack of oversight allows legislators to abandon their districts' wishes on key pieces of legislation, as long as they stick with their districts most of the time. As we saw in chapter 2, assembly members during the cross-filing era frequently joined bipartisan blocs on votes for Speaker—blocs that were often bankrolled by wealthy lobbyists from the oil, liquor, and banking industries, among others. The Speaker then had the power to distribute committee chairs and to assist or kill pieces of legislation at the behest of the lobbyists supporting these blocs. Although these legislative blocs held sway on several administrative and substantive roll call votes over multiple consecutive sessions (Buchanan 1963), they never appeared on a ballot and rarely even showed up in newspapers. Even if a legislator was acting as a moderate Republican or a moderate Democrat most of the time, he could take part in one of these totally unaccountable blocs on occasion, and these blocs made all the truly important decisions.

In this sense, the weak party system, although appearing on the surface to be good representative government, was, in fact, the opposite. The vital decisions of the state were being made by invisible voting coalitions backed by shadowy groups of lobbyists. If a voter wanted to hold his elected official accountable, he would need not only to closely follow roll call voting in Sacramento but also to have access to data on campaign finance transactions and other transfers of favors and wealth. Even if those data were available, probably fewer than one voter in a thousand would avail herself of them. The legendary liquor industry lobbyist Artie Samish, who brokered more than a few legislative votes outside of the limelight, was once asked how he and others like him could be gotten rid of. Samish replied, "There is one way. The people must take more interest in the men they elect" (1971: 151). Under the Progressive regime, that simply wasn't going to happen.

Quite near the opposite system came about within a few short decades after the death of cross-filing, and it remains vibrant today. Under the current regime, as we saw in chapter 3, legislators are almost completely unresponsive to district sentiment; they vote with their fellow partisans. Informal party organizations and the ideological activists who run them ensure that relatively extreme candidates are nominated and that those nominees, once elected, hew to a strict party-line agenda, regardless of the district's ideological preferences. The district's partisan balance will, of course, determine whether it is represented by a Democrat or a Republican in the legislature—much better than it did during cross-filing—but after that, a Democratic assembly member from a moderate district and one from a liberal district will vote nearly identically. District-level representation is essentially dead; voters are dependent upon the parties for representation.

It should be noted that this strong-party system doesn't cure a democracy of all the unseemly practices of the Progressive Era. There are still powerful, wealthy special interests whose hired-gun lobbyists try to ply legislators with money, food, liquor, favors, prostitutes, and everything else at their disposal. But today's legislators have much less freedom to maneuver than their predecessors did. It's dangerous for modern legislators to disappoint their activist backers, because those backers, unlike general election voters, have the time and resources to track legislative activity and hold them accountable. As a result, legislators today are much more likely to do what they were elected to do, and are much less likely to be bought. Lobbyist money becomes much less powerful when legislators know that they'll lose their jobs for deviating from their party's agenda. Today, just one bad vote can end a career. Former Fresno assemblyman Mike Briggs's crime of supporting Governor Gray Davis's 2001 tax increase continues to haunt him—it cost him the nomination for a congressional seat in 2002, and it likely prevented him from winning back his old assembly seat in 2004 (Fitzenberger 2004).

Paradoxically, even though the activists that run party primaries would seem to be in charge today, average voters have more power than they used to. This is because the party label is much more meaningful today than it was under cross-filing. Because it is essentially impossible to buy someone's vote across party lines, virtually all transactions occur within a party. The centralization of campaign funding within informal party organization, which began under Speaker Jesse Unruh and has become standard operating procedure today, all but ensures that favors are distributed in a partisan manner. Individual voters may not be able to easily track who votes for what in the legislature or how much money a legislator receives from whom, but they can see the result of these efforts in the form of a legislative party agenda. And if they don't like the agenda or the way the legislators are following through on it, they can vote that party out of office. It is much easier to affix responsibility and blame today than it was under the Progressive regime.

Should voters grow disgusted with the majority party, there is another very distinct party prepared to take over the reins of government. Again, this differs strongly from the cross-filing era, when it was very difficult to distinguish between the two parties and their agendas. The existence of a minority party, as V. O. Key noted in *Southern Politics* (1949), is essential for accountability:

> The lack of continuing groups of "ins" and "outs" profoundly influences the nature of political leadership. Free and easy movement from loose faction to loose faction results in there being in reality no group of "outs" with any sort of corporate spirit to serve as critic of the "ins" or as a rallying point around which can be organized all those discontented with the current conduct of public affairs.... In those states with loose and short-lived factions campaigns often are the emptiest sorts of debates over personalities, over means for the achievement of what everybody agrees on. (304)

In his study of the one-party systems of the South, Key found another problem: a lack of concern for citizens at the lower end of the economic spectrum. Politics, he argues, is generally a struggle between the haves and have-nots, and an organized party system is an enormous aid to the have-nots, a finding that has been echoed in other research (Bowman and Kearney 1986; Karch and Deufel 2003; Schattschneider 1960). Simply having competitive, distinct parties forces office-seeking politicians to address the needs of the have-nots, if for no other reason than to win their votes:

> Over the long run the have-nots lose in a disorganized politics. They have no mechanism through which to act and their wishes find expression in fitful rebellions led by transient demagogues who gain their confidence but often have neither the technical competence nor the necessary stable base of political power to effectuate a program. (Key 1949: 307)

Although Key's statement was written with regard to Southern politics, he may as well have been describing such "transient demagogues" as Democrats Upton Sinclair, the failed gubernatorial candidate of 1934, and Culbert Olson, who had a famously incompetent tenure as governor from 1939 to 1943. It is no coincidence that New Deal-style legislation largely failed in California during the cross-filing regime. Notably, advances on civil rights, education, and other issues that gave California its liberal reputation did not begin until the early 1960s, after the death of cross-filing.

So is the modern strong party system the apotheosis of representative democracy? Not if you ask voters. Interestingly, since the National Election Studies began asking "feeling thermometer" questions about political parties in 1978, the two parties have steadily lost favor among the American public. During a time when the national parties have, by virtual consensus (see, e.g., Poole and Rosenthal 1997), become more polarized, disciplined, and responsible, approval of them has dropped by roughly 5 points. Disciplined parties may be making Americans feel less efficacious and less confident in their governing institutions, even as they make those institutions more accountable to them and more likely to produce policies in line with their preferences, at least in the aggregate.

SOME EXAMPLES FROM THE TWO EXTREMES

A few examples of political life under these various regimes will shed some light on the advantages and disadvantages of each. The first example comes from the mid-1930s, during which time the cross-filing regime and Progressive rules were in full effect. With the two parties weak and devoid of legislative leadership, other agents willing to provide legislative direction stepped into the leadership void. One such agent was Artie Samish, the chief lobbyist for the California State Brewers Association. By taking a five-cent cut from every barrel of beer sold in the state and distributing that money to political candidates on the basis of need and acquiescence, Samish managed to accrue a great deal of power over legislators—power that he needed only exert on a few key votes per session to serve his clients (Rusco 1961).

Several of those key votes came up in 1936. In the absence of strong parties, one of the main political cleavages in the state was between "Wets" and "Drys" on the subject of prohibition. Although the Drys were on the defensive in the wake of the Twenty-first Amendment's passage, they came up with the idea of "local option" in several states. In California, local option came as a state constitutional amendment initiative, proposing that every city, town, county, or territory should have the power to regulate, zone, or prohibit the sale of alcoholic beverages. As Samish rightly noted, "There would have been towns all over the state that the Drys would have been able to close up for liquor sales. We had to fight that" (1971: 67).

With his Sacramento connections—Samish was a major backer of Secretary of State Frank Jordan—he used several political maneuvers to ensure that the Dry initiative wouldn't pass. The first was to advance an opposition bill to appear on the same ballot, based on the notion that voters would become confused or irritated and reject both measures. The second was to make sure that the opposition bill received a higher ballot placement than the Dry measure; Samish felt that propositions with lower numbers had much better chances of passing than ones further down the ballot. In the end, Samish's measure, which he funded heavily, became Proposition 3; the original Dry local option measure became Proposition 9. Both lost; Samish and the brewers had won.

The Drys tried again in 1948, and Samish met them with yet another opposition initiative that mysteriously received a higher ballot position. He also used a statewide billboard campaign to advance his Proposition 2, one designed less to inform than to confuse. As Samish described the billboard campaign:

> I got a picture of a mother—the most beautiful mother you ever did see. She was wearing a gingham dress and holding a broom in her hand. The slogan

said: LET'S CLEAN THEM OUT—VOTE YES ON NUMBER TWO! That didn't have a damn thing to do with the proposition, but it sure as hell attracted a lot of sympathy. (1971: 68)

Again, both initiatives lost. Tired of battling the Drys through the initiative process, Samish pushed for a new law that sharply curtailed the signature-gathering period for new initiatives. This ensured that only very wealthy and organized interests could get propositions on the ballot, which, explains Samish, "is why the beverage industry was never threatened by local option thereafter" (1971: 69).

With parties weak, one of the major cleavages that emerged under the Progressive regime concerned liquor sales—an issue that divided both major parties internally. It was difficult for voters to demand either Wet or Dry laws from their state representatives or to elect Wet or Dry legislators since the labels *Wet* and *Dry* did not appear on the ballot. The only way for voters to make themselves heard on this matter would have been to enact local laws favoring one policy or another. Samish, operating behind the scenes, rigged the legislative machinery to make sure that people never had that option. Regardless of the merits of Wet or Dry legislation, it would be hard to call this state of affairs representative democracy. The one group that did well by this system was the brewers. They did not have to try to influence scores of legislators from different regions and with different personal agendas. Rather, they invested all their efforts in one agent, Samish, who did the research and advocacy for them. Their five-cent-per-barrel investment surely paid off for them.

The local option story shows what one powerful person can accomplish when parties are weak. By contrast, events of 2003 and 2004 in California showed just how limited a powerful person can be when parties are strong. Actor Arnold Schwarzenegger was elected governor in the recall election of 2003 amid one of the worst state budget crises in American history. His mandate (he received 49 percent of the vote in a field of 135 candidates) was to do something—anything—to solve the state's systemic budget deficit. His standing with the voters remained strong for months after taking office. Just prior to the March 2004 primaries, despite facing the same sort of fiscal crisis that finished off his predecessor, Schwarzenegger boasted a 65 percent approval rating, putting him ahead of Democratic senator Dianne Feinstein as the most popular politician in the state (Finnegan 2004). The easy victories of two initiative campaigns and two primary candidates he championed further suggested the new governor's clout with voters.

Yet despite his popularity and his mandate for action, Schwarzenegger remained significantly constrained by the disciplined Democratic Party, which maintained control of the legislature, and the disciplined Republican Party, of which he was a member. A survey I conducted among several journalists, consultants, and staffers closely familiar with Sacramento politics suggested that Schwarzenegger, given the chance, would have solved the state's budget problems through large cuts in social programs, a flattening of the tax code, a reduction in state pension payouts, and a renegotiation of state union contracts. Were the Democratic Party disorganized, as it was under cross-filing, a popular governor could probably have enacted much of that agenda. In 2003 and 2004, that proved impossible; Democrats largely held the line against Schwarzenegger's proposals.

Schwarzenegger's relative impotence in dealing with the Democratic Party was revealed in the November 2004 elections. Throughout the election season, the governor denounced recalcitrant Democrats as "girlie men" and threatened to "terminate" them by campaigning against them in their districts (Marelius and LaVelle 2004). Furthermore, he endorsed candidates in ten open-seat legislative races in an attempt to increase Republican numbers in the Capitol. These ventures proved fruitless. None of the ten districts in which he endorsed candidates went Republican, and the three Democratic legislators he targeted for termination (state senator Michael Machado and assembly members Barbara Matthews and Nicole Parra) retained their seats. Despite considerable expenditure of effort and money, Schwarzenegger went into the 2005 legislative session facing the exact same balance of Democrats and Republicans he had previously inherited.

Schwarzenegger was similarly constrained by partisans on the right. If he had his druthers, my respondents suggested, the governor would have eliminated the two-thirds vote threshold for the approval of new state bonds, freeing his hand to borrow more funds, but the ideologues that controlled his own party wouldn't have stood for that. In other words, although Schwarzenegger's approval rating was nearly four times that of Governor Gray Davis's prior to his ouster, his hands were equally tied when it came to dealing with the state's considerable financial difficulties. It is telling that Schwarzenegger's first move to address the fiscal crisis was to champion a $15 billion bond initiative that effectively deferred some of the crisis into the future without getting into revenue increases or spending cuts.

Was this a good thing? There is no easy answer to that. Perhaps, if the parties were weak, the governor would be able to resolve the fiscal crisis more readily, setting the state on surer financial footing sooner than he otherwise will be able to do. Doing that, however, would certainly force a few groups—union laborers, retirees, students and faculty of the state's university system—to absorb most of the blow. Unable to do that, the governor has been forced to defer some of the pain and to spread it out more evenly. That is certainly a fairer outcome, but it may doom the state to fiscal irresponsibility (and a low credit rating) for years to come. And that will exact its own price on the California dream.

WHAT CAN BE DONE?

It should not be assumed that our political system is incorrigible. Indeed, although the strong party system is frustrating to citizens and to moderate legislators, it does seem to produce the most representative government and, in the long run, the most good for the state. With a few reforms, the current system could be substantially less frustrating and more effective.

In California, one relatively small change that would tremendously advance the cause of responsible party government would be the removal of the two-thirds requirement for passage of budgets. This requirement is an oddity among state governments—only Arkansas and Rhode Island have similar statutes—but its existence is a massive hindrance for party government and probably the lead cause of legislative gridlock. As former Speaker Willie Brown explains, "It's the 100 percent reason why we're in the mess we're in. The advent of term limits and the latest reapportionment help get us here, but the two-thirds requirement for budget passage is the trigger that has the state in a crisis" (Evans 2003). If not for the two-thirds requirement, a Democratic majority—even a narrow one—could create new social programs *and* raise the taxes necessary to pay for them. A disciplined minority Republican Party could be the outlet for voter anger over the raised taxes, and if there was enough anger, the Democrats could lose majority status. In other words, there would be both a balanced, timely budget and accountability. In the current system, however, the Democrats fight tooth and nail for their social programs, and the Republicans refuse to support a budget with tax increases. The result, as we have seen in several recent budget cycles, is a stalemate, followed by a budget deficit, and no real accountability.

That suggested reform is obviously quite specific to California. More generally, though, states interested in securing some of the benefits of strong party systems without some of the drawbacks should consider doing away with term limits. Reasonable people may disagree about whether lifelong legislators are a good thing or if politicians become more corrupt the longer they spend in office. However, since the imposition of term limits in several states in the early 1990s, we have learned two important truths about their function. First, term limits do not turn over politics to amateurs. They do force career politicians to jump from office to office quite frequently, but because those politicians are well ensconced in informal party organizations, they are usually secure in a job. At the end of 2004, state senator John Burton (D-San Francisco) was retiring from public life, and Willie Brown had just completed two terms as San Francisco's mayor—fourteen years after reformers passed term limits in an effort to drive these very people from power. And as I demonstrated in chapter 5, some 90 percent of California's current officeholders came to power through the aid of an informal party organization. In addition, recent studies suggest that incumbents are just as safe as they were prior to term limits, and that campaign spending is just as high (Masket and Lewis 2007). Quite simply, the amateurs are not in charge.

A second lesson about term limits is that they have the perverse effect of protecting incumbents until those incumbents are termed out. Potential challengers see little value in going after an incumbent in either the primary or the general election because that incumbent will be gone in another two or four years anyway. Even if that incumbent is obviously incompetent, he or she will be protected, because it is far less costly for a challenger to seek the seat when it is an open one. Thus, even if the incumbent is incompetent, venal, or otherwise embarrassing to the party, term limits ensure that the incumbent will remain in office until he or she is termed out. The removal of term limits could change this. It would still be risky to take on an incumbent in a primary, but if that becomes the only way that a challenger's ambition can be sated, then weak incumbents will be challenged and will occasionally fall.

CONCLUSION

The reforms suggested here would tend to bring politics more in line with the principles of responsible party government. They assume, of course, that citizens would prefer the strong-party system currently on display in California, several other states, and the U.S. Congress to the weak-party one of the Progressive years. This assumption should not be taken for granted. A California proposition to create multipartisan, Louisiana-style primaries, with the top two candidates (regardless of party affiliation) advancing to a runoff election, garnered Schwarzenegger's endorsement and 46 percent of the vote in November 2004. Its narrow loss was likely attributable to the presence of a countervailing initiative—with higher ballot placement—placed on the same ballot, à la Samish, by incumbents of both parties. A similar reform was approved by nearly 60 percent of voters in the state of Washington that same year. Nonpartisanship still has a strong hold on the public's mind. There is no clear consensus among voters as to whether the strong-party or weak-party system is better.

However, those who rail against today's intractable parties should remember that the alternative is not necessarily sanity and moderation, but more often corruption and unaccountability. Similarly, those activists who continue to demand ideological fealty from the elected officials they back have made compromise nearly impossible, and compromise is sometimes exactly what's needed in public life. All would-be reformers must recognize that, no matter how they seek to purify the system, *somebody* is going to organize politics, and they're going to bring money. The people are not capable of running politics on their own. On this point, I cannot improve on Schattschneider (1942):

> The immobility and inertia of large masses are to politics what the law of gravity is to physics. This characteristic compels people to submit to a great channelization of the expression of their will, and is due to *numbers,* not to want of intelligence. An electorate of sixty million Aristotles would be equally restricted. (52)

Someone will intercede between the government and the governed, and whoever does it will demand a price. The people merely get to decide what system they want, and what price they are willing to pay.

APPENDIX

List of Interviews

ORANGE COUNTY

Roger Faubel	Lobbyist	1/29/2003
Gil Ferguson	Former Member of the Assembly	2/26/2002
Amy Inaba Freyder	Press Secretary, former Rep. Chris Cox	3/1/2004
Kelly Hart	Field Representative, former Rep. Chris Cox	3/2/2004
Beth Holder	Executive Director, Lincoln Club	3/24/2003
William Buck Johns III	CEO, Inland Group	2/28/2002
Stan Oftelie	President and CEO, Orange County Business Council	2/28/2002
Eileen Padberg	Political Consultant	3/8/2002
Jean Pasco	Orange County Writer, *Los Angeles Times*	11/2/2001
Curt Pringle	Mayor, City of Anaheim	3/6/2002
Tom Rogers	Former Chair of County GOP	3/8/2002
Chris St. Hilaire	Executive Director, New Majority	12/11/2001
Charles Smith	Orange County Supervisor	1/9/2002

ALL LOS ANGELES

Bill Boyarsky	Former City Editor, *Los Angeles Times*	9/29/2003
Todd Flora	Government Affairs Officer, First Five LA	7/6/2004
Fernando Guerra	Professor, Loyola Marymount University	7/10/2002
Sherry Bebitch Jeffe	Scholar, USC	12/23/2003
Matthew Klink	Vice President, Cerrell and Associates	4/10/2003
Keith Parker	Assistant Vice Chancellor, UCLA	5/5/2003

SOUTH LOS ANGELES

Bobbie Anderson	President, New Frontiers Democratic Club	5/14/2002
Mervyn Dymally	Assembly Member	6/17/2002
Chris Hammond	Capital Vision Equities	2/28/2003
Reggie Jones-Sawyer	Secretary, California Democratic Party	5/28/2002
Kerman Maddox	Campaign Consultant	6/11/2003
Eric Shabsis	Staff, Office of Mayor James Hahn	2/11/2003
Stanley Sheinbaum	Donor and fund-raiser	4/14/2003
Ken Spiker	Lobbyist	1/31/2003
Don Stephenson	Voter Empowerment Coordinator, Western Region 1, NAACP	5/17/2002

EASTSIDE LOS ANGELES

Dan Farkas	Staff, State Sen. Gil Cedillo	5/8/2003
Victor Griego	Campaign Consultant	5/28/2002
Mike Hernandez	Staff, L.A. City Councilmember Nate Holden	5/7/2002
Henry Lozano	Campaign Chief of Staff, Rep. Xavier Becerra	5/8/2002
Jorge Morales	District Aide, former Assembly Member Marco Firebaugh	2/17/2004
Frank Quevedo	Southern California Edison	7/11/2002
Jaime Regalado	Director, Pat Brown Institute, Cal. State Los Angeles	5/13/2002
Miguel Santana	Staff, Supervisor Gloria Molina	12/20/2002

WESTSIDE LOS ANGELES

Burt Margolin	Former Assembly Member	2/27/2004
Rick Tuttle	Former Los Angeles City Controller	3/8/2004
Henry Waxman	Member of Congress	5/8/2002

FRESNO

Juan Arambula	Fresno County Supervisor	1/10/2003
Mike Der Manouel Jr.	President, San Joaquin Valley Insurance Associates	1/9/2003
John Ellis	Political writer, *Fresno Bee*	1/15/2003
Coke Hallowell	Donor and fund-raiser	1/23/2003
Will Hensley	Staff, Rep. Cal Dooley	1/9/2003
Deborah Hurley	Staff, Rep. George Radanovich	1/9/2003
Nathan Magsig	Clovis City Councilmember	1/22/2003
Henry T. Perea	Fresno City Councilmember	1/10/2003
Debbie Poochigian	Wife of State Sen. Chuck Poochigian	2/24/2003
Steve Samuelian	Assembly Member	1/10/2003
Earl Smittcamp	Donor and fund-raiser	1/23/2003
John Wallace	Former broadcast news journalist	1/25/2003
Wendy Warfield	Fund-raiser	1/28/2003
Sarah Woolf	Staff, Rep. Cal Dooley	1/9/2003

REFERENCES

Abramowitz, Alan. 2004. *Voice of the People: Elections and Voting in the United States.* New York: McGraw-Hill.

Abramowitz, Alan I., and Brad Alexander. 2004. "Incumbency, Redistricting, and the Decline of Competition in Congressional Elections: Evidence from the 2002 Midterm Election." Paper presented at the annual meeting of the Western Political Science Association, March 11–13, Portland, OR.

Abramowitz, Alan, John McGlennon, and Ronald Rapoport. 1983. "The Party Isn't Over: Incentives for Activism in the 1980 Presidential Nominating Campaign." *Journal of Politics* 45 (November): 1006–15.

Achen, Christopher, and Larry Bartels. 2002. "Blind Retrospection: Electoral Responses to Drought, Flu, and Shark Attacks." Paper presented at the annual meeting of the American Political Science Association, August 28, Boston.

Aistrup, Joseph A. 1993. "State Legislative Party Competition: A County-Level Measure." *Political Research Quarterly* 46 (2): 433–46.

Aldrich, John H. 1983. "A Downsian Spatial Model with Party Activism." *American Political Science Review* 77 (December): 974–90.

Aldrich, John H. 1995. *Why Parties?* Chicago: University of Chicago Press.

Aldrich, John H., and James S. Coleman Battista. 2002. "Conditional Party Government in the States." *American Journal of Political Science* 46 (January): 164–72.

Aldrich, John H., Michael Brady, Scott de Marchi, Ian McDonald, Brendan Nyhan, David Rohde, and Michael W. Tofias. 2007. "Party and Constituency: How Constituents Influence Conditional Party Government and Roll Call Voting." Paper presented at Politics through the Lens of Parties, a conference in honor of Leon Epstein, April 27, Madison, WI.

Aldrich, John H., and David W. Rohde. 2001. "The Logic of Conditional Party Government." In *Congress Reconsidered,* ed. L. C. Dodd and B. I. Oppenheimer. Washington, DC: Congressional Quarterly.

Ansolabehere, Stephen, James M. Snyder Jr., and Charles Stewart III. 2001. "Candidate Positioning in U.S. House Elections." *American Journal of Political Science* 45 (January): 136–59.

APSA (American Political Science Association). 1950. "Toward a More Responsible Two-Party System: A Report of the Committee on Political Parties." *American Political Science Review* 44 (September).

Bailey, Eric, Peter M. Warren, and Dexter Filkins. 1996. "GOP in O.C.: Setting Sights on the State." *Los Angeles Times*, July 7, 1.

Banfield, Edward C., and James Q. Wilson. 1965. *City Politics*. Cambridge: Harvard University Press.

Bardella, Kurt. 2004. "Battles in Bakersfield." *California Journal*, August 1, 38.

Bartels, Larry M. 1998. "Electoral Continuity and Change: 1868–1996." *Electoral Studies* 17 (3): 301–26.

Bartels, Larry M. 2000. "Partisanship and Voting Behavior, 1952–1996." *American Journal of Political Science* 44 (1): 35–50.

Bawn, Kathleen. 1999. "Constructing 'Us': Ideology, Coalition Politics, and False Consciousness." *American Journal of Political Science* 43 (April): 303–34.

Bawn, Kathleen, Marty Cohen, David Karol, Seth Masket, Hans Noel, and John Zaller. 2006. "A Theory of Political Parties." Paper presented at the 2006 annual meeting of the American Political Science Association, September 2, Philadelphia.

Bean, Walton. 1952. *Boss Ruef's San Francisco: The Story of the Union Labor Party, Big Business, and the Graft Prosecution*. Berkeley: University of California Press.

Berinstein, Jan G. 1986. "Realignment and Political Party-Building in California, 1952–1963." Ph.D. dissertation, Political Science, Cornell University, Ithaca.

Bernstein, Jonathan. 1999. "The Expanded Party in American Politics." Doctoral dissertation, Department of Political Science, University of California, Berkeley.

Blair, George S., and Houston I. Flournoy. 1967. *Legislative Bodies in California*. Belmont, CA: Dickenson.

Bowman, Ann O'M., and Richard C. Kearney. 1986. *The Resurgence of the States*. Englewood Cliffs, NJ: Prentice-Hall.

Boyarsky, Bill. 2008. *Big Daddy: Jesse Unruh and the Art of Power Politics*. Berkeley: University of California Press.

Brambor, Thomas, William Roberts Clark, and Matt Golder. 2006. "Understanding Interaction Models: Improving Empirical Analysis." *Political Analysis* 14:63–82.

Broder, David S. 1972. *The Party's Over: The Failure of Politics in America*. 1st ed. New York: Harper and Row.

Broder, David S. 2003. "Million-Dollar Recall." *Washington Post*, July 30, A19.

Brownstein, Ronald. 2003. "In the Political Arena, the Gladiators Are Now Engaged in Total War." *Los Angeles Times*, July 28, A8.

Buchanan, William. 1963. *Legislative Partisanship: The Deviant Case of California*. Berkeley: University of California Press.

Bullough, William A. 1979. *The Blind Boss and His City: Christopher Augustine Buckley and Nineteenth-Century San Francisco*. Berkeley: University of California Press.

Burnham, Walter Dean. 1965. "The Changing Shape of the American Political Universe." *American Political Science Review* 59 (1): 7–28.

California Journal Editors. 2002. "*CJ*'s District-by-District Analysis—Assembly." *California Journal,* December 1, 27.

California Journal Editors. 2004. "Election 2004—Assembly Hot Races." *California Journal,* October 1, 17.

California Journal Staff. 2002. "Primary Election Results—Congress and the Legislature." *California Journal,* April 1, 29.

California Legislature. 1951. *Journal of the Senate.* Sacramento: California State Publisher.

Campbell, Angus, Philip E. Converse, Warren E. Miller, and Donald E. Stokes. 1960. *The American Voter.* New York: John Wiley and Sons.

Canes-Wrone, Brandice, David W. Brady, and John F. Cogan. 2002. "Out of Step, Out of Office: Electoral Accountability and House Members' Voting." *American Political Science Review* 96 (1): 127–40.

Cannon, Carl M. 2002. "California Divided." *California Journal,* January, 8–14.

Cannon, Lou. 1969. *Ronnie and Jesse: A Political Odyssey.* Garden City, NY: Doubleday.

Cannon, Lou. 2003. Interview with author. Los Angeles, August 25.

Carney, Francis. 1958. "The Rise of the Democratic Clubs in California." New Brunswick, NJ: Eagleton Foundation.

Carney, Francis. 1964. "The Decentralized Politics of Los Angeles." *Annals of the American Academy of Political and Social Science* 353 (May): 107–21.

Carr, Elston L. 1997. *Oral History Interview with Mervyn M. Dymally.* Sacramento: California State Archives.

Carsey, Thomas M., and Geoffrey C. Layman. 2005. "'Conflict Extension' in American Party Politics." *Vox Pop: The Newsletter of Political Organizations and Parties* 24 (summer): 1, 6.

Chinn, Ronald E. 1958. "Democratic Party Politics in California, 1920–1956." Ph.D. dissertation, Department of Political Science, University of California, Berkeley.

Christensen, Terry, and Larry N. Gerston. 1984. *Politics in the Golden State: The California Connection.* Boston: Little, Brown.

Clark, Peter B., and James Q. Wilson. 1961. "Incentive Systems: A Theory of Organizations." *Administrative Science Quarterly* 6 (September): 129–66.

Clucas, Richard A. 1995. *The Speaker's Electoral Connection: Willie Brown and the California Assembly.* Berkeley: Institute of Governmental Studies Press.

Cohen, Marty, David Karol, Hans Noel, and John Zaller. 2008. *The Party Decides: Presidential Nominations before and after Reform.* Chicago: University of Chicago Press.

Cohen, Marty, Hans Noel, and John Zaller. 2004. "How Politicians Act When Voters Are Left in the Dark: The Effect of Local News on Quality of Political Representation." Paper presented at the annual meeting of the Western Political Science Association, March 11–13, Portland, OR.

Coleman, John. 1996. "Party Organizational Strength and Public Support for Parties." *American Journal of Political Science* 40 (3): 805–24.

Cornwell, Rupert. 1995. "The Old Man of War Is Still a Sure Shot." *The Independent,* July 22, 17.

Cotter, Cornelius P., James L. Gibson, John F. Bibby, and Robert J. Huckshorn. 1984. *Party Organizations in American Politics.* New York: Praeger.

Cox, Gary W. 1987. *The Efficient Secret: The Cabinet and the Development of Political Parties in Victorian England.* Cambridge: Cambridge University Press.

Cox, Gary W., and Mathew D. McCubbins. 1993. *Legislative Leviathan: Party Government in the House.* Berkeley: University of California Press.

Cox, Gary W., and Mathew D. McCubbins. 2005. *Setting the Agenda: Responsible Party Government in the U.S. House of Representatives.* Cambridge: Cambridge University Press.

Cresap, Dean R. 1954. *Party Politics in the Golden State.* Los Angeles: Haynes Foundation.

Dahl, Robert A. 1961. *Who Governs? Democracy and Power in an American City.* New Haven: Yale University Press.

DiCamillo, Mark, and Mervin Field. 2003. "Voters Very Dissatisfied with State Budget Negotiations. Blame Davis and Both Parties in the Legislature. Three in Four Fear the State Is Seriously Off on the Wrong Track." San Francisco: Field Research Corporation.

Dionne, E. J. 1991. *Why Americans Hate Politics.* New York: Simon and Schuster.

Doherty, Joseph William. 2006. "The Candidate-Consultant Network in California Legislative Campaigns: A Social Network Analysis of Informal Party Organization." Ph.D. dissertation, Political Science, University of California, Los Angeles.

Dominguez, Casey Byrne Knudsen. 2005. "Before the Primary: Party Participation in Congressional Nominating Processes." Doctoral dissertation, Department of Political Science, University of California, Berkeley.

Douglass, Enid Hart. 1988. *Oral History Interview with Victor V. Veysey.* Sacramento: California State Archives.

Downs, Anthony. 1957. *An Economic Theory of Democracy.* New York: Harper and Row.

Dvorin, Eugene P., and Arthur J. Misner. 1966. *Introduction to California Government.* 2d ed. Reading, MA: Addison-Wesley.

Ehrenhalt, Alan. 1991. *The United States of Ambition: Politicians, Power, and the Pursuit of Office.* New York: Times Books.

Eilperin, Juliet. 2003. "Fundraising Focus Earns DeLay Wealth of Influence." *Washington Post,* July 22, 1.

Eilperin, Juliet. 2006. *Fight Club Politics: How Partisanship Is Poisoning the House of Representatives.* Lanham, MD: Rowman and Littlefield.

Eilperin, Juliet, and Albert B. Crenshaw. 2003. "The House That Roared." *Washington Post,* July 19, 1.

Epstein, Leon D. 1958. *Politics in Wisconsin.* Madison: University of Wisconsin Press.

Erickson, Robert S. 1971. "The Electoral Impact of Congressional Roll Call Voting." *American Political Science Review* 65 (December): 1018–32.

Espino, Rodolfo, and Matthew Hindman. 2007. "Parties? We Don't Need No Stinkin' Parties! Roll Call Voting in the Non-Partisan Arizona Territorial Legislature." Paper presented at the annual meeting of the Western Political Science Association, March, Las Vegas.

Evans, Jim. 2003. "The Two-Thirds Vote." *California Journal,* August 1, 18.

Fenno, Richard. 1978. *Home Style: House Members in Their Districts.* Boston: Little, Brown.

Findley, James C. 1959. "Cross-Filing and the Progressive Movement in California Politics." *Western Political Quarterly* 12 (September): 699–711.

Finnegan, Michael. 2004. "The Times Poll: Schwarzenegger Widely Popular; Pessimism About State Declines." *Los Angeles Times,* February 26, 1.

Fiorina, Morris P. 1977. *Congress: Keystone of the Washington Establishment.* New Haven: Yale University Press.

Fiorina, Morris P. 1994. "Divided Government in the American States: A Byproduct of Legislative Professionalism?" *American Political Science Review* 88 (2): 304–16.

Fiorina, Morris P. 1999a. "Further Evidence of the Partisan Consequences of Legislative Professionalism." *American Journal of Political Science* 43 (3): 974–77.

Fiorina, Morris P. 1999b. "Whatever Happened to the Median Voter?" Paper presented at the MIT Conference on Parties and Congress, October 2, Cambridge, MA.

Fitzenberger, Jennifer M. 2004. "Tough Decisions Await Valley's Winners: Assembly Candidates Hope to Advance to General Election." *Fresno Bee,* February 27, 1.

Ford, Henry Jones. 1909. "The Direct Primary." *North American Review* 190 (1): 1–14.

Fowle, Eleanor. 1980. *Cranston, the Senator from California.* Los Angeles: Jeremy P. Tarcher.

Fowler, Linda, and Robert McClure. 1989. *Political Ambition: Who Decides to Run for Congress.* New Haven: Yale University Press.

Gaylord, Edward H. 1977. "History of the California Election Laws." In *West's Annotated California Codes,* Section 1, 1–53. St. Paul, MN: West Pub.

Gendzel, Glen. 2003. Progressives in California, Email correspondence with author, July 24.

Guerra, Fernando. 2002. Interview with author, July 30.

Halper, Evan. 2003. "Careers at Stake, Brulte Tells GOP." *Los Angeles Times,* June 5, 1.

Halper, Evan, and Nancy Vogel. 2003. "Lawmakers See Slim Chance of Meeting Budget Deadline." *Los Angeles Times,* June 11, 1.

Hetherington, Marc J. 2001. "Resurgent Mass Partisanship: The Role of Elite Polarization." *American Political Science Review* 95 (3): 619–31.

Hichborn, Franklin. 1911. *Story of the Session of the California Legislature of 1911.* San Francisco: Press of the James H. Barry Company.

Hichborn, Franklin. 1922. *Story of the Session of the California Legislature of 1921.* San Francisco: Press of the James H. Barry Company.

Hichborn, Franklin. 1959–60. "The Party, the Machine, and the Vote: The Story of Cross-Filing in California Politics." *California Historical Society Quarterly* 38–39 (December, March): 349–57, 19–34.

Hicke, Carole. 1987. *Oral History Interview with Gordon A. Fleury.* Sacramento: California State Archives.

Hopper, Stanley D. 1975. "Fragmentation of the California Republican Party in the One-Party Era, 1893–1932." *Western Political Quarterly* 28 (2): 372–86.

Jackley, John L. 1992. *Hill Rat: Blowing the Lid Off Congress.* 1st ed. Lanham, MD: Regnery Gateway.

Jacobson, Gary. 2001. *The Politics of Congressional Elections.* 5th ed. New York: Longman.

Jacobson, Gary C. 2004. "Explaining the Ideological Polarization of the Congressional Parties since the 1970s." Paper presented at the annual meeting of the Midwest Political Science Association, April 15–18, Chicago.

Jacobson, Gary C., and Samuel Kernell. 1983. *Strategy and Choice in Congressional Elections.* 2d ed. New Haven: Yale University Press.

Jamieson, Kathleen Hall, and Erika Falk. 2000. "Continuity and Change in Civility in the House." In *Polarized Politics: Congress and the President in a Partisan Era,* ed. J. R. Bond and R. Fleisher. Washington, DC: CQ Press.

Jeffe, Sherry Bebitch. 2003. "The Day of the Long Knives." *Los Angeles Times,* July 6, 3.

Jenkins, Jeffrey A. 1999. "Examining the Bonding Effects of Party: A Comparative Analysis of Roll-Call Voting in the U.S. and Confederate Houses." *American Journal of Political Science* 43 (October): 1144–65.

Jenkins, Jeffrey A. 2000. "Examining the Robustness of Ideological Voting: Evidence from the Confederate House of Representatives." *American Journal of Political Science* 44 (4): 811–22.

Johnson, William Carl. 1960. "The Political Party System in the 1959–60 California Legislature." Master's thesis, Political Science, University of California.

Karch, Andrew, and Benjamin J. Deufel. 2003. "The Missing Link: Party Competition and the Political Process." Paper presented at the annual conference of the Midwest Political Science Association, April 3–6, Chicago.

Kent, Frank R. 1924. *The Great Game of Politics: An Effort to Present the Elementary Human Facts about Politics, Politicians, and Political Machines, Candidates and Their Ways.* Garden City, NY: Doubleday, Page.

Key, V. O., Jr. 1949. *Southern Politics.* New York: Vintage Books.

Key, V. O., Jr. 1952. *Politics, Parties, and Pressure Groups.* 3d vol. New York: Thomas Y. Crowell.

Kiewiet, D. Roderick, and Mathew D. McCubbins. 1991. *The Logic of Delega-*

tion: Congressional Parties and the Appropriations Process. Chicago: University of Chicago Press.

King, David C. 2003. "Congress, Polarization, and Fidelity to the Median Voter." Unpublished manuscript, Cambridge, MA.

Koger, Greg. 2000. "Speaker Elections in the U.S. House, 1899–1998: Some Policy Consequences of Partisan Organization." Paper presented at the annual meeting of the American Political Science Association, Washington, DC.

Koger, Gregory, Seth E. Masket, and Hans Noel. 2009. "Partisan Webs: Information Exchange and Party Networks." *British Journal of Political Science.*

Krasno, Jonathan S. 2007. "Political Parties in the Money-Driven Campaign Economy." Paper presented at the annual meeting of the Midwest Political Science Association, April 14, Chicago.

Krehbiel, Keith. 2000. "Party Discipline and Measures of Partisanship." *American Journal of Political Science* 44:212–27.

Layman, Geoffrey C., and Thomas M. Carsey. 2002. "Party Polarization and 'Conflict Extension' in the American Electorate." *American Journal of Political Science* 46 (fall): 786–802.

Leary, Mary Ellen. 1957. "The Two-Party System Comes to California." *Reporter,* February 7, 33–36.

Lee, Frances E., and Bruce Ian Oppenheimer. 1999. *Sizing up the Senate: The Unequal Consequences of Equal Representation.* Chicago: University of Chicago Press.

Lewis, Jeffrey. 2003. "Voting in Low Information Elections: Bundling and Non-Independence of Voter Choice." Paper presented at Yale University, April 25, New Haven.

Los Angeles Times Staff. 1940. "Peek Ousted as Speaker in Fast Assembly Move." *Los Angeles Times,* January 30, 1–2.

Los Angeles Times Staff. 2005. "Times Endorsement: A New Political Landscape." *Los Angeles Times,* October 23, M4.

Lynch, Jeremiah. 1889. *Buckleyism: The Government of a State.* San Francisco: Blake.

Macartney, John David. 1975. "Political Staffing: A View from the District." Doctoral dissertation, Political Science, University of California, Los Angeles.

Mann, Thomas E. 1978. *Unsafe at Any Margin: Interpreting Congressional Elections.* Washington, DC: American Enterprise Institute for Public Policy Research.

Mansfield, Harvey. 1965. "Political Parties, Patronage, and the Federal Government Service." In *The Federal Government Service,* ed. W. Sayre. Englewood Cliffs, NJ: Prentice-Hall.

Marelius, John, and Philip J. LaVelle. 2004. "Governor's Celebrity Outshines Budget Plea." *Copley News Service,* July 22.

Marshall, Joshua Micah. 2003. *Talking Points Memo* [Web log], posted May 14, 12:23am. Available from http://talkingpointsmemo.com/archives/147163.php.

Masket, Seth E. 2007. "The Needs of the Many: An Examination of the Link between Size of Place and Partisanship." Paper presented at "Politics through the Lens of Parties, a Conference in Memory of Leon Epstein," April 27, Madison, WI.

Masket, Seth E., and Jeffrey B. Lewis. 2007. "A Return to Normalcy? Revisiting the Effects of Term Limits on Competitiveness and Spending in California Assembly Elections." *State Politics and Policy Quarterly* 7 (1): 20–38.

Mason, Mary Ann. 1994. "Neither Friends nor Foes: Organized Labor and the California Progressives." In *California Progressivism Revisited,* ed. W. Deverell and T. Sitton. Berkeley: University of California Press.

Mayhew, David R. 1974. *Congress: The Electoral Connection.* New Haven: Yale University Press.

Mayhew, David R. 1986. *Placing Parties in American Politics.* Princeton: Princeton University Press.

Mayhew, David R. 2000. "Electoral Realignments." *Annual Review of Political Science* 3:449–74.

Mayhew, David R. 2004. *Electoral Realignments: A Critique of an American Genre.* New Haven: Yale University Press.

McGirr, Lisa. 2001. *Suburban Warriors: The Origins of the New American Right.* Princeton: Princeton University Press.

McHenry, Dean E. 1946. "Cross-Filing of Political Candidates in California." *Annals of the American Academy of Political and Social Science* 248 (November): 226–31.

Meyerson, Harold. 1994. "The Liberal Lion in Winter." *Los Angeles Times Magazine,* December 4.

Miller, Gary, and Norman Schofield. 2003. "Activists and Partisan Realignment in the United States." *American Political Science Review* 97 (2): 245–60.

Monroe, J. P. 2001. *The Political Party Matrix: The Persistence of Organization.* Albany: State University of New York Press.

Morris, Gabrielle. 1987. *Oral History Interview with Jerome R. Waldie.* Sacramento: California State Archives.

Mowry, George Edwin. 1951. *The California Progressives.* Chicago: Quadrangle Books.

Nicholas, Peter, and Evan Halper. 2003. "Assembly Rejects GOP Budget Plan." *Los Angeles Times,* July 7, 1.

Noel, Hans. 2001. "The New and Improved Party ID (Now with More Meaning!): Party Identification and Ideological Realignment since 1954." Paper presented at the annual meeting of the Midwest Political Science Association, April, Chicago.

Oppenheimer, Bruce I. 2005. "Deep Red and Blue Congressional Districts." In *Congress Reconsidered,* ed. L. C. Dodd and B. I. Oppenheimer. Washington, DC: Congressional Quarterly Press.

Orange County Register Staff. 2001. "California Gets Car Tax Fever." *Orange County Register,* December 13.

Owens, John R., Edmond Costantini, and Louis F. Weschler. 1970. *California Politics and Parties.* London: Macmillan.

Patterson, Samuel C. 1968. "The Political Cultures of the American States." *Journal of Politics* 30 (February): 187–209.

Pollard, Vic. 1999. "Legislator Cultivates Reputation for Integrity." *Bakersfield Californian,* August 28.

Poole, Keith T., and Howard Rosenthal. 1997. *Congress: A Political-Economic History of Roll Call Voting.* New York: Oxford University Press.

Posner, Russell M. 1957. "The Progressive Voters League, 1923–26." *California Historical Society Quarterly* 36 (3): 251–62.

Pringle, Curt. 2002. Personal correspondence with author, November 12.

Raftery, Judith. 1994. "Los Angeles Clubwomen and Progressive Reform." In *California Progressivism Revisited,* ed. W. Deverell and T. Sitton. Berkeley: University of California Press.

Reid, T. R. 2003. "GOP Redistricting: New Boundaries of Politics?" *Washington Post,* July 2, A04.

Reiner, Rob. 1995. *The American President.* Produced and directed by Rob Reiner. Castle Rock Entertainment.

Reinhold, Robert. 1988. "Bradley Quest for 5th Term Puts End to Epitaphs of '87." *New York Times,* August 20, 6.

Reinier, Jacqueline S., ed. 1987. *Oral History Interview with Hon. Lloyd W. Lowrey.* Sacramento: California State Archives.

Reynolds, John F. 2006. *The Demise of the American Convention System, 1880–1911.* New York: Cambridge University Press.

Richardson, James. 1996. *Willie Brown: A Biography.* Berkeley: University of California Press.

Riordan, William L. 1963. *Plunkitt of Tammany Hall: A Series of Very Plain Talks on Very Practical Politics, Delivered by Ex-Senator George Washington Plunkitt, the Tammany Philosopher, from His Rostrum—the New York County Court House Bootblack Stand.* New York: Dutton.

Roderick, Kevin. 1988. "Yaroslavsky Must Shed Anonymity to Defeat Bradley." *Los Angeles Times,* November 13, 1.

Rogin, Michael Paul, and John L. Shover. 1970. *Political Change in California: Critical Elections and Social Movements, 1890–1966.* Westport: Greenwood.

Rohde, David W. 1991. *Parties and Leaders in the Postreform House.* Chicago: University of Chicago Press.

Rohde, David W., and Kenneth A. Shepsle. 1987. "Leaders and Followers in the House of Representatives: Reflections on Woodrow Wilson's *Congressional Government.*" *Congress and the Presidency* 14 (3): 111–33.

Rood, W. B. 1978. "Speaker of Assembly: From the Power Flow the Political Funds." *Los Angeles Times,* October 3.

Rosenthal, Alan. 1984. "If the Party's Over, Where's All That Noise Coming From?" *State Government* 57 (1): 50–54.

Rowe, Leonard. 1961. *Preprimary Endorsement in California Politics.* Berkeley: Bureau of Public Administration, University of California.

Royko, Mike. 1971. *Boss: Richard J. Daley of Chicago.* New York: New American Library.

Rusco, Elmer Ritter. 1961. "Machine Politics, California Model: Arthur H. Samish and the Alcoholic Beverage Industry." Ph.D. Dissertation, Department of Political Science, University of California, Berkeley.

Samish, Arthur H. 1971. *The Secret Boss of California: The Life and High Times of Art Samish.* New York: Crown.

Schattschneider, E. E. 1942. *Party Government.* Westport, CT: Greenwood.

Schattschneider, E. E. 1960. *The Semisovereign People: A Realist's View of Democracy in America.* Fort Worth: Harcourt Brace Jovanovich College Publishers.

Schlesinger, Joseph A. 1985. "The New American Political Party." *American Political Science Review* 79 (December): 1152–69.

Schwartz, Mildred A. 1990. *The Party Network: The Robust Organization of Illinois Republicans.* Madison: University of Wisconsin Press.

Schwartz, Thomas. 1989. "Why Parties?" Unpublished manuscript, Los Angeles.

Seney, Donald B., ed. 1989. *Oral History Interview with John E. Moss, Jr.* Sacramento: California State Archives.

Shaw, Stanford C. 1988. *Oral History Interview with Stanford C. Shaw.* Sacramento: California State Archives.

Sittig, Robert F. 1997. "Nebraska." In *State Party Profiles*, ed. A. M. Appleton and D. S. Ward. Washington, DC: Congressional Quarterly.

Skelton, George. 2001. "Riordan Loves the State—the Way It Used to Be." *Los Angeles Times,* November 8, B8.

Skerry, Peter. 1993. *Mexican-Americans: The Ambivalent Minority.* New York: Free Press.

Snyder, Elizabeth. 1996. *A Ride on the Political Merry-Go-Round.* Los Angeles: Silverton Books.

Snyder, James M., Jr., and Tim Groseclose. 2000. "Estimating Party Influence in Congressional Roll-Call Voting." *American Journal of Political Science* 44 (June): 193–211.

Sonenshein, Raphael Joel. 1984. "Bradley's People: Functions of the Candidate Organization." Doctoral dissertation, Department of Political Science, Yale University, New Haven.

Sonenshein, Raphael J. 1993. *Politics in Black and White: Race and Power in Los Angeles.* Princeton: Princeton University Press.

Sorauf, Frank J. 1960. "The Silent Revolution in Patronage." *Public Administration Review* 20 (winter): 28–34.

Squire, Peverill. 1992. "The Theory of Legislative Institutionalization and the California Assembly." *Journal of Politics* 54 (4): 1026–54.

Stokes, Donald E. 1966. "Spatial Models of Party Competition." In *Elections and the Political Order,* ed. A. Campbell, P. E. Converse, W. E. Miller, and D. E. Stokes. New York: Wiley.

Stone, Clarence N. 1989. *Regime Politics: Governing Atlanta, 1946–1988.* Lawrence: University Press of Kansas.

Stone, Walter J., and Alan I. Abramowitz. 1983. "Winning May Not Be Every-

thing, but It's More Than We Thought: Presidential Party Activists in 1980."
American Political Science Review 77 (December): 945–56.

Stonecash, Jeffrey M., and Everita Silina. 2005. "The 1896 Realignment: A Reassessment." *American Politics Research* 33 (1): 3–32.

Sundquist, James L. 1983. *Dynamics of the Party System: Alignment and Realignment of Political Parties in the United States.* Washington, DC: Brookings Institution.

Suskind, Ron. 2003. "Why Are These Men Laughing?" *Esquire,* January 1.

Suskind, Ron. 2004. "Without a Doubt." *New York Times Magazine,* October 17, 44–51, 64, 102, 106.

Tichy, Noel M. 1981. "Networks in Organizations." In *Handbook of Organizational Design,* ed. P. C. Nystrom and W. H. Starbuck. London: Oxford University Press.

Turner, Henry A., and John A. Vieg. 1967. *The Government and Politics of California.* 3d ed. New York: McGraw-Hill.

VandeHei, Jim. 2006. "Funding Constrains Democrats." *Washington Post,* October 18, A12.

Vásquez, Carlos. 1987. *Oral History Interview with Thomas M. Rees.* Sacramento: California State Archives.

Volden, Craig, and Elizabeth Bergman. 2006. "How Strong Should Our Party Be? Party Member Preferences over Party Cohesion." *Legislative Studies Quarterly* 31 (1): 71–104.

Waldie, Jerome. 2001. Interview with author, August 12.

Walsh, James P. 1972. "Abe Ruef Was No Boss: Machine Politics, Reform, and San Francisco." *California Historical Quarterly* 51 (spring): 3–16.

Ware, Alan. 2002. *The American Direct Primary.* New York: Cambridge University Press.

Wasserman, Jim. 2001. "California Budget Standoff Continues into the Weekend." Associated Press, July 21.

Waters, Maxine. 2004. "The Crumbling Credibility of the Bush Administration." Press release, February 14. Washington, DC.

Werner, Erica. 2004. "Republican House Primary Pits Two Party Powerhouses." Associated Press, January 25.

Wilson, James Q. 1966. *The Amateur Democrat: Club Politics in Three Cities.* Chicago: University of Chicago Press.

Wilson, James Q. 1973. *Political Organizations.* New York: Basic Books.

Wolfinger, Raymond E. 1972. "Why Political Machines Have Not Withered Away and Other Revisionist Thoughts." *Journal of Politics* 34 (May): 365–98.

Wright, Gerald C., and Michael B. Berkman. 1986. "Candidates and Policy in United States Senate Elections." *American Political Science Review* 80 (2): 567–88.

Wright, Gerald C., and Tracy Osborn. 2002. "Party and Roll Call Voting in the American Legislature." Paper presented at Midwest Political Science Association, Chicago.

Wright, Gerald C., and Brian F. Schaffner. 2002. "The Influence of Party: Evidence from the State Legislatures." *American Political Science Review* 96 (2): 367–79.

Wright, Gerald C., and Jon Winburn. 2002. "Patterns of Constituency-Legislator Policy Congruence in the States." Paper presented at the Second Annual Conference on State Politics and Policy, May 24–25, Milwaukee.

Zaller, John R. 1992. *The Nature and Origins of Mass Opinion.* Cambridge: Cambridge University Press.

INDEX

Note: Numbers in *italic* indicate pages with figures or tables.

Miller, Gary, *172*
Mills, James, 113
moderate officeholders and candidates, 141–43
Molina, Gloria, 15, 122, 130, 152, 156, 169, 180, *181*
Morales, Jorge, 135, 155
Moss, John, 69–70
multipartisan primary elections, 203

Nakano, George, *172*
national political machines, 14
National Science Foundation, 55
Nebraska state legislature, 17–18, 88
network analysis, 21–22
New Deal, partisanship during, 104, 105, 197
New Frontiers Democratic Club, 119, 131, 139
New Jersey direct primary system, 60
New Majority, 118–19, 141
New Mexico politics, 6
Nixon, Richard, 49
nomination-centered politics, 17–20, 85, 115, 128–29
nominations
    activists' control of, 28–29, 43, 75, 78–80, 84–85, 106–7, 110–11, 188–89, 192–93
    cross-filing and control of process, 11, 58–59, 76–80, 86
    IPO control of process, 17–19, 33, 43–44, 45–50, 53, 86, 128–29, 157, 165–67, *166*
    local party organization's role in, 8–9
    political machine's control over, 26
    primary election battles, 9, 10
Nunes, Devin, 2, 32, 126, 127, 139

Occidental Petroleum, 154
officeholders and candidates. *See also* incumbents
    accountability of, 21, 49–50, 194–96
    candidate selection, 50–52, 135–36, 141, 145–51, 159, 161–63
    career path in politics, 35
    character of, 6, 12–13, 23–24, 54–55
    as creatures of parties, 80–85, *82, 84,* 105–6, 157–58, 189
    demand for party organization, 35
    discipline enforcement, 27, 48–49, 52–53, 126–27, 129, 151–53, 192
    fund-raising abilities of candidates, 146–47

goals of, 33
ideologically extreme candidates, 9, 24–25, 41–42, 43, 51–52, 140–43, 185–86, 195
incentives for working with IPOs, 16–17, 49
IPO control over, 9–10, 19, 185–87
moderates, 141–43
nomination battles, 9, 10
parties as creatures of, 13, 26, 105–7, 157, 186, 188–89
payment of, 105
political machine's control over, 13, 19, 26–27
power as reward, 34, 130
relationship with IPOs, 41, 129–32
relationship with parties, 12–13, 26–27
resources for, 9, 10, 43, 159, 176
responsiveness to donors, 133–34
routes to office, 21, 167–76, *169, 172–73, 175*
term limits, 10, 11, 50, 202
terms of service, 105
TPO control over, 13–14, 19, 187
voting behavior and cross-filing, 63–71, *65, 67, 68,* 80–85, *82, 84,* 91–93, *92,* 104, 105, 193–94
voting behavior and outside coalitions, 95–104, *97, 99, 101, 103,* 194–95
Oklahoma politics, 6, 60
Oller, Rico, 32
Olson, Culbert, 71, 104, 197
O'Neill, Thomas P., 3
Orange County
    candidate selection, 146, 149–50, 186
    Central Committee, 139–40
    cross-government alliances, 155
    Democrat, election of, 80
    demographics of, 119
    discipline enforcement, 152
    elite endorsements, 176, *177,* 182–83, *183*
    IPO control in, 186
    Lincoln Club, 14–15, 116, 117–19, 132, 133–34, 136–37
    New Majority, 118–19, 141
    political bosses, 117, 119, 158
    routes to office, 168–69, *169,* 170–75, *172–73, 175*
organizational routes to office, 168–75, *169, 173, 175*
out-party primaries, 75
outside elites, 28–29. *See also* activists; elite endorsements

Pacheco, Nick, 169
Pacht, Jerry, 114
Padberg, Eileen, 146
Parker, Keith, 130, 134–35, 156–57
Parks, Bernard, 150
Parra, Nicole, 135–36, 200
partisanship. *See also* party coherence
  in California, 1–3, 10, 75–76, 85, 190–93
  cross-filing and, 20, 63–71, *65, 67, 68*
  incentive to avoid, 69
  increase in, 4–6, *5,* 24–25, 105–6, 190–93
  IPO control over politicians and, 9–10,
    32–33
  less populous political communities and,
    128
  literature on, 6
  majority party size and, 66, 91
  during New Deal, 104, 105, 197
  nonpartisanship preference of voters, 203
  party organizations responsibility for, 3
  professionalization, 65–66, 112
  Progressive movement and, 54–55
  reasons for, 11
  redistricting efforts and, 6
  reelection of incumbents and, 7–8, 25–26
  in U. S. Congress, 3, 4–6, *5,* 87–88, 189,
    191
  voting behavior and, 90–94, *92, 93, 94*
party-centered politics
  candidate selection and, 161–64
  IPO control of process and, 157–59
  party dynamics, 186–87
  Progressive Era reforms and, 105–6
  responsible party government model,
    80–85, *82, 84*
  tests to determine, 164–65, 185–86
party coherence
  cartel theory, 25–26, 85–86
  cross-filing and, 74–75, 80–85, *82, 84,* 105
  discipline enforcement, 27, 48–49, 52–53,
    126–27, 129, 151–53, 192
  influences on, 27–29
  outside coalitions and, 95–104, *97, 99,*
    101, 103, 107
party organization. *See also* informal party
  organizations (IPOs); local party organizations; traditional party organizations (TPOs)
  agenda of vs. district opinion, 80–85, *82,*
    84, 86, 93–94, *94,* 106, 188–89, 192
  alternative to, 203
  approval of, 197
  bill passage, 25
  in California, 3–4, 14, 88

  as creatures of politicians, 13, 26, 105–7,
    157, 186, 188–89
  cross-filing and, 19–20, 59, 74–75, 85–86
  definition of party, 10, 45
  gatekeeper role of, 9
  goals of, 18, 33
  patronage, 11, 36–40
  politicians as creatures of, 80–85, *82, 84,*
    105–6, 157–59, 189
  realignment theory, 27–29, 43
  relationship with politicians, 12–13, 26–27
  responsibility for partisanship, 3
  state party systems, 17–18, 44–45, 88
  strong, 167–68, 193, 195–97, 199–202,
    203
  supply and demand and, 33–36, 109, 113
  weak, 23–24, 125–28, 167, 175–76,
    193–95, 197–99
Pasco, Jean, 137, 139
passive endorsements, 178–79, *178*
patronage, 11, 36–40, 114–15
Patterson, Jim, 127
Peek, Paul, 71, 89, 104
People's Party (Populist), 98, 99
Perea, Henry 153–54
Pescetti, Anthony, 2
Plunkitt, George Washington, 36, 162–63
Polanco, Richard, 121–22, 130, 156, 180,
  181
polarization process, 4–6, *5,* 49, 88, 190–91,
  193
political parties. *See* party coherence; party
  organization
politicians. *See* officeholders and candidates
Poochigian, Chuck, 16
Poochigian, Debbie, 151
Poole, Keith, 64, 65, 89
Populist revolt, 98, 99
power, 34, 113, 130
primary elections. *See* elections, primary
Pringle, Curt, 118, 152, 182, *183*
professionalization, 65–66, 112
Progressive Era, 188–89. *See also* cross-
  filing
  acceptance of reforms in California, 11
  direct primary system, 58, 59–61
  initiative process, 72–73, 198–99
  nonpartisan elections, 58
  reforms to rid corruption, 58, 109–10,
    188–89, 193–94
  repeal of reforms, 17, 87
  survival of, 61
  takeover of California government by,
    54–55, 57–58